D1520086

PSEUDO

Dorothy Speak

stories

 FriesenPress

One Printers Way
Altona, MB R0G 0B0
Canada

www.friesenpress.com

ISBN
978-1-03-912298-7 (Hardcover)
 978-1-03-912297-0 (Paperback)
978-1-03-912299-4 (eBook)

1. LITERARY COLLECTIONS, CANADIAN

Distributed to the trade by The Ingram Book Company

for my sisters

Also by Dorothy Speak:

The Counsel of the Moon

Object of Your Love

The Wife Tree

Reconciliation

The author would like to thank The Canada Council,
The Ontario Arts Council and The City of Ottawa
for their financial support.

Table of Contents

Rock Paper Scissors

MOST EVENINGS, AXEL and I walk in the narrow park that runs beside the river, a few blocks from my house. Most evenings, now that winter is dying -- or rather is *wearing away* -- we are drawn over there. It is mid-April but all of our nights and most of our days here are still too bitter for the snow to shrink. But people have shattered it on the paths, smashed its glassy surface to brilliant diamonds with the teeth of their winter boots, they have assaulted it with their demand for spring. Light hangs longer in the sky now, and the crystals bite the eyes and the ice under foot is in places transparent blue, or, depending on the sun's angle, it is pink or mauve or yellow. Beside this glacier pulses the dark river, a living vein that seems to absolve and restore us. Some people would not call this a park at all. It is more a forgotten, wild corridor that nobody ever did anything to, a narrow strip of patchy grass and shabby bushes and pockets of broken forest. But it is a place beloved by locals for its raw, shabby splendour. Everything here is natural and gentle, everything unfolds in the fullness of time.

Axel and I pursue the meandering paths. We watch the water's eddies and dark reflections and listen to its murmur. In our ease with each other, we are like an old couple, though I am sixty and he is twenty-five and my son. At the moment, he lives with me. Many people disapprove of this. They say I should kick him out, but I tell them I do not see the urgency, there is too much urgency in this world.

Axel is tall and slender as an arrow and has black curly hair and a long, deeply pockmarked face. His teeth are small and cramped in front. Still, he is handsome in his darkness and his height and his grace and also, to me, he is appealing in his self-doubt and his desire for more than the obvious path in life. His mouth droops down on one side because he was a forceps birth and, so, he came into this world with a black eye and a welt the size of a pancake on one side of his face and a red bruise on the other cheek, shaped like the forceps loop. Once these wounds healed, it was clear that the forceps had severed a nerve and now he has a crooked smile. Axel isn't ready to leave home, just as he wasn't ready at nine months to be born. I like to hear his soft movements in the house, the scrape of a drawer, the creak of bed springs, the groan of a floorboard, the sound of running water. What do they mean to me? It's not that I'm lonely at all. I don't need anyone to live with, now or ever. But when I hear his footsteps overhead, his quiet intimacies with the house, it's as though he has not left my womb. I still have a chance, I still have a chance to nourish him. I like to believe that he's strengthening himself, that he's getting ready to emerge. More than that: I like the idea that he is searching for something and that he is still becoming.

My ex-husband, Rex, sometimes appears at my door and accuses me of weakening Axel by sheltering him. He says I am afraid to cut the umbilical cord. Just as I had not birthed Axel successfully, now I refused to push him out of the house. Down the three porch steps and across the sidewalk, in their idling coupe, his wife Helga, a round, pink, blunt-snouted woman resembling a certain farm animal, lowers her window and shrieks across my small lawn, her voice shredding the air like a chainsaw, "Where was the mother? Where was the mother when that little shit went wrong?" Rex casts a fugitive look over his shoulder, threatened as a man with bloodhounds at his heels. By the time he left me, he was bleeding at the throat from drink. Now, he attends AA every night, while Helga hits the bottle at home. Sometimes on the weekends, he escapes to AA three times a day because he married his own demon. He sits in cold church basements in a circle of hard stacking chairs, searching for himself in the faces of strangers just as bankrupt as he.

After Rex leaves, Axel comes downstairs, pale and shaken. "What did he say? Did he mention me?"

"Not this time."

"Don't ever tell him I'm depressed. Don't ever say he means anything to me."

"*Does* he mean anything?"

"Don't let on I even think about him."

"I won't."

Recently, I moved my mother here from Montreal and installed her in a nursing home on a manmade island. It's a salmon-brick tower with glass cupolas on its four corners, meant to make it look like a palace. It is strange for me now to walk to the end of our park and look across the boiling river and to know that she is living there, just a stone's throw away, for when I was a child, she was unreachable. At first, she thought the home was a psychiatric ward.

"No," I told her, "this is a different place." And she said, "Then why is everybody here crazy?"

"They're just old," I told her.

She gave me a withering look. "I know a crazy person when I see one."

In my teens, I stopped bringing friends home from school because we would often arrive at our handsome stone house in Mount Royal to find my mother still in her nightie, passed out on the black and white hall floor tiles, reeking of booze, a bruise on her forehead or cheek, an empty bottle of Johnny Walker clutched in her hand. We'd grab her by the arms and legs and drag her onto the living room couch. At first, this spectacle hurt and embarrassed me. Gradually, I became indifferent. I swung her body onto the sofa with no more feeling than if she were a vagrant from the street. Her behaviour has made it easy for me to move on quickly from disappointment. Nothing touches me now, nothing sticks to me.

My mother lived in bed for sixteen years, incapacitated by a mix of drugs prescribed by six doctors unknown to each other. People got away with that sort of thing back then, before proper records were kept. She washed the pills down with tumblers of scotch. Every now and then she checked herself into a psychiatric ward, as though it were a spa. It was something many middleclass women did in those days to escape a housewife's madness. There, she was stricken by a painful clarity. When I visited her, she ranted like a suffragette. "I was a gold medalist in engineering," she'd cry, "I was on my way up when I met your father. To marry, I was forced to choose between a career and him. I shouldn't have had to do that."

"This is the king of nursing homes," I told her the first day at the home. Each floor has a vast sitting room with fat white Doric columns, a grand piano, Persian carpets, a wood fireplace, expensively upholstered sofas, vases of fresh flowers. "It's like a five-star hotel," I said.

"I never liked hotels," she answered dryly. I wheeled her out onto one of the big curved balconies off the lounge. "It's very windy out here," she complained, cringing, her hair blowing straight up from her brow, which has shrivelled, like one of those dolls with a head made from a dried apple.

"Look down," I told her. "See the view? Isn't it beautiful? The river flows all the way around the building. I had to take a bridge to get here. It's like you're living in a castle."

"Or Alcatraz." Her ears have become large, elaborate works of engineering, with deep caverns and dark tunnels and ridges gleaming like marble. She plays with her hands like an infant discovering her fingers for the first time. She worries the wool blanket spread across her lap, braiding and unbraiding its long fringe. Her knuckles are jagged as stones, her fingers twisted like weathered branches, both powerful and feckless. Her small wheelchair traps her body, pushing all its components together like a landslide, her breasts, her stomach, her thighs. She is a big mound of flesh, wrapped in mohair. This confinement has captured her in the role I always wanted her to play, it has forced her to become the accessible woman I needed as a child.

On my lunch break, I leave the tall, narrow red-brick Victorian house that holds the legal offices where I work and I walk two blocks to the canal to sit on a bench under a sugar maple. The still waters tremble and shine. The clouds and the blue sky float on the transparent surface. Bicycles spin by on the path, their wheels glittering like stars. I open my novel. Now and then, some man in a business suit, a young or middle-aged or even an older man, will come along and pause before me, politely say some version of the following: "I've noticed you here before. Many times. Always reading.

You seem very contented. At one with yourself and with life. It's unusual. I must say, I envy you this tranquillity. Would you consider telling me your secret?" This is not some sexual come-on. They are genuinely seeking help, because we have become a society with many questions but no answers. They pull at the strangulating knots in their ties, shove their hands into their trouser pockets, shuffle restlessly, look at me with lost eyes, a childish hunger. What can I answer? *Want what you have.* But I smile and reply, "If I knew why I was happy, I'd sell the reason and become a millionaire."

I take my friend Frank to meet my mother. He bows like a gentleman and shakes her silky hand. She isn't fooled. "You are very thin," she says with a penetrating look. She narrows her eyes with prophecy. "I'll outlive you," she says.

On the way back to the car, Frank predicts, "Someday you'll look like her. You'll look like your mother. I can see it. I won't know you then."

That night, she phones me. "He looks like a marked man. Are you in love with him? I hope not. It wouldn't surprise me, though. You always excelled at making bad decisions." She adds, "He has very bad skin. I have never seen such bad skin on a grown man." I know she hasn't forgiven me, the daughter of a gold-medalist, for dropping out of university, so that I could gallivant with an assortment of boys around France, where we slept on park benches, survived on baguettes and wine and sex. I was supposed to have the career she was denied.

I ask Axel when he's going to move out and a black cloud drifts across his face. We are sitting in the living room, which is crowded with many chairs, some of them torn. His expression reminds me of the fear I noticed each day I sent him off to primary school, where the other boys tore at the corners of their mouths and called him *The Big Mistake*. "Mom," he answers, "I feel safe here. When I'm alone, I go to a dark place. I'm scared that if you make me leave, I'll want to kill myself."

"What do you desire in life, Axel?"

I can see he's disappointed that I would once more ask him this facile question. He replies patiently, as though I am a half-wit, "I don't know, Mom. I'm thinking."

"What are you interested in? Are you interested in anything?"

"I'm looking, Mom, I'm looking."

He knows that I wonder what he does all day while I'm at work.

"What if I told you I was writing a novel?"

"Are you?"

I hold up a book, "I'm reading these short stories." I keep a stack of library books on the coffee table. On the weekends, I plough through five or six of them, sitting on my couch at the front window where the sun pours in. Right outside, city buses stop, their powerful air brakes wheezing, their rubber-lipped doors flapping open and closed, their tires churning up clouds of dust, their very weight shaking the house. The window pane behind me shivers and sings as though alive. "In this collection, some of the stories are better than others," I tell Axel. "Do you want me to show you which ones I like best?"

"No."

Frank Furnace and I have not had sex since he found out he has cancer. Sex seems irrelevant, I tell him, in the face of things.

"Irrelevant!" he cries. "Sex is all I have left!" He lies on the sagging leather sofa in the dark kitchen at the back of my house, his long legs draped over the arm rest. It is late one afternoon in July. "I never would have got cancer if you'd agreed to marry me," he insists. "Stress causes cancer, everybody knows that now. My longing for you ate a hole right through my liver."

"You don't think it could have been your toxic lifestyle," I suggest. "Your drinking and your smoking and your drug use." I hand him a piece of buttered toast. He looks at it critically. "Do you always have to burn it? For five whole years you've been burning my toast. Burnt food has carcinogens!"

"So, which is to blame for your cancer?" I ask. "Stress or burnt toast?"

"Both."

"I have deliberately been trying to kill you."

He finishes the toast, then looks down at the empty plate. "Is this a meal?" he says wildly. "Is this supposed to be a repast? Sick people need sustenance. Crumbs! All I have left are crumbs! I'm running out of time."

"You never knew what time was," I say unfeelingly. It's true. He always slept in, opened a beer at noon, sat and smoked all day, later stumbled to a bar.

We met in a Red Lion five years ago. His ravaged bad-boy looks, his destroyed complexion appealed to me. His leather jacket had a big slash in the sleeve from a knife fight. I told him I was a skilled mender, that I could do a tidy repair for him. I took him home that night, a totally inappropriate man fifteen years my junior, a high school dropout with a cocaine habit, a struggling photographer not struggling hard enough, as far as I could see, to do more than scrape by. Poking around my bedroom the following morning, fingering my Chanel suits, my silk stockings, picking up my tortoise shell hair combs, he said, "You don't screw like a rich broad."

"I'm not rich."

"What about that private school you mentioned?" he said, because I'd already divulged the details of my childhood. "What about golfing with your father? What about the tennis club and the summer cottage in the Laurentians? That sounds rich, to me."

However: my narrow half-double is on a graceful passage to ruin. I don't replace the broken porch boards or repair the faulty door lock or paint the peeling gable or rescue the dying garden or redo the lifting kitchen linoleum because I believe this organic deterioration must be respected. When I point out to Frank that I live without a dishwasher or food processor or the internet, he calls me a *poverty fraud*. A dabbler, a hobbyist. He says that choosing to *look* poor is not the same as *being* poor. I do not have the scars of a poor person, he says. I have not paid the price.

My boss, Larry Dark, calls me into his office first thing in the morning. We are up on the fourth floor of the Victorian house, under steeply sloped ceilings. My desk is on the small landing and his office is in a back room, with a fire escape descending past his window. This used to be the servants' quarters of this old house. The further up they put you in this place, the less productive a lawyer you've been. This is an obscure law firm of not very ambitious, not very successful lawyers getting by on modest billings.

"Close the door?" Larry pleads, his eyes swimming with panic. I shut the door and sit down, a pencil poised over my steno pad, ready for dictation.

"Put that down," he tells me. Then he blurts out, "I'm having another breakdown." Twenty years my junior, tall, handsome and vain, he's a serial cheater. Last month, his wife, Sheila, got wind of the latest affair and kicked him out.

"Get a psychiatrist," I say.

"I'd rather talk to *you*. You know a lot about life."

"If I'm going to be your shrink too, I ought to get a raise."

"I'll give you a raise."

"Liar."

"I didn't sleep all last night. I couldn't stop thinking about Sheila."

"You never wanted her when you had her."

"I wanted her. I just wanted other women too."

"Greedy pig."

"I know. I know it's my fault. But now I'm a fucking mess. I think of killing myself."

"You're a big, philandering baby."

"I'm lonely."

"Commit the crime, do the time."

"I could fire you, the way you talk to me."

"Go ahead."

He begins to cry. "Tell me what to do. How can I fix this? I'm ready to change."

"I don't believe you."

"You have to. I need someone to believe in me. That's what I'm paying you for. Help me write a letter to Sheila."

"Just put down what's in your heart of hearts."

"I have no heart. You told me so yourself."

"Then, be authentic."

"I don't know how. Teach me. Teach me to be good."

My daughter, Matilda, her curvaceous form packed into a sky-blue business suit, her long strawberry blonde hair spilling over her shoulders, has walked over from a large government estate bordering our neighbourhood, enclosed by miles of fine iron and stone fencing. There, she is executive assistant to a high-ranking quasi-regal official. She was no genius in school, but I'm told she landed this job because of her beauty, her charm, her ability to go in for the kill. She lives on these public grounds rent-free in a field-stone cottage, amid rolling lawns, forests, cricket fields, ceremonial guards in crimson jackets and tall furry hats, the music of bagpipes, a sentry at the gates. She has accompanied her boss on diplomatic missions to India, China, Australia.

Tonight, she bursts through my front door without knocking, though she hasn't lived here for ten years. From the expression on her face, I know immediately that she's got her period again: once more, the artificial insemination has failed. She flops down on my couch, unbuttons her suit jacket, pulls up her white cotton blouse, pinches the soft flesh of her stomach and sticks a long hypodermic needle in, her injection of hormones.

"If I don't have a baby," she tells me angrily, "I'm going to spit blood."

"Maybe it'll happen next month," I say.

Overhead, the sound of Axel crossing his room. He no longer comes downstairs when Matilda is here, though as children they were close. She raises an eyebrow critically at me.

"When's he going to get a job?" she demands.

"He's writing a blog or something," I say.

"That's a virtual life, Mother."

"I give him the classifieds to look over."

"The last time I saw him, he was reading a comic book. What's he qualified to do?"

"Make up your mind what you want from him."

In high school, Matilda was a champion partier, every Sunday morning leading a different boy downstairs from her bedroom. Quarterbacks, skiers, bartenders, drummers. At the time, she said marriage was for losers. When, one day, she brought home Felix, a librarian, and told us they were engaged, you could have knocked Axel and me over with a feather. Today, in the doorway, there stands Felix, breathless from trying to keep up with Matilda as she hastened down the street, her heels murdering the sidewalk.

Felix pursues me to the kitchen where I go to make tea. "I've lost control of my life," he whispers intensely, as I put the kettle on. He is small, fine-boned, fragile enough for Matilda to knock down with one blow. He has pale skin and a neat goatee. "We agreed when we married that we'd talk about having children," he says in low tones, following me as I get the tea bags out, the cups. "*Talk.* You understand? I never signed up for this insemination shit. The whole process is unnatural. Then they go and tell me my sperm can't swim. I didn't need to hear that. She keeps saying to me, 'This is a human being we're creating, don't you understand? *A human being.*' I don't see why it's my responsibility to put another person on this catastrophic planet. And, anyway, she works seven days a week, she's away half the year, so who's going to take care of this kid? All I want is a room where I can sit in peace at night and read Dickens. I've decided that next month, I'm going to refuse to give my sperm."

"What if she just finds a donor?" I ask.

"Then, it won't be my kid, will it?"

Frank has arrived at my house at five o'clock, unannounced. He is very thin now. He lost pounds and pounds before the diagnosis. How could he not have known that unexplained weight loss meant cancer? Doesn't everybody know that? He asks me if I'll go to his doctor's appointments with him, to take notes in case he forgets what he's told, but I point out I'll be at work.

"Don't they give you family leave? Just for a couple of hours?"

"But you're not family."

"You never loved me," he shakes his head tragically.

"I did *like* you, though. Sometimes that's harder."

"You could just say *love*, before it's too late. Words are cheap."

"Not *that* word."

"You only have so much time left to say nice things to me."

"I'm not going to start to lie just because you're dying."

I'd never thought of him as a boyfriend and he'd never acted like one. He came and went as he pleased. Sometimes

I wouldn't hear from him for weeks. Now that he's dying, he wants to make a romance of our story.

"Does he have to be here all the time, now that he's kicking the can?" Axel asked me today. The first time he met Frank, Axel said, "Let me know if you ever need me to knock his block off." Later, he handed me a box of condoms. "Times have changed, Mom," he said. "You can't go around anymore, sleeping with every Tom, Dick and Harry. I don't want to have to tell people my mother has AIDS."

Tonight, Axel, passing the kitchen door, throws Frank a knife-like look. After he's gone upstairs, Frank asks me bitterly, "Does he think I'm worse than his father, that drunk you married? Does he think I have any less value than a twenty-five-year-old mama's boy?"

"Let's go outside and see the ducks," I tell my mother.

She shivers and frowns. "I don't want to be cold." I wrap her in blankets and we go down to sit in a wooden gazebo right beside the river.

"Isn't it pretty here?" I say.

"Take me home with you," she pleads, her words slurred, like a drunk. In the mornings she tries very hard to speak clearly, she is like an immigrant focused on pronouncing a new language, but as the day wears on, she forgets, her tongue will not perform.

"What's wrong?" I ask her. "The care here is good. Isn't it?"

"I'm lonely."

"Mother, I work, remember? Who'd take care of you all day? Who'd feed you?"

"I don't need much. A cracker to eat."

"And my old house. You couldn't climb the stairs to bed or to the bathroom."

"I'd sleep on the front couch. I'd use a bedpan. I'm not proud. Please."

"I'm sorry," I say. "Let's talk about now. What can I do for you today?"

"Take my mind. Feed it to the ducks."

"They are vegetarian."

"Kill me, then. Get a hold of some pills. I'll administer the dose myself."

The ducks swim in circles on the glassy water. "Do you want to go to heaven?" I ask her.

"Yes," she says, then adds quickly, contradicting her wish to die, "but not right now."

"What's to live for?"

"Loving you." I look at her but can't tell if this is truth or manipulation.

We admire the ducks' mahogany heads, their purple wings. After a while, she tries again, "Please don't take me back in that place."

"Alright, I won't." She sighs with happiness, trust. Soon, as I expected, she's fallen asleep, lulled by the babble of the river. I wheel her back along the path and we whoosh up in the elevator. Then I drive home, guiltless. By the time she wakes up, she'll have forgotten what she begged me not to do.

One Saturday in September, Frank crosses the park to where I'm reading on a bench beside the black water. The ground is uneven and he nearly trips, for he is weak, wispy as a twig, pale as a ghost. I rise, grasp him by the elbow, steer him across the grass. "Let's go back," I say. "I'll make you a cup of tea."

On the way, he says resentfully, "I deserved to live longer."

"Nobody wants to admit that people die," I say.

"But, I'm not people."

The hot and wild and lying winds of autumn twist past my open kitchen door. The trees writhe, screaming their beautiful messages. From time to time, a car grinds slowly down the narrow back lane, tires gnawing on the gravel, crying on the jagged lips of potholes, tearing the air. On the porch, the Virginia Creeper is shot with colour, its blood-red fingers curling around the posts.

"Can I die here?" Frank pleads from the kitchen couch.

"What?"

"I don't want an institutional death."

"I wouldn't know what to do for you."

"Then I'm going to have to go in."

"In?"

"I have no one. No one to take care of me. I have to go in."

"Would you tend to Mother if I brought her here to live with us?" I ask Axel. We are sitting in an intimate alcove in the dim part of the living room, watching my old-fashioned television set.

"*Mom.*"

"Well, I just wondered. Since you aren't doing anything."

"What makes you think I'm not doing anything?"

"Come to my apartment tonight," begs Larry Dark, late one Friday afternoon.

"Dream on," I tell him, closing up my desk.

"I know you love me."

"Sure, I do."

"I'll fix you supper."

"Like fun. I know what you're looking for."

"You're like a big sister to me."

"Big sisters don't sleep with their brothers."

I had sex with him once, a few years back. It was on a night when I'd stayed late to complete some urgent documents. Sheila was at a spa in California. "Spending my meagre earnings," Larry said glumly. The office had emptied out. We were alone up on the third floor. When he came in the following Monday morning, he was frisky, hovering around my desk like a child looking for candy. I put him in his place.

"That was a one-off," I told him without looking up. "I must have been out of my mind."

Axel comes to me on Saturday morning. I am on the couch, reading in the sun. He shuffles awkwardly on his feet.

I glance up from my book.

"I know a girl who's pregnant," he says.

"I'd give her a wide berth if I were you," I advise him. "Girls like that are usually trouble."

"I can't."

"Why?"

"I'm the father."

I didn't know he even knew any girls. "What about those condoms you told me about?" I ask him. He smiles, shy, proud, happy.

She is someone he met at a bar down on the corner and had sex with the same night, pressed up against a brick wall in the alley outside, because she told him his crooked smile turned her on. Now, the thought of being a father suddenly has him whistling about the house, a spring in his step. He has put away his torn t-shirts and sweatpants, and wears pressed trousers, a crisp shirt. I see him at the kitchen table, the newspaper spread out before him, circling notices in the employment ads.

Frank says to me, "He looks pretty goddamned full of himself, now he's got a bun in that chick's oven."

"For a change," Axel tells me, "for a change, something is happening in my life." He wants to bring the girl home to meet me. "Her name is Mary but she goes by Amber," he says.

"Mary is a nice name," I reply.

"Don't ask about her mother. Don't ask where she lives. Don't ask how much school she's got. Don't ask what she does all day," he cautions me the Sunday she's coming for supper.

"What am I supposed to talk to her about?"

He borrows my coupe to fetch her from the west end, where the local gangs are headquartered and all the city's knifings and murders occur. My heart sinks when she walks in, a short, sullen girl with hostile, darting eyes. It saddens me to think that Axel should set his sights so low. But he is happy and anxious for the evening to go well. He springs about endearingly, pouring drinks, carrying the plates earnestly to the table. I've prepared the simplest meal I can think of. Chicken, broccoli, an apple pie. But she says she does not eat vegetables or cooked apples, she does not like wine. "Is there any pasta?" she asks. "Is there beer? Is there ice cream instead?" She's twenty-one. I'm surprised she hasn't got pregnant before this. I try to imagine her holding a baby, I try to imagine Axel holding a baby. I wonder what kind of job Axel might get to be able to feed and clothe and shelter this baby and this Mary/Amber. They know it's going to be a girl. They've already decided to call her Alice. On his return from taking her home, Axel asks me eagerly, "What did you think of her?"

"You need someone happy at your side."

"She was just shy. She was just nervous."

"You'll be able to teach her some table manners. How to hold a knife and fork."

"*Mom*," he says, wounded. Then he adds, "She's not *common*."

"I didn't say she was."

"Well, I know you like that word."

October comes. I drive Frank to his place to fetch a few things. He lives in a tenement house in a poor and crime-ridden area of beggars and thieves and drug pushers and hookers and shootings and people smoking on their front porches all day long in their housecoats. He is so weak that it takes him ten minutes, sweating and trembling and gasping for breath, to climb with me up to the third floor. I wait for him, step by step, supporting his elbow, saying I could go up alone. But he says, no, he wants to see the place one last time. When we get there, I can't see anything worth collecting. All we can find to put into a paper bag are a toothbrush, a hair comb, a razor. This beggary is harrowing for both us, in different ways.

"If Axel has a baby and I don't," says Matilda, "I am going to murder someone. He just pulls out his dick and, *bingo*, he's got a kid on the way. That burns my ass. How will he be a father, anyway? What does he have to offer a child? He can't even take care of himself. He doesn't deserve it."

"What does *deserve* mean?" I ask her.

"I don't see why you're not upset about this."

"Do you want me to be?"

At the hospice, volunteer women, all of them round and heavy, mop the hallways, weed the gardens, bring glasses of apple juice, packaged cookies. They toil slowly along the hallways, rocking on their painful hips. They have asked Frank if he'd like to sing hymns. They have offered him bibles, devotional readings, crucifixes. Down the hall is a niche with a statue in it of the Blessed Virgin Mary, her face passive, her plaster hands and feet small as a child's. Rays of gold shoot from her fingertips. Frank calls her *the BVM*. "Don't take me past that creepy BVM," he warns me when I put him in a wheelchair. The day he was admitted here, they laid him on a gurney and wheeled him down the hall under a ceiling of fluorescent stars meant to suggest heaven. "They freaked me out, those bloody stars," he told me. "Whose goddamned idea was that?" The volunteers keep asking him if he'll donate his organs, they have the forms to sign in their hands. Finally, he tells them, "I'll give you my liver. The doctors say it's a beauty." We were told this was the finest palliative care facility in the city. We were told this was a place of joy.

"Joy!" Frank spits out with disgust.

Mary/Amber phones to inform Axel that he's not the father. He comes to me, weeping, and says he wants to hire a lawyer to force a DNA test to determine paternity. He wants to go for joint custody. "To live *here*?" I say, wondering how I'll pay for the lawsuit, the diapers. For a while, the thought of being a father had made Axel's hands stop shaking, but now I notice them trembling again.

Every day, a square white truck pulls up beside the hospice to deliver oxygen tanks. A fat boy unloads them clumsily, the heavy aluminum clanging loud as canons. "What is that god-damned racket?" cries Frank, tossing in his bed. To escape this noise, I take him out back, where we sit on a cracked patio and look across a deep sloped lawn toward ancient willows trailing in the water. "Isn't this the same bloody river that goes past your place?" asks Frank. It is not the same river. In this watery city, there is a mighty river and this sweet, smaller river as well as a manmade canal. "Jesus," says Frank, "you can't get away from rivers in this town. Water everywhere, washing away at the edges of our lives! These goddamned rivers will drown you!" Swans, released every summer, float by. There are a dozen white ones and a black one that no one ever sees. "Why do they put these death houses in the middle of places that are beautiful and heartbreaking?" Frank complains. "Hospices should be built beside coal heaps and garbage dumps."

A note flutters through the letter slot onto the torn foyer carpet. Axel tears it open, leaning against the bulky coats on hooks there, where a draft sweeps in around the old front door. It is from Mary/Amber, telling him she has lost the baby.

"Do you think she had an abortion?" he asks me in the living room. He is not crying now, he is becoming hardened by the facts of life. I see this as progress. He looks around for a place to sit down. He's so tall that he must fold, bend his long body like a jack-in-the box to fit into the living room chairs I took from my mother's house. Even then, he looks uncomfortable, displaced. "Is there a way to find out?" he asks me.

"What would you gain from that?"

"You're glad, aren't you?"

"No, I'm not glad," I lie unconvincingly.

"This is wrong. If she wanted an abortion, I should have had a say. Doesn't she need the father's signature for that? It was my kid too. That baby was part of *me*."

"I don't think Mary/Amber was good enough for you," I say.

"Why? Because she uses her fork wrong?"

"Because I know what you're worth."

It is mid-November now and there is still no snow. Every day, sunshine and warm confusing winds, like May. No one understands this but everybody is happy about it, except Frank. This is cruel, he says, this is mockery, for nature to hold forth such heresy, such spring-like promise of rebirth.

He has become dry and brittle, hollow and weightless, like a mannequin. The hefty women here effortlessly toss him around as though he were a piece of tinder. Beneath the thick blanket covering him, his legs are smooth and hairless as an old woman's. Gone is his look of gangsterism and criminality. He is cleaner than ever before, fresher somehow, as though ready for an important journey. Six months ago, he was mounting me on the hood of my car. I do not even like to think about this anymore. The average stay in this hospice is two weeks. "Two weeks!" he cries. Already, he's been here that long. "That means, at most, I have two more weeks to live. If you do the math," he tells me. I say those are just statistics. "There's no oxygen in my room," he complains. "No oxygen. They suck it out while I'm sleeping. Their job here is to finish you off." If not with the air, then with the food. They serve shepherd's pie, stew, moussaka, chili. It's all the same dish, he says, just different names.

He asks me if I'll adopt his cat. I say no, it would scratch my furniture. "Say you'll take her just to make me feel good. Drown her in the toilet after I die. I'll never know."

"Ok, I'll kill your cat for you."

Then he confides that he's going to leave me the diamond stud he has in his ear.

"It's glass," I tell him.

"It's a *symbol*," he says impatiently.

He adds bitterly, shaking his head. "Just toss me in that dumpster out there when I'm gone."

"That's against health laws."

"I don't want a funeral or a grave. I don't want prayers or hypocrisy. I don't want ashes or an urn. I've got no friends.

I'm forty-five and you're the only one I've got. All I've got. How did this happen?"

"Easy come, easy go," says Matilda smugly when she learns of Mary/Amber's termination. "This is nature taking over. Protecting the helpless."

"Do you have to look so happy about it?" I ask her.

On my way out of the hospice, I'm intercepted by the manager, a man awkward, shy and lonely looking.

"Are you getting through this OK?" he asks.

"Oh, yes."

"Do you have everything you need? Does your husband have everything he needs?"

"He's not my husband."

"Oh."

"I hardly know him. He's practically a stranger."

"Did you visit Mother?" I ask Axel.

"Yes."

"You didn't tell me that."

"You didn't know I could do good works?" he raises his eyebrows at me. "I'm disappointed in you." Then, at supper, he says, "I told Grandma about the baby. She said she would have liked to hold it. She said it would have been her first great-grandchild. It wasn't just some idea to her. It was *real*. You know what else she said? She said I had a brilliant face."

Recently I read a theory that, though babies are born at the end of the third trimester, they would be happier with three more months in the womb. They cry for the warm amniotic fluid, the sound and vibration of the mother's heartbeat, the swing and sway of her movements. They are not ready to suck, breathe, wail, be bombarded by light or exposed to cold, to uncurl their legs and fists.

One day when I arrive, Frank reports, "That fucking black swan is hanging around now. He's out there every day. Why can't he get lost? Black! You know what that means, don't you? That means curtains for me." His skin has grown waxy, like the other patients in this place. I glimpse them through their doorways, lying in bed, half-covered, their legs bare, their chests. They are not troubled by this exposure. They no longer respect their bodies because they have been utterly betrayed by them.

But Frank does not die. Not yet. When I go in on the first of December, he tells me, "I feel calmer now. I feel like a new person." He does indeed look different. His face is less lined, less dark, his forehead smooth, his neck not so ropy, his hands calm. "I'm prepared to die," he says. "No guff. I've accepted it. I think this cancer is a good thing, in the end. I don't think I was very happy with my life. I don't think my life was very useful. It's too late now to repair that. So, I might as well let it all go. These people did that for me. They opened me up. They made me see it." So: I have been replaced by these heavy, sexless women, I see. These women are now more important to him than I. It shows in his expression when he looks at me. Triumph. Repudiation. Revenge. "But, now that I'm at peace, I sense a new longevity, an energy burst," he tells me with sudden optimism, his eyes shining. "I'm going to try to last until the twenty-fifth. My death will be my Christmas present to you."

"Funny."

"I'm going to instruct the nurse to put a great big red bow on my corpse."

From upstairs, at times, comes a great shuddering sigh so powerful it seems to shake the air in the house. Axel's room still has the faded green paisley quilt we bought when he was nine, and the yellowed rock star posters from his adolescence. His room is on the back of the house with a small door leading outside to a rickety balcony. Sometimes I hear him open it and step out onto this upper porch, where he lingers for many minutes. A cold river of air sweeps down the stairs and with it the smell of the coming winter. I wonder what Axel thinks when he gazes down on the all too familiar tangle of lilac bushes in the long, broken back lane, the battered aluminum trash cans, the cats creeping in the bull thistle, where as a child he once played with a ball. Sunshine pours in onto my shoulders, through the front window. I feel the weight of my library book and the lives described in it heavy in my lap, the rough texture of its pages, the rub of the wool blanket thrown across my knees.

The hospice calls on December third to say Frank put me down as next of kin. They say I must come at once, as they need Frank's bed for a new patient. Also, there are papers I must sign.

"I have no authority," I tell the nurse. "I'm nobody."

She says there are Frank's personal effects to pick up.

"It's just a few worthless toiletries," I say.

"And the clothes he was wearing when he came in here."

"Couldn't you just burn it all?" I ask.

"We're not permitted."

"Isn't there a sister somewhere?"

"Please. Come. Out of respect."

"He never bathed enough," says Matilda when I tell her Frank has died.

Axel says, "So this means I'll never get to bust his nose."

For a long time, without knowing it, I've felt I was carrying around a heavy object. Now my arms feel so weightless that sometimes, standing up, I nearly lose my balance.

In our park, I have sometimes walked on spring or summer or fall evenings, on the dusty path so narrow and aimless that it looks accidental, though many people use it, it is the primal route. One season, I passed a certain man on this path many evenings and then one night, as it was darkening, we stepped wordlessly together into the thin birch wood and lay down on the bed of dead leaves and silently made love. The same thing had happened with another man and another, in other years and seasons. I got up with bits of crushed leaf in my hair. The next morning, I sometimes had to go back to search for a lost earring. I wondered what it was in my expression -- a fracture, a crack in my look of contentment with life, a glimmer of doubt or despair -- that would make a man think I was game for such recklessness, hungry for fulfillment or self-destruction.

Felix calls me from a tiny village in the purple hills, where he is now in charge of the local one-room library. He tells me he has a small flat, an armchair, an old tub on legs, a view of the river, of the dark, forested slopes, all he professed to need.

"Are you lonely?" I ask.

"No," he answers, but his voice quivers, then breaks and over the line I hear the deep, ragged *huh, huh* of his sobs.

"We all have the potential to be better people," Frank told me toward the end. "Even you."

During her last years in Montreal, my mother had begun to call me nearly every day. She'd claim she was having arrhythmia, she had shingles, congestive heart failure, pneumonia. I'd rush down to Montreal for nothing. False alarms.

Confusion. Lies. Trickery. The vivid imagination of an old woman. Then once, at midnight, she phoned to say she thought she was having a stroke. I was in bed with Frank. I didn't want to get dressed and drive two hours in the dark on another wild goose chase only to find that she was simply lonely, a friendless woman who'd never cared about anyone but herself. That night, I promised her I'd be there right away. Then I hung up the phone and went back to sleep. But this time it wasn't a ruse. The following day, her cleaning woman discovered her, half-paralyzed, on the bedroom floor. We have never spoken of my lie, and my failure to come to her rescue. Like so much in our history, it is unspeakable. I do not know if she remembers what happened or if she's forgiven me for letting her down or if she always considered me capable of nothing better or if she'd been waiting all her life for me to pay her back. This weighs heavily on my mind. Every day, I think I will probe her memory, apologize for my betrayal. But then I come upon her in the nursing home, locked in her layers of wool, and I think that calling up the past would merely bring her anguish.

"They are going to bury Frank," I tell Axel when we are walking in the park. It is December fourth. The path is rigid and lumpy with frost, the lawns brittle as glass, the blades crackling and breaking off when we cross it, leaving our ghost-like footprints behind us. As the sun sets, a skin of pink ice floats on the river. Ducks swim round and round in a small black pool in the centre, where the water will not freeze, even in February.

"Who is?" asks Axel.

"First, the funeral parlour works on him and then the public trustee takes over and they bury him in some worthless place that nobody wants. What they used to call a potter's field. Because he has no money for a proper grave and no family to step in. They said they could let me know when the interment happens. Do you think I should go? Would you come with me?"

"How can someone not have one single relative who cares?"

When Frank got sick, I'd said to him, "What about your brother? What about your sister? They live only a day's journey away by train. They must love you."

He shook his head, smiling, both bitter and boastful. "No one in our family ever loved anybody." It was after he'd got religion at the hospice. After they convinced him that all the important things happen in heaven.

Axel lies on his stomach on the living room carpet with one of my novels, turning the pages.

"I thought you weren't interested in my books," I say.

"I'm only reading it to make you happy."

"I want to leave you my camera," Frank had told me. "I want you to have it."

"I don't take photos."

"But you can't give it to Axel. If you give it to Axel, I'll come back from my grave and kill you."

"How?"

"I don't know. With a gun?"

"I'll get out my bullet-proof vest."

My mother tells me, "I outlived your lover. Now it's time for you to start caring about *me*."

Rex is at my door again, still on a search for himself, like a detective out to find a missing person. He peers past my shoulder into the dark hallway and the rooms beyond, as though he pictures himself there. I have never let him cross this threshold. He seems to think that, twenty years after our divorce, he should be forgiven and welcomed in like a family member.

He'd been furious first about the pregnancy, then about the idea of Axel wanting custody. But now that the baby is lost, he says to me sadly, "So. No grandchild for us."

"There *is* no *us*," I tell him.

This time he has come alone. In his eyes, I see the panic of a drowning man. "I heard you had a fellow and he died," he tells me. "I'd give anything to turn back the clock." He searches my face, hopefully. "If there were any chance you'd…take me back…?"

Axel has been job-hunting. He comes downstairs wearing a suit and tie, looking handsome, tragic and fine. He says that, until Frank died, it never occurred to him that he himself wouldn't live forever. "I don't want to be a loser like him," Axel tells me. "Thanks for dating the kind of man I would never want to become."

While he's out at his interviews I go to his room, searching for the novel he was supposed to be writing. But all I find, in his night table drawer, is the note that came through the letter slot, now wrinkled and soiled from repeated handling and rereading. *The babys ded. A miss karidge. So get lost. Yer ugly anyhow. I never want t see u again. If u dropt dead I'd laff.* I consider taking the note downstairs, burning it in the kitchen sink. But then, I think: maybe this message is working the opposite of its intent. Maybe it's helping Axel believe in himself, so I put it back where I found it.

"Are you sad about Frank?" Axel asks.

"I'm sixty," I tell him. "I don't have enough time left to be sad."

The canal freezes over. The workers drill holes in it, pump water out from underneath the ice, fan it across the surface. The gates are opened for skaters, the green flags go up. At lunchtime, I leave the office and venture over there, carrying the ancient white skates of my adolescence, their leather cracked now, the toes scuffed and torn. I lace them on, stroke down the dark, scarred ice, my blades cutting the surface, setting the air singing. A slender figure shoots toward me, makes a smart-aleck hockey stop right at my feet, spraying my ankles with shaved ice, nearly knocking me over. It's Larry Dark. He catches my elbow to keep me from falling.

"What's the matter?" I ask. "You look happy."

He holds up his cell phone like a trophy. "Sheila just called. She says she might be able to love me again."

"Ring her back," I say, holding out my hand to take his phone. "I want to talk to her."

He slips it into his pocket. "You showed no pity for me in my hour of need," he says, aggrieved.

"You had to face the music."

I am covered in a carapace that all the assaults of life, the heat and ice and storms thrown at me from the skies cannot damage. This troubles me. Within this shell, I dare not move for fear of bruising myself. I must hold perfectly still.

Axel has landed a job as a junior photographer for the city paper. They were impressed when he walked in carrying Frank's expensive camera. "What if I stay at that level? What if I'm never anything more than a junior?" he asks me anxiously.

"What if you are? What would be wrong with that?"

"What would Dad say?"

"Who?"

"Someday, I *will* move out," Axel promises, his face asking forgiveness. There are granite lines carved around his mouth now. I'd never noticed this before.

"Take your time," I tell him, patting his hand.

We are eating supper at the back of the house, at an old scarred table in a small room that was once a summer kitchen and is now my dining room. I turn my head and look at the worn couch where Frank used to lie to watch me work my old-fashioned toaster, with the sides that fold down. It is December twenty-fourth. To save money, I have not yet turned on the furnace, so we shiver a little out here, surrounded as we are on three sides by dark windows showing us the quiet laneway, the broken fences, the stripped bushes.

Axel raises his head, looks out with anguish at the first snow, flakes large as goose feathers turning in the air, perfect and pure.

"Alice," he murmurs, a whisper soft almost as the falling snow.

"Yes," I say.

Wilderness

I NEVER TIRED of that view. For me, it provided all the necessities of life: colour, texture, line, composition. There at the living room window, I could set up my easel and make a hundred paintings, every one of them different. We had built the house ourselves, a simple cabin. Four rooms in a straight line: living room, kitchen, study, bedroom. Then the garage, quickly converted by me into a studio. All with their windows opening onto the forest and the steep slope tumbling down to the cobalt river, flashing far below. We chose a humble pine for the floors, for the woodwork, because we wanted to honour the natural world around us. We'd brought with us only our Danish furniture, which, being sleek, understated, blended seamlessly with our adopted home. We were whittled to our core here, panned down to the gold.

At first, the house smelled of sweet timber and fresh paint, everything virgin, and it seemed like we too were new. There was no taint of the world's anguish here, no loss or betrayal or disappointment, no memory, sorrow, obligation, guilt, no past or future. We had shut the door on all that. We had come here to live in the moment, we would merely *be*. It was all I desired. I was eighty-five. I believed the struggle of life was behind me. Now I was entering something much more profound: existence. Of course, Beryl did not like to hear me say this. She was not ready for life to end.

Through the open windows entered the smell of sticky pine sap trickling down heavy bark, of the springy, nettle forest floor, of black acid earth, even of the weedy perfume of the river, clinging to the wind as it rolled up the hill. We heard the *ssss* of the leaves twisting in the birch, the lush, primal moan of the stirring pine branches. Breezes murmured in our ears, lifted the hairs on my arms as I painted at the window. From that height, we witnessed storms approaching down the river valley, black clouds boiling toward us, we were struck by sudden cool gusts laden with moisture. After the rain, pink or orange sunsets bled across the sky. Powerful smells and sounds stunned our senses, suspended us in the *now*. It gave me life, *life!* It was all so pure, *we* were pure, the earth had become our skin. There were only these scents and sensations, mixed with those of my viscous paints as I pressed my brush to the canvas. Below us, ancient tree roots and lichen-clad boulders shouldered our house aloft, solid on the ridge. In the evenings, the murmur of Beryl's leather slippers sliding over the pine floorboards and the turning of my brittle poetry book pages carried on a dialogue with the trees, the wind. The perfume of the swift, cold river, the whisper of small creatures foraging in deep seas of dry leaves, the silver gloss that the full moon laid over everything in sight.

The land around us was carved like the human body – hills, valleys, ridges, cavities. We would live sheltered within its folds, like children cradled by their mother. The roads were winding, and rolling or steep, they wove sometimes along the river, sometimes between pink granite walls, through woods, past lakes thick with ducks, past crashing waterfalls, stone ruins, cabins with stacks of firewood piled up higher than their roofs, like pioneer dwellings. In the beginning, we drove frequently through this country for pleasure, we found it steadfast, true. Sometimes the coloured leaves sliced the air like shards of stained glass, or great snowflakes braided themselves into ropes, raking our windshield, or the sun shone, the air glittering with diamonds of rain.

But after the dog died, we no longer made these drives. After the dog died, we did not find the landscape inspirational. "Please stop calling her, '*the dog*'," Beryl told me. "Her name was *Precious*. She wasn't an *object*. She was a *sentient creature*." I noticed that Beryl had suddenly aged. To be sure, I am old, but she all of a sudden looked shrunken and fragile. So, it seemed to me that it had been only the dog that had sustained her. She had never needed *me*. When she adopted it ten years before, a puppy, she named it *Precious*. "I thought *I* was your precious," I said, jealous, and she only grunted, "*Huhhh*." In time I told her, "Really, this is a very dumb dog."

And she said, "Maybe that's why I love her. She listens to me. She's sensitive. I value empathy over brains."

When we moved up into the wilderness, when we landed high on that saddle, Beryl told me, "You have come back to your origins, like a homing pigeon. You are right back where you began," she said, knowing full well how angry this would make me, how it would call up unwelcomingly in my mind's eye the house on the mountain where my mother, a powerless and witless woman, had failed in the single most important task she'd been charged with: to shelter her children. "Just because you've read Neruda," said Beryl, "doesn't mean you're superior to your siblings or changed fundamentally from where you started out."

When Precious died, Beryl warned me that she did not want to hear any of my "fake sympathy," my "phoney grief," she called it. It was true. I didn't give a damn about that animal. I was glad it was gone. Because, Beryl would go for a walk in the hills, in the woods with Precious but she would not go with me and I did not even have to be leashed. "I need time to think," was her excuse. "I need *space*." And wasn't it perfectly fine for that dog to follow her everywhere, right on her heels, but when I got up each morning and approached Beryl, needily, like a child, I admit, to ask, "What are we doing today?" I'd see her wince, hear her sigh with resentment?

When I met Beryl, I told her in no uncertain terms that I wouldn't consider having more children. I already had two sons of my own, more than I wanted. Eventually, she paid me back by adopting Precious. "She was my *child*," Beryl said, the day the dog died. She stood in the kitchen, weeping over that creature, over the condition of the doghouse, which, when she'd cleaned it out that day, she'd found it crawling with armies of beetles, spiders and for this she could not forgive herself. But I could not understand, I could not understand. The fact was: I had two children to my credit and she had none. Sixty-five now, and she had nothing. And I may even have said, that doghouse day, "What was that animal useful for, when you come right down to it? She was brainless." And Beryl said, "What did you want from her? Poetry?" I was pleased that there were just the two of us now. Beryl would have no one but me. Of course, she knew that's what I was thinking.

After that, she did sometimes permit me to go with her on her walks. One time, we came upon a great turtle slowly crossing a path, trying to reach a lake, its long yellow nails clawing the powdery earth. "That old turtle," observed Beryl, "that's you."

"What?"

"Every time anything threatening comes along" she said, "feelings for example," she said, "you pull your head and limbs into your hard shell and wait until the danger has passed."

An old turtle!

I told Beryl that was when it had all started, the coughing. Later, much later, that is, I proposed that the dust and the insect droppings and the dog dandruff and microscopic hairs that flew into the air the day Beryl swept out the dog-house, had invaded her lungs, implanted a disease. Beryl suddenly leaving the supper table coughing, out on the deck coughing, coughing. I am sure I remember that. But she said I was getting the order of things mixed up, that my claim was impossible, that I was looking for some way to blame her sudden illness on Precious. If she'd been sick, Beryl pointed out, she wouldn't have been able to pack up everything in the country – *all by herself,* she noted, while I sat out on the deck above the forest, above the river, frozen with self-pity, grieving for the house, for the impending loss of my new-found existential life, for nature itself, at times weeping – she wouldn't have had the stamina to do it, if she'd already been sick, that is. I insisted that the death of Precious, the filthy doghouse triggered her illness, and was the reason she'd suddenly become obsessed with tearing us out of our paradise on the ridge, shifting us into the city because she knew the medical care there, in the hills, was inferior. She said, "No it wasn't. It was months after that, when the coughing began. Months." And I answered, "You were asleep, so how would you know? I heard you. All night long, coughing, coughing." It was all part of the same thing, I said.

The towers of cardboard boxes filling up with crockery, books mounted around us like an invading army. I told her this move was killing me. "Killing *you!*" she cried, bitterly amused. "You haven't lifted a finger!" She said, "There is nobody keeping us here but you." And it was true. When she'd proposed we meet people, ask our neighbours over, find a community up there, I'd said I didn't want to get to know anyone. I was not interested in strangers. People lived in the hills for privacy, I lectured her. I wanted to be solitary, like a pine in the forest.

So, before we knew it, we were looking no longer at the trees, the hills, the river but at a forest of apartment towers, at pavements, artificial lights, smog, not a single thing in sight worth painting. It seemed to happen in an instant, abandoning the woods, landing in the soulless city. Wilderness to wasteland. My heart was broken. Now, here was our fine Danish furniture turned ugly, wedged into tiny rooms, my easels and paints shoved into a dark corner, my inventory packed away in a wire cage filled with dust and fumes in the carpark. Disoriented, we tripped over each other in the apartment hallways, lost our balance, knocked against walls like drunks, paced with restlessness and claustrophobia, gasped for oxygen, sickened with loss. That, at least, was how I felt. Beryl could not feel anything, for already she was wracked with spasms.

There was no arguing about her illness now. We wondered if it might be caused by something in the apartment – asbestos, off-gassing, mould -- or in the environment -- pollution, the air-born filth of the city. Beryl wouldn't let me go along with her to her appointments. And I'm ashamed to say I was just as glad because her breath had changed, soured, turned rotten, sick, and I didn't want to be sealed in a car with her. I called her doctor one time, when she was out. "I will be honest with you. Beryl is not going to get better," he told me. "But will she get worse?" I asked. "Of course," he said.

It took until winter to get an appointment with the respirologist. This time, I insisted on going. We parked in an icy lot, fought our way through a heavy snowfall into the clinic. This doctor said that Beryl had a serious lung disease to be sure. In response to some injury, some invasive substance, her body's repair process had gone into overdrive, so that her air sacks had become so scarred and thickened that they could no longer expand or contract properly. They could not fully fill with air and they could not completely expel it. One version of this disease was the rapidly advancing kind, and yes, she did indeed appear to have this unfortunate strain. "How long before I'm dead?" she asked the doctor flatly. He blinked. "Maybe two years?" he said, "If you're lucky. With medication. A lot of morphine at the end to keep your lungs out of paroxysm. Oxygen all the way along to avoid a stroke or a heart attack." *Dyspnea, hypoxemia.* Breathlessness, low blood oxygen. Dizziness and exhaustion. These were what she could expect.

Back at the apartment, she said, "You were supposed to die first, not me."

I told her, "Maybe I will, I'm eighty-five."

She said, "They don't know for sure what caused it, they say probably exposure to toxins. Such as the fumes from your paints, which I've been inhaling all these years. You have killed me," she said passionately.

And I answered, "You are joking, right?"

She said, "Maybe not."

"What about *my* lungs?" I protested. "I breathed even more of those fumes than you and I have no problem."

And she said, "This is not about *your* lungs, it's about *mine*. For once, for once the subject of conversation is *me*."

Now, she was a prisoner of this unproductive cough, her whole body wracked with spasms. My own body stiffened, ached, watching her, sometimes I felt myself holding my breath until I too felt dizzy. The oxygen tank now perpetually at her side, like a pet, like Precious. A rubber mask hanging around Beryl's neck by a flimsy piece of elastic. Finally, actually more and more frequently, she would have to go and lie down, drained. Her body was now her enemy. As soon as she lay flat, it started up again, the hacking, and I rushed to bring more pillows, prop her up, sat there and held her hand until she fell asleep. Then, I went to my recliner and slept too, as worn out as if I'd run a marathon. It seemed all we did was sleep. It seemed like time stood still. But of course, it was not standing still, it was hurtling us faster and faster toward Beryl's end!

I was fourteen when my father enlisted. My mother waited for his service cheques to arrive and when they didn't, she called up the army payment office, but they said they'd never heard of her. My father had signed up as a single man and there was no way, without his signature, that she could get her hands on his earnings. We were living in a wooden house in the mountains of northern British Columbia. My father had brought us there with some idea of adventure but it had turned out to be folly. Soldiering was more romantic than feeding a wife and six children off that unyielding land. He wanted adventure, travel, freedom. We kept a few chickens and we had a milking cow. My father had been working on the only goat ranch in the district. My mother sent me over there to replace him but the rancher ran me off the property. In the cabin doorway leaned his young wife, who, it turned out, had had something in common with my father: a wandering eye. Balanced on her hip was a baby with my father's unmistakable red hair.

We lived a cash-less life. Once a month, my mother sent me fifteen miles on foot into the nearest town, my father having ridden off on our only horse. At the general store I signed a chit for a sack each of flour and sugar, promising that our bill would be paid soon. I hauled the sacks back in a child's wagon, along the dirt road, up the steep, bumpy foot-path to our house. We survived on eggs, milk, butter, flour and sugar, vegetables from our garden and whatever game I could bring home: rabbits, groundhogs, birds. I enjoyed hunting because it was an escape from my mother, and it taught me how to get along by my own wits.

Sometimes, returning home, I'd pause in the pines above the house, my gamey catch, reeking of blood and fur, heavy in an oil cloth sack thrown over my shoulder, and I'd think: why has this become my life? Toil, hunger, scrounging and begging to feed children who were not even the fruit of my own loins, never having more to hand than you could put in your mouth? One day, the general store owner refused me more credit and slammed the door in my face. My mother had made a liar and a beggar of me. I trudged home empty-handed and humiliated.

That very week, our landlord appeared, demanding our overdue rent. He said, "I been distracted by other things but now I had my limit. I been patient enough." My mother told him we'd no place to go, we wouldn't leave and he couldn't make us. He said, "We'll see about that." The next day, he returned with horse and wagon, bringing with him a pry bar, a hammer and nails, pliers, a stack of lumber. First, he lifted the front door off its hinges and nailed half a dozen boards crosswise over the opening so we couldn't get out to interfere with his attack on the house. He commenced to pry off the windows, one by one, barring them with more two-by-fours.

Inside the house: bedlam. The children screaming, crying, right up to the thirteen-year-old, while the tearing wood of the window frames shrieked and the splinters flew and the glass shattered and sprayed and the mountain wind rushed in. The children ran in circles, they ran from room to room, knocking over chairs, slamming doors behind them, crashing into each other, falling down, tearing at my mother's skirts, bawling into her apron. All the while, my mother was shouting at the landlord, "You can't do this! It's inhuman. Look at us! Have some pity!" But he played deaf. She turned to me. "What's the matter with you? Why don't you do something? Stop him!" she cried. "Get at him as soon as he takes a window off," she told me, but he cut in, "You keep your distance, boy, or I'll put your eyes out with this bar." He had a savage, pock-marked face, a mouth like a hack saw. His neck, dark as leather, glistened with sweat as he hammered away. My mother hurled things at him, a butcher knife, a cast iron pan, boiling water. The littlest children mimicked her, throwing their dolls, their trucks toward him. He climbed a ladder and pulled off the upstairs windows. Now we were both exposed to the elements and prisoners in the wind-swept house.

At the end of the day, after stacking the windows on his flatbed truck, he said, "I'll leave ya one room 't sleep in t'night. I'll give ya that much, outa decency. But I'll be back t'morra t' finish 'er off. That's when the last window comes out. The bloody wind'll clean ya out, alright." He added, "Ya been livin' offa me free fer near a year. I been too good 't ya. How much more did ya think ya was gonna get outa me? Ya'd best start packin."

He left and we were all shaking, the smallest ones still sniffling. It was August and frigid at night in the mountains. My mother said, "I need a few hours to think. In the morning I'll know what to do." We pulled the mattresses off some beds and fitted them side by side on the floor of the sole enclosed room. Finally, we lay down, exhausted from our trauma, the seven of us huddled together under blankets, like refugees. The air grew thick with our breath. The youngest whimpered in their sleep.

I woke before midnight, realizing I'd already made my plan. There beside me lay my hapless siblings, sound asleep, their arms thrown across each other's necks. For the first time, I saw how thin we'd all grown from our meagre diet. I may have loved them. I don't remember.

But I did not love my mother, for she'd become a dead weight around my neck. In the darkness I peered over at her. If she'd ever been pretty, you couldn't tell now. The curl I thought I remembered was gone from her hair. Her cheekbones looked hard as iron, her lips bore scabs and cracks, her neck was ropy and her breasts sagged as she lay there, her mouth open, bubbles forming in its corners. I saw a woman entirely broken, with nothing ahead of her but hardship and bad luck. I had no use for her. I hated her just as much as I hated my father, maybe more, because he'd had not only the sense to escape but the wherewithal, whereas she was weak, passive, trapped. I wanted to be more his son than hers. I would not replace him, I would not pay for his sins or for her mistakes.

My mother had started packing that evening, weeping as she opened our bags. I saw her take a framed photograph of my father down off the bureau and kiss it before putting it in a suitcase. That was the last straw for me. Now, I did not regret the attack on the house because it had pushed me to a decision. That door the landlord had torn off had opened wide an escape for me. I was nearly sixteen now. I believed I was destined for greater things. If I didn't seize the moment, I was doomed.

With just the clothes on my back, I quietly loosened some of the two-by-fours downstairs, squeezed through them and ran hard until I could no longer see the house. A full moon lit my way down the mountainside. Without regret, I threw it all away, the lakes and waterfalls, the Engelmann spruce and red cedar, the yellow columbine and glacier lily and Indian paintbrush, the powerful scent of pine sap, familiar to me as the smell of my own sweat. The shadow of the dark mountains, their crushing weight, fell off my shoulders like a heavy winter coat. I walked forty miles, down through the softening foothills until I reached the highway. Without a penny in my pocket, I hitchhiked south, the sight of the Pacific flashing from time to time on my right, filling me with hope. In three days, I'd reached Vancouver.

Somehow, I knew to get to the docks. There I got a job as a stevedore. The salt smell of the ocean, its luminosity, the moist air and temperate winds, the longer days, the infinite view to the horizon, money in my pocket, all of these thrilled me. A kind body shop owner let me sleep at night in a car in his garage and use the little sink in the employee bathroom to wash up. For six months, this served as my home, until I had enough money tucked away to rent a room in a tenement house. At a local community centre, I enrolled in an art course. I spent the evenings in my room, drawing. Soon, I landed a scholarship to college.

I did not miss my brothers and sisters or wonder where they'd landed. I did not think about my mother. In my heart, a metal door had clanged shut. Years later, one of my brothers recognized me on a city street. He told me that my father had met a woman in France during the war. He married her and never returned to Canada. I did not care. I could not even remember what he looked like.

At the Hospice, the rooms beyond the open doors, up and down the hallways, were silent. The patients were silent. Most of them were women. They had all survived their husbands. So, Beryl was right. I should have died first. Here I was, eighty-five, and she only sixty-five, and the one dying. The average stay there was two weeks. Every other day, nearly, someone died. We did not see them pass by in the hallway, the deceased, covered with a sheet. It was as though they disappeared into thin air, had never existed, and this was even more frightening.

When we arrived at the hospice, when we got there in May, the Siberian iris in the courtyard garden were in tight blooms. We thought Beryl would last just long enough to see them open. But they came and went, followed by lupins, then poppies, then peonies, then phlox, foxglove, anemone. May, June, July. Beryl lasted more weeks than was allowed. It was a place where you were supposed to die. The doctor asked Beryl, "Who let you in here? You are not dying. You're not declining. If you continue to remain stable, I'm going to have to discharge you."

He confronted me in the hallway. "She can't stay here. She's not going downhill. People here die between one and thirty days of arrival. Nobody is here longer."

"But she's already on morphine," I pointed out.

"That could go on a long time. Months. She must go to a nursing home."

"She's afraid of those places. You read in the papers so many terrible stories …"

"She's taking up a precious bed," he cut in.

"I'll pay more. Anything you want. Give me a figure."

"Money has nothing to do with it. We are not a holding place. We are not an alternative to long-term care. We have special skills to help people die. We can't squander them on the living."

The doctor was handsome, slender and fit, fresh out of medical school, young enough that he would not die until the next century. Why would they send such a doctor here? So certain of himself but knowing nothing about life.

"How will you make us leave?" I asked him.

He looked astonished by my question. I could see he didn't understand anything about old people.

"This is an abuse of our services," he said.

"You have made us hate you," I told him.

He blinked. "Mr. Bragg," he said. "Luther – may I call you that?"

"No."

I was shocked and frightened when, one day, Beryl presented to me the signed forms. Even though we had read in the newspapers that it was coming, Assisted Medical Death, that the bill had finally been passed by Parliament. But that was for other people, I had thought, not for us.

"What are you trying to do to me?" I demanded. "Couldn't you hold on longer?" Here she was, sitting up in bed, thinner, to be sure, but carrying on a conversation as though she was perfectly healthy. Yes, able to do that, all there, mentally, engaging with me, giving me emotional support. She wasn't finished, not cognitively. So why would she choose death? She was being selfish. She might have another six months in her, for all we knew, so I could spend every day here, talking about – well, many things. To rob us of those months together was unfair. Why did she want to leave me alone now? I wasn't ready. Two years were not enough. I realized I'd been in denial all this time.

"You're fine at the moment," I told her.

"*At the moment*," she emphasized. "But we both know what's coming."

"Is it that doctor chasing you out of here? Come back to the apartment," I begged her. "I'll hire a nurse. I'll spend every cent I have to keep you comfortable."

"I'm weak," she said. "I've been in bed for four months. Just getting into an ambulance would kill me."

She said, "I don't want to go downhill, to deteriorate so much that I'm unable to sign, no longer permitted to sign. I don't want to become pitiable and helpless. I am already in despair. I have no life, I'm practically a corpse. I'm pressing them for a firm date."

I went out and got into my car, pounded the steering wheel, which only exhausted me. I could never forgive Beryl for choosing to die. How does a person decide to die? It was monstrous. All because of that damned dog. Precious, Precious. That dog had killed her. But this was mad thinking, I knew, sitting there in my car, in the hospice parking lot, surrounded by a dark palisade of Ponderosa Pines. I had no one to call. No one. I couldn't phone my sons. Beryl and they had never got along. She thought them selfish and had told them so. "We are only following our father's example," they retorted. "We are only doing what he did to us, walking out when we were little, his father's son, that is plain to see, with no thought for anyone but himself." So, of course, it would have been useless to turn to them.

We waited for a date for the procedure. The days passed. Beryl seemed happier, at peace, now that she'd made this decision. I sat on the edge of her bed and tried to put my arms around her. But she'd shrunk so small, to the size of a child. It wounded me to touch her. She'd lost fifty pounds, maybe more. She was just melting away before my eyes. It was frightening.

"You're going to have to be nicer to people," she said, "if you aren't to spend all your time alone." Nicer. How was I going to do that? I did not even know what it meant. "I am who I am," I told her. "No, you're not," she answered. Somehow, she had a new authority, lying in that bed. She had turned into a prophet because she no longer had a stake in life, in this earth, she was dwelling on another plane. She had reached the last chapter. She had read the ending that none of the rest of us had read. She had embraced some truth I could not see.

Who? Who was there to be nice to?

"You have the people in the apartment building," she said.

"I don't know any of them."

"You could introduce yourself. Start with that."

"I have nothing in common with them. I have nothing in common with anyone in the whole world."

She said, "You don't see people when they're right in front of your face. You only see things you can paint. How you can turn them into a picture. All your life, you've chosen images over relationships. Your ambitions over real life."

"I know I am not a naturally lovable person."

We were tender. We treasured each other more, but it was too late. We had injured, denounced each other so often in the past, we had squandered our finite time together. *Unsuited*, she'd once said about us. *A bad match.* Something she'd heard, she admitted, from a counsellor. A person who'd never even met me, so how would they know? Now we came together. We could see nothing wrong with each other, almost. We were one being. Moments became important. There were hardly any moments left. She grew more and more gentle with me and this was how I could tell the end was near.

Back at the apartment, I began to go through old photographs, to collect pictures to flash up on a screen at the memorial service. This was killing me! Why did people expect this? Snap shots of Beryl wouldn't bring her back! They would only drive the knife deeper into the heart! The photos fell from my trembling hands. Dizzy with nostalgia and regret, I leaned over my knees, covered my face, rocked, moaned, called softly: *Beryl, Beryl.* My words fell into what seemed a black canyon, the sole answer the echo of my own voice, hot and corrosive, mocking me.

The evening before the procedure, we ran out of things to talk about. Or, out of respect for what was coming, we did not speak. Nothing was important anymore. Nothing was relevant. But I would still be here after it was done, I would be left with the irrelevance! A volunteer came, ludicrously offering Beryl supper. I wanted to shout at her to go away! Beryl let her put the tray before her, then covered it with her napkin after the woman left.

It is one thing to see a person die naturally, to be at their side when they slip away, their body making its own decisions, one organ after another methodically shutting down, like dominos. This, one can accept. But it is quite another to know the exact moment of the exact hour of the exact day on which your wife will die. It is not right. It is not something you can actually comprehend. Execution. I could not stop thinking of it this way. That night, I stayed with Beryl until darkness fell. Finally, I got up and walked toward the hallway with as much dignity as I could muster. I trembled and felt faint. Every fibre of me cried out against what was to take place, but I was a weak old man, powerless to stop it. In the doorway, I turned and looked at Beryl, sitting upright in the bed, so alive, her white hair filled with light, her eyes so intelligent, dazzling. The illness had made her skin thin, transparent, but now it had turned unexpectedly radiant again, her cheeks pink as a girl's. I wanted to say, "You are young. You are the picture of yourself when I met you." Our eyes locked but we'd become strangers. I will never forget that moment. It is not fathomable to me.

The next day was all business. They had bathed Beryl and washed and fixed her hair and put on a fresh gown, though I could not understand the point of this, I thought it absurd. Her eyes were fiery, as though she had a fever or had seen some supernatural vision. The night before, she'd told me, "Don't come early. We've said everything there is to say. If you're upset, it won't help me." I promised her, "I won't be upset." But, out of dread or cowardice, I actually arrived late, or just in time. They were waiting for me in the hallway, pacing impatiently. A heavy, flat-footed social worker who'd been sent to support me, though I had not asked for anyone, and the same young doctor. I said to the social worker, "Could it not be another doctor? A deeper, more compassionate one? More authentic? This one has a conflict of interest. This one always wanted her dead." He heard what I said, I made sure of that. Still, he stood there, self-righteous, entitled, clutching his wrapped instruments. I did not like the idea of him touching Beryl. I thought she would feel the same way, for often we had spoken of him with such bitterness and contempt. But she did not seem to care anymore.

I sat beside the bed and held Beryl's hand, which had grown light as a piece of driftwood. Beryl wouldn't look at me, she stared straight up at the ceiling. I thought she might have changed her mind. I could feel her pulse, her heart racing. "She's frightened," I told them but they didn't listen. The doctor was taking the hypodermic needles out of a bundle concealed in white cloth. I thought there would be only one, but there were six. He laid them out on a small, paper-lined table. Everything was unfolding too quickly and I could not stop it. The social worker asked Beryl if she wanted me to stay. I felt very angry that she would ask such a thing. I felt insulted. As though I wasn't essential here. As though we were no longer part of each other, one spirit! They asked her if she was comfortable. Comfortable! What a ridiculous question!

I felt like a child, trembling with fear and ignorance. When the doctor plunged the first needle into her vein, an involuntary wail flew out of me. "Aahhh!" The social worker seized my arm roughly, hissed. "Don't do that!" But I couldn't help it! I felt like I was dying too! It was horrible, horrible! I had to cover my eyes. I couldn't watch the rest of the needles go in, but within seconds, I felt the life go out of Beryl's hand. Finally, the doctor pressed his fingers to her neck, her wrist, her ankle. "She's gone," he told me. "Are you sure?" I asked, hoping it wasn't true. He said, "We'll leave you alone now."

There was a look on Beryl's face I'd seen before, her feelings all gathered into herself. The part of her she would never let me touch. It had always been there, I now realized. I bent over and pressed my cheek to hers, smelled her freshly shampooed hair, the hospice soap on her skin. I don't know how long I stayed there. I was afraid to go. Not to leave her alone but to be alone myself. What would they do with her now, I wondered? Maybe I'd already been told this. Then, I remembered: they'd asked for the name of the funeral home.

Finally, I got up and crossed the room shakily. The social worker hung in the doorway. I could not get past her. She put her hand on my shoulder and said, "I am so sorry." Sorry! She didn't even know Beryl! She didn't know me! Empty words, hypocrisy. And what right did she have to touch me? I shrugged her off.

The doctor waited a few steps away. His face was smooth now, he no longer looked annoyed at the very sight of me. He'd got what he wanted. He would not have to see me coming here anymore. Perhaps this thought was unfair, perhaps it wasn't. His eyes were expectant. But I would not speak of my feelings, least of all to him. I turned in the other direction, fled blindly down the hall, and pushed at a back door.

I had never been out in this garden before. Black-eyed Susan, red hot poker, Gay Feather. Tables and chairs, a stone Japanese lantern, a buddha in fake bronze. A gracious lawn, wide and green, gently descending. Tears burning my throat, I stumbled down the rolling slope. Through pools of dense shade beneath two-hundred-year-old elms, creaking overhead in the wind, stiff as old men, their thick bark impenetrable as stone. I gazed up and, though more ancient than I, there were their branches, fanned out gloriously against the blue sky. The sight took my breath away. Somehow it gave me hope.

Then: the river. Of course. Why had I not known it was there? And a haphazard path through high grasses, through wildness, thistle, daisies, Virginia Creeper, taking me right to the pungent water's edge, rich with bright green algae, bull rushes, water lilies. A stagnant, splendid home for ducks, geese, frogs. Miraculous light. The utter silence of a sanctum. A rank and rotting smell. Then, a small island where birds rested.

And old turtles.

I could still feel the social worker's hand on my shoulder, hot as coals. No one would ever touch me again, I vowed. I would be like that pine in the forest.

I began to drive up into the hills to paint. Otherwise, there was no point in living. Painting was all I had, all I had left. I turned off the highway and took a dirt two-wheel track, then jounced over a bumpy tractor path into a meadow. I got out and opened the car trunk. There lay Beryl's ashes in a white cardboard box, nestled beside my paints and canvases. I lifted the lid, placed my hand flat on the powdery ash. Then I swung my easel out, wrestled with its legs, set it up where I could look over and see Beryl. I thought about what she must have felt when Precious died. At the time, I'd belittled her grief, dismissed it. *Shame on me.* I left the lid off her ashes. From time to time, the wind caught at them and lifted small clouds into the sky and blew them across the grasses and the milkweed and goldenrod and sunchoke and aster. Once the ashes were all gone, then – then I would have to accept her death.

Those hills to which I ran should rightly have enfolded me, like a mother's arms. Hadn't I had loved them, every contour and rise, every rock and tree? So, surely, they must love me. But, no. I sat very still and I smelled the pungent earth and the dead leaves and the bittersweet perfume of fall, but these did not offer succour. I found the hills an alien host. They would swallow me up, as they would the rot, the decay of autumn.

They judged me, accused me of – what? Of surviving? Surviving who? Beryl? Maybe, maybe not. For, had I not deserted my little brothers and sisters in the mountains of BC, slopes of rock and forest, just like these hills, damning in their silence? Had I not refused to feed and shelter them, though they were young and tender and helpless to fend for themselves? The image of them huddled on the floor beside me, in the hours before I walked out on them, tore at me. "It's alright, what you did. You were just a kid. They knew you had to. They would have done the same. They've forgiven you." This was what Beryl had told me, alive or in a dream -- I did not know which or whether to believe it.

In the beginning, on these expeditions, my painting arm felt so leaden I could scarcely raise my brush to the canvas and when I managed it, my hand shook. I feared I'd been struck by a palsy. It was September, the air crisp. I shivered. Landscape had always been my subject but what I saw now did not speak to me. Day after day, I struggled, came up empty-handed, packed my paints and canvases and my stool back into my car and slunk back to the city, full of self-loathing. But I had to keep returning because I had nothing. Nothing else.

Then one morning after I'd set up my easel, something happened. Without even thinking, I began to paint a house tilting on a mountainside, a wooden shelter, raw and fragile, tall and narrow, haunted. Where there should have been doors and windows, only dark openings, like gaping wounds. A black hole like a wailing mouth. Behind this house, the mountains thundered, a dark army. My hand trembled, my whole body quaked as though resurrected. The house on the slope swayed and twisted, the wind was a snake coiling around and through its openings, but still it stood strong. I recalled my mother's last words to me: "In the morning, I'll know what to do." I needed to believe she had.

Half-Boy

THE PLACE THEY moved to in the country was only half a house. They couldn't afford to live in the whole thing. Behind blank walls lay unheated, unwired spaces, with concrete floors, exposed beams, raw studs, boarded up windows. Once a month, his mother unfurled the house blueprints on the dining room table before his father, who promised her that if such and such a client came through with a retainer or if such and such a deal closed or if such and such a merger was successful or if such and such an arbitration proved profitable, they could go ahead and gradually break through the walls into the ghost rooms. At these meetings, his father sweated and flushed and trembled as though this unfinished business would destroy them all. The set of drawings kept springing back into a roll, as though alive, and this set him cackling madly, as if it were some sort of prophecy. Eventually, there were to be a games room, a library, a movie theatre, a formal living room, a conservatory. The boy's mother had written her Masters' thesis on Art Deco and she could not live without an Art Deco house. Though not an architect, she'd designed it herself. She pointed out to the boy the ten-foot ceilings, curved walls and mouldings, stretches of glass block, iron grillwork. He did not understand how these things could be important.

Now, they'd lived there for four years and nothing had changed. They still inhabited only the few, sparsely furnished rooms. The spectral space haunted the boy. He feared the threat of squatters, imagined he could hear the movements of another more radiant, more authentic family thriving righteously, beyond the barrier walls. He dreamed of this proxy family, imagined its conversations, longed to be adopted. He suffered the contiguous vacuum deeply, deeply. A hollowness within, echoing the unembraced spaces, a schizophrenia his parents had set upon him. Until the orphaned side of the house was recovered, he could never be whole. He was powerless to complete himself, doomed to be unrealized, a half-boy living a half-life in a half-house. What he further feared were isolation, irrelevance. There were no other children hereabouts. The town buses came this way infrequently and his friends' parents refused to drive them out this far and one of them had remarked, "My mother says your house is pretentious."

"It's Art Deco," the boy replied feebly.

The boy's mother had promised him that he would fall in love with the country. But the view from his bedroom window pierced his soul. The sight of the rutted road, the heavy clods of turned earth in the brutal fields, the odious smell of birth in the April air, the vulnerable green shoots struggling suicidally through the horrid soil, the autumn leaves dropping sickly from the treacherous elms, the cold drifts of snow invading the wretched furrows, the desperate farm houses, death in the sinister barns -- all of this filled him with ennui. He told his mother that he hated it out there. She replied that hate was a very strong word, that the only four-letter word they had in this house was *love*. He wanted to shout at her: what about *shit, hell, kill, pain, balls, tits, rape, fire, guts, puke, weep, rage, piss, dick?*

His parents had met unluckily at some university. Michigan? His mother studying art history, his father the law. His father had intended to teach. But, after graduation, the boy's mother bullied the father back here, to her birthplace, outside a town lacking a university. Now, he was with a private firm. The practice of law, he complained, was a rat race. The boy's mother told the boy, "Your father thinks he's an intellectual, he sees himself as cerebral. But now that he has a family, he has to step up to the plate. He needs to haul in the big bucks." Why had his father ever agreed to this? Because he was born and bred on The Rock, the son of a Newfoundland parson, schooled to serve, forgive, absolve others. *Fool!*

Behind the house grew a thin birch wood, the sole buffer against the grandfather, a dark figure dwelling in a gloomy bungalow on the banks of a creek in which the boy's mother had waded and fished and on which she'd skated as a girl. The grandfather had brow beaten her into believing it was her duty to return here to succor them, she being an only child who owed them her very existence. She'd escaped to college and then hived back here like an inmate to a prison. These two acres on which they were trapped had been severed from the grandparents' property and given to the boy's mother on her wedding day to trap her. But the grandfather offered both the boy and the boy's father a cold welcome. He'd never asked for a son-in-law or a grandson. All he wanted was his daughter back. Nevertheless, they were obliged to troop over to the bungalow every Sunday to attend lunch, which dragged on until four in the afternoon, the entire day destroyed. The boy's father called the grandfather *the old bugge*r under his breath and privately said to the boy, "I hope to *god* you never become the grandson he will find useful."

There was a crack between the boy's parents and there was a crack between the occupied and the phantom rooms. There was a crack between the town and the country and between normal people and his parents and between their house and the grandparents' house. There had been one bankruptcy for the boy's parents and that year they'd suffered a great deal of silence in the house and they had not had Christmas or birthday gifts. But then his mother began to work the credit card game. She fanned out a dozen pieces of plastic in her hand like a card shark. She paid one card off using another, somehow dodging the banks, all the while telling the boy, "I am not a materialist, you know. I am not a person who cares about possessions." *Lies!* Then there was a second bankruptcy because his father's billings were not up to scratch, he was not a hustler, not a barracuda, he couldn't bring out the knives. As the need for money mounted, they seldom saw him. He worked late into the evenings and every weekend, trying to rack up the billings, sometimes sleeping on his office couch, becoming a half-father. The boy's mother, in turn, never held a job. She lunched with her friends, belonged to three book clubs, a film club, a lecture club. She believed she'd hit pay dirt when she married the boy's father. She would be a law-yer's wife.

Now it was winter and something more was happening to his parents. He could feel it in the air's wattage, the atmosphere's vibration when they were in the same room together, the floor seeming to tremble as from a tectonic shift. He saw his father begin to unravel. He moved heavily, he perspired and shook and muttered to himself, a five-foot-tall man clown-ish in off-the-rack suits comically baggy in the leg, long in the jacket. His little round head and his flat-combed black hair and his heavy moustache gave him the appearance of a Mexican drug dealer. All the things he'd guaranteed the boy's mother were fiction. It was just a poppycock story to get her off his back. He'd been born in a tiny fishing village on a blasted shore, torn and scoured and fired by a regimen of prayer, self-denial, punishment, guilt and criminal weathers.

It was an existence at one with the treeless, soilless ground of Newfoundland, lived out in a peeling wooden house worried by cold, salty, iniquitous winds.

More and more, the father let slip mutinous comments to the boy.

"Once your mother gets an idea into her head, you can't knock it out."

"Your mother seems to think I'm her beast of burden."

"Your mother wants to mould me in her own likeness. I am not her clay."

"When I met your mother, I didn't know she had a few screws loose."

One day in January, when working at his math after school, the boy saw his father's car swerve unexpectedly into the driveway. His father never came home at this time of day, four o'clock. From his bedroom window, the boy observed his father wrestle, under a heavy snowfall, with suitcases, garbage bags bulging with soft items, shirts, still on their hangers, dancing in the wind, blankets and pillows, all of which he stuffed recklessly into the car. Cold air from the open front door blasted up the stairs to the boy's desk. Finally, his mother's coupe swung into the drive and, recognizing his father's great escape for what it was, she floored it, fish-tailed forward in the deep snow, then slammed on the brakes just in time to collide with his bumper. She got out and began to lecture him calmly, with soft persuasive gestures. But this time his father was not to be sublimated. He belched thick clouds of steam, snorted like a bull, lowered his head and dove for her keys. She whipped them away, sprang aside, suddenly nimble as a cloven-hooved gazelle, pranced round him, trotting through the deep snow towards the house. Murderous, he followed, roaring at her back. Now they gained the circular foyer, with its acoustics to rival a concert hall, their amplified voices sliding like canon round and round the curved walls.

By the time the boy had pulled on his pea jacket and pounded down the stairs, his parents were wrestling like children over the keys. The two of them smelled of winter, hatred and homicide. His mother turned and started to call the boy *Buttermilk* and *Lamb Chop* and other enraging pet names. He snapped that he was heading out to the *rotten* creek with his *blasted* skates. He shot through the kitchen, drove his feet into his boots, tore at the back door and vaulted out into the snow.

The storm had died and already the high brittle notes of a shovel scraping ice rang across the silent afternoon, sending shivers of dread down the boy's spine. Moments later, he hovered unnoticed above the creek. From his shoulder hung the skates. He'd asked for a *skateboard* for Christmas but had instead been given these *ice* skates, in deference to his grandfather's demands. Now, he observed the old man, a friendless, corroded figure in heavy gloves, a mediaeval wool coat, galoshes from another century, with rusty fastenings, a man who begged for life to thwart him so that he'd have something to howl against. Fifty years ago, he'd purchased these ten worthless acres outside town at a time when normal people did not do such a thing unless they were hippies and god knew he was no hippy. Locked now in this shallow creek bed about which he boasted as though it were the mighty St. Lawrence River and not some nameless trickle that ran to nothing half a mile from here. He'd shovelled its ice for his daughter to skate on and he would clear it for his grandson and, by god, the boy would use it every winter day, while showing the proper gratitude.

Finally, the grandfather noticed him. "Lace those skates on now," he ordered, but the boy resisted, for the grandfather would tell him he couldn't skate worth a damn, instruct him to soften his knees, square his shoulders to the ice, stop flailing his arms about like a marionette, cease destroying the surface with his goddamned hockey stops or he would get what was coming to him.

"I think I'll go inside," said the boy, dashing toward the door.

"What?"

"I'm coming down with something. A cold."

The overheated house was fragrant with the smell of butter, brown sugar, cinnamon. His grandmother was making Chelsea buns. "Want to finish the job?" she asked, handing him a knife, and together they glanced furtively out the window at the grandfather, who condemned the boy's interest in baking, predicting that it would turn him into a goddamned fairy. The boy stood close to his grandmother, for she was like a still pond. Only when he was with her did he feel happiness. He loved her thick support hose, her puffy ankles, the radiant warmth of her soft body.

"I think Dad's flown the coop," he confided.

"Oh?" she said lightly.

"Why would he do that?"

She turned toward the kitchen window. "I guess some people don't like to be managed," she mused, and he realized she must have witnessed the entire spectacle through the window, the packing of the car, the skirmish over the keys, his father finally ploughing aside his mother's car, tearing her fender off. He thought he detected a small stirring within her, desire, as she lifted her eyes to the country road, watched it disappear into the distance.

Soon the grandfather burst into the house. "Are you going to get on that ice, young man?" he growled, as though he couldn't remember the boy's name. "I didn't clean that creek for the fun of it."

"He's feeling under the weather," said the grandmother.

"The boy's malingering!"

Recently, the grandmother had taken up volunteer work at a palliative care home two miles away. The grandfather refused to drive her there, saying she had no business leaving him here to fight with the wood stove alone. "Your grandmother suddenly thinks she has to save the world," he'd told the boy sarcastically. "And the peculiar thing is, up to now, she's had nothing at all to do with the world." Which wasn't true, the boy reasoned. She'd been a chambermaid when his grandparents met. Wasn't that the world?

"It's just a few poor women needing someone to talk to," explained the grandmother.

"They're *dying*. What use is *talk*?"

The back door flew open and out of the darkness appeared the boy's mother. He abhorred the sight of her and his revulsion corrupted his face. "Why, Pudding, what's the matter?" she simpered, and she came and stood behind him, smiling, her hands, trembling, resting on his shoulders. He sensed the monstrous lie in them. He wanted to shake them off, they enraged him so. He'd never asked for her murderous love. This interference of hers, this mealy-mouthed control would destroy him.

"Wells seems to have moved into the city for a spell," she told her parents lightly. "It's a temporary thing. Nothing to worry about." Her expression was cheery but to the boy she looked crazed.

"What's the bastard up to?" shouted her father from his tweed chair. "Who will pay for that? He's always been an imbecile with money. He couldn't manage his way through a five-dollar bill. I never trusted that character," he said, as though the father were a figure in a play. "Some people don't care about doing the right thing," he said.

HALF-BOY

"Of course, doing the right thing doesn't always make a person happy," said the grandmother. No one heard her.

"Mark my words! We won't see him again!" predicted the grandfather gleefully.

"Dad," said the boy's mother patiently. "You're not helping."

"He's burned a serious bridge now!" he cried with relish. Then, he snapped his thumb on the TV remote. The national news, which was apparently more important than their own, leapt into the room.

"Can I stay here tonight? Sleep over?" the boy begged his mother.

"Now, Honey, why would you want to do that?"

"A coward's move!" the grandfather roared at their backs as they slipped out the door.

"Why did Dad take so much stuff with him if he's coming back?" the boy asked, following his mother as they picked their way through the snow, between the glimmering birch.

"Your father loves to act out. I'm letting him have his childish drama."

In the moonlight, between the white tree trunks, the boy's shadow shot away, leaping like a renegade over the crisp hillocks of wind-hardened snow. Envious, he watched it cavort. Whatever its knavery, it thrilled him.

Now, his mother wept on the family room couch through the weekends, a box of donuts balanced on her knee. The haunting whisper of tissues pulled from a box drifted through the

77

house, like a dying person's sighs. She wanted his father back, though she called him *a little strutting marionette*. "Mr. Such and Such," she dubbed him, because of his posturing about billings, professional coups. In no time, she packed on thirty pounds. She'd never been at all pretty or feminine. She wore men's trousers, shapeless cardigans in colours the boy could not even name. Puce? Bile? Excrement? Now, he recognized everything about her that was worthy of abandonment, repudiation. He hated her. Yes, it was true. He hated her and hate was a very strong word.

Early in March, he abandoned his skates in town. It was a *fun day* at school and they'd gone to the arena. When the city bus pulled up at four, he set the skates down on a stone wall as though in a trance, and climbed the bus steps. From his seat, he looked down at them, heady with the liquor of revolt. Of course, that evening, his grandfather said that losing the skates was totally irresponsible.

"Totally irresponsible!"

"Anyone can make a mistake," said the grandmother, but she was ignored.

"That was no accident! You've got savings," he ordered the boy, "you'll buy a new pair."

But, at home, the boy shouted at his mother that he wasn't buying any goddamned skates.

"Anger is a very ugly emotion," she told him.

Any *fucking* skates was what he'd wanted to say.

His father demanded access. His mother tried to block it, believing it would force his father home. Finally, the boy told her, "I'm not your pet monkey."

"Monkey?" she said, feigning innocence.

One Saturday morning in April, he went up to his father's apartment, only to find him pacing, his coat on, briefcase in hand. He said he had pressing work at the office.

"Then, what am I doing here if you're going out?" the boy asked.

"This is my weekend to have you, you know that perfectly well. Your mother and I have a legally binding agreement. Just keep busy with your homework."

He considered calling his mother to come and fetch him but then he realized that, of course, she didn't want him either. She had her weeping for company.

He sat at the kitchen table and reluctantly opened his textbooks, one hand fishing in a bag of marshmallows, the only edible thing he could find in the apartment. Once the bag was empty, he, to his own surprise, began to cry. He put his hands over his face and let himself sob for a minute or two, his shoulders shaking, the sugary powder from his fingers streaking his cheeks. Finally, he stopped and wiped his nose on the back of his sleeve.

He'd come to his father's apartment initially expecting a cool bachelor pad. But it was a very shoddy place, a mattress on the bedroom floor, bean bag chairs. "Your mother is trying to drain me dry," his father had told him. "Your mother is a vampire. She wants to suck every drop of blood out of my veins. Yes, if she can't have me, she'd make me a corpse."

The boy went out and down the street to a corner store to buy himself a Coke. On the way back, he detoured through a large park. Presently, he came upon a middle-aged couple shamelessly embracing on a bench, half-screened by a lilac bush. It turned out to be his father, ardently kissing a small-boned woman with olive skin, jet-black hair down to her elbows, large dark eyes, a red mouth. Her clothes were dazzling. A short, tight, lime-green skirt, a bright yellow jacket, a lustrous shawl the colour of the Pacific Ocean. The pretty curves of her bare brown legs shook the boy.

Instantly, he saw that, compared to his mother, this vivid woman was wildly exotic. He thought: Fiji, Polynesia, some paradisiacal resort island. She'd slipped his father's glasses off his face and she held them folded in her child-sized hand. This left the boy's father blind as a mole. By the time the boy had absorbed all this, he was upon them. His father didn't see him, for now his face was buried in the woman's thick hair. He gave out a low, carnal moan, his hand fumbling inside the yellow jacket. The woman's dark eyes caught those of the boy for an instant but of course she didn't know him from a stray dog. His heart pounding with shock, confusion, he made a sharp left, darting into some thorny bushes, which tore at his jacket sleeves, his face. Back at the apartment, he rammed his belongings into his duffle bag and waited an hour for his father's return, pacing and beating the thin walls and shouting profanities.

As soon as his father came in, the boy yelled, "Pressing business my eye! I saw you in the park. With – with that – that slut!"

"Hiroko," said my father calmly, his lips swollen and red with lipstick.

"Kissing in broad daylight. Who do you think you are -- some kind of – of playboy?"

"That's *my* business. Now stop shouting. What's that white stuff on your face? What are those scratches?"

"You said there was no one else! You told Mom there was no other woman."

"There wasn't. Not then. Not back in January."

"You're a liar!" He was shaking and sobbing, a viscous rope of snot swinging from his nose, enraged with himself, for he'd intended to confront his father man to man, not like a blubbering child. "You're a bloody fake!" he sobbed. Here he was, ignored and diminished, a half-boy, an impotent ward of his parents, while his father was cruising about, sowing his seeds like some kind of Casanova.

"Settle down," his father told him. In the close apartment, the woman's perfume hung on him, sweet and powerful as paper whites. The boy longed to kiss a woman so beautiful, to lose his fingers in her dense hair, to absorb her smells and textures. He felt jealousy and injustice, for he feared he'd never land a woman like that, he'd be forced to settle for

PSEUDO

some wooden, style-less, sexless girl, like his own mother. He felt desire, the stirrings of an erection, and this made him wild with dismay. Before he knew it, his hand had hardened into a fist and he'd thrown a terrifically accurate punch at his father's nose. He heard a *snap*, watched his father stagger backward, blood spraying against the wall.

Seizing his bag, the boy thundered along the hall and leapt down the echoing stairwell, two steps at a time. By a stroke of luck, a city bus rolled up just as he burst outside. At the transfer point, with no connection in sight, he walked a mile or so out of town, then stood on the shoulder of the muddy road with his thumb out. A woman with a toddler in the back stopped and he got in. They bumped along into the countryside. He kept his eyes fixed on the horizon. *Oh. Oh.* You could drive and drive out here on this miserable road and come up with nothing, nothing. *Oh.* The woman kept turning to him and smiling brightly, her face curious and nurturing. He did not need this stranger's infernal love. He detested these murderous mothers. Their buckets of sickening concern. You would drown in it.

They drew up before his house. Getting out of the car, he spotted his grandmother standing over on the bungalow porch, a suitcase on either side of her. Troubled, he went over to ask her where she was going. As he came close, he could see that she was a different person from the woman he knew, optimistic, alive.

82

"I'm moving into town," she said, incredulous. "When your father left, it finally dawned on me how simple it was to make a break for it. How obvious. Your grandfather is at his bridge game, so I'm making my exit. I've left him a casserole for dinner."

Did you lace it with arsenic? he wanted to ask. There were subtle changes in her: a greater height, a softening of her jaw, a breath of youthfulness, her cheeks flushed, wonder shining in her eyes. His mind instantly flew back to the previous week. He'd been over at the bungalow following school. There'd been a lengthy phone call for his grandmother. "Are you sure about this? Are you sure she meant *me*?" she kept asking before hanging up and turning to them as though in a dream. The grandfather demanded irritably, "Now, who was that? Who in god's name was that?" He did not like the phone to ring. He did not like people calling her. He was in his putrid corner chair, cheating at the day's crossword puzzle. The creek had melted, the shovels were stored in the shed. Every morning, he went out to the garden, shouted at the buried tulip bulbs to grow.

"I've been left a million dollars," his grandmother answered, dazed. A patient at the hospice, whom she'd companioned for months, had, lacking heirs, bequeathed her life's savings to her. The boy's gaze met his grandmother's and, in her eyes, he read deliverance.

"At last, I've got the means to escape," she told him now, on the porch. "I'm rich. Rich as I ever need to be." She'd rented an apartment on a park, she said. A beautiful place with walls of glass.

His heart broke. "I wish I could go with you."

She smiled. "I was hoping you'd say that. I picked a two-bedroom on purpose. Come with me. You and I can bake our hearts out."

"But I belong to Mom and Dad," he told her. "I'm in their contract."

She touched his cheek. "We'll see what a judge has to say about that. Now, your mother's out. This is your chance. Run and throw a few things together. Hurry. The cab will be here any moment. But I'll wait." He looked at her papery cheeks, at the waterfall effect of her neck, at her chest – a wondrous cliff. She was magnificent. He loved her. Only her. He had to go. If he didn't, he'd perish.

He ran, then, tripping ecstatically over his own feet, his heart exploding. Chunks of mud flew, the birch wood parted, made a path for him. He tore open the back door and there lay the divided house, where for so long he'd been exiled from his true self, split from the boy he wanted to be. Now he would be entire.

Lake of Many Islands

IT WAS THANKSGIVING weekend and they had all come up here to help Clive and Dixie close up the cottage. This lakefront plot was bought when the four children were under six and, with the exception of Hilda, there wasn't a summer yet when they hadn't spent time together here, Miranda and Eve and Chip, with their spouses, and, once in a blue moon, Hilda. This rocky property plummeted vertiginously to a sheer shoreline, as lakes did in this part of eastern Ontario, in the Precambrian Shield. It was set on a high point and right in front was a pine-covered island they used to sail around on the Sunfish. Beyond that, other islands lay like a giant's stepping stones across the water.

Hilda had felt a chill descend on the group when she appeared unexpectedly at the corner of the cottage and looked down the hill to where they were all seated below at the picnic table, eating hot dogs for Saturday lunch. To break the ice, Chip, slightly drunk though it was only noon, sprang up from the picnic table and bounded up the hill with a bear-like roar and swept her up into his meaty arms and whirled her round and round while she threw back her head and laughed, longing to believe they wanted her there. Chip cried, "You surprised the *shit* out of us, Girl!" He had Clive's big head and handsome square face but he was Dixie's son through and through, schooled in her sense of humour, with her always-mischievous expression, her mouth twitching with irony, her blue eyes searching for the next joke. He was the reincarnation of Dixie, had got away with murder all his childhood because her reflection in his face helped her believe she hadn't lost herself.

"You could have told us you were coming," Miranda said with irritation when they all slid over so Hilda could sit down with them.

"Aren't there enough beds?" Hilda answered lightly, taking up a hotdog. "So, what's the problem?" No one asked how she'd got there, no one wanted to know what stranger she'd hitch-hiked with or who in god's name she'd prevailed upon or how, being no doubt penniless, she'd repaid such a favour.

This cottage was fifty years old and at the time it went up it was called a *log cabin*. Back then, it hadn't looked as fake to them as it did now. The timber was factory-milled, not hand-hewn. On the outside, the logs were stripped, sanded, stained red-brown and shellacked, but inside they'd been left their soft blonde colour, and the floor was the same light wood laid down in wide raw planks. The living room had the original colonial furniture from their childhood, its flowered upholstery now faded and threadbare, the oval rag rug full of holes. There was a certain air of defeat here, everything, inside and out, looked like it was going to wrack and ruin. Once you stepped off this great room, things got very dark. A narrow log-lined hallway with just a bare sixty-watt light-bulb hanging down to light the way and off this, two rooms with bead curtains for doors and just enough space to pass between bunk beds, four sleeping spots in each room, with a battered dresser under a small window for clothes. Then, the bathroom, and finally, at the end, the master bedroom.

They ate supper on Saturday night at the maple table in a corner window, where Clive liked to watch the orange descent of the sun. He was a tall, handsome, broad-shoul-dered, impressive man with a square, dignified face and now, at eighty, a quiet authority, though they remembered how he'd bullied them like a general, up here when they were kids. "You leave that screen door open one more time, Buster, and I'll have you court-martialled!" he'd shout, the colour rising in his fair face. "Hang up that wet towel, Private, or I'll slam you in solitary!" "One more smart remark out of you, Soldier, and you'll be peeling potatoes in the kitchen for a week!" "What are you doing having a shower, Trooper, when there's perfectly good water down in the lake?" They knew he was more bark than bite. Still, they'd feared him. He'd been an RCAF pilot during World War II, so handsome the Air Force put his face on their recruitment posters. He was decorated. More crosses and stars than you could hang on one chest. Distinguished Flying Cross. Victoria Cross.

Europe Star. Atlantic Star and a dozen others. After the war, he remained in the Forces. When he retired at a mere fifty, an Air Chief Marshall, promoted for his physical stature, his penetrating eyes, his leadership, his love of his men, Dixie had threatened to shoot him if he didn't stay out from under her feet. He'd felt more wounded by that than by anything he'd experienced in the war.

"I never should have had to stop working after I married," declared Dixie that night at supper, determined as always to be the centre of attention. The dark and freckled skin on her chest twisted down between her great breasts like a vortex. Fat swung from her neck. She had a jolly body, soft rolls around her waist, chubby feet.

"Oh, Mom," groaned Miranda. They all looked over at Clive, who smiled stoically, to assure them that what Dixie said didn't smart.

"I was a star nurse," said Dixie. "I gave that up to marry a bore."

"Well, boring or not, he's a fine man," said Eve, the pretty daughter, second-born. She had sweet dimples, a fine nose, long-lashed eyes. To be sure, Miranda was the bolder looking of the two, with her red hair and freckles and ruddy face and flashing green eyes, backed up by a pushy, big-sister way of talking that commanded attention, but Eve was the one people preferred to look at.

Dixie had been fired at age twenty-three, the day she got pregnant. She had enjoyed the science of nursing, she liked the doctors flirting with her. They appreciated her impish face, the way she made them laugh with her bawdy jokes and her cruel mimicry and her childish pranks, welcome comic relief in a hospital. They all requested she be assigned to their ward, and she was accustomed to such attentions. Growing up, the only girl in a houseful of boys, she'd been spoiled by her father, himself a notorious practical joker. He had put her on a pedestal and she intended to stay there.

She met Clive at an officer's dance. She was petite and pretty in a frothy dress, flashing her calves. She married him because he ranked a Lieutenant, called her *Miss*, was a foot taller than she, was bound to give her good-looking children. Clive was a lot like Dixie's father – firm, authoritarian, worshipful, eager to take care of her. As for Clive, he was taken by her small, explosive figure, her ribald sense of humour, the dirty jokes she'd picked up from her brothers, the way she played hard-to-get. He could see she was a fighter, and he knew about fighting. "I've met a girl," he grinned proudly at his buddies back at the barracks. "She's a handful." After the war, they moved all over. The officers' wives told themselves that they held the real power on the base, but all they were in charge of was picnics, children's birthdays, booze parties. Dixie gained fifty pounds in two years. Since then, she'd been on one fad diet after another, the grapefruit diet, the watermelon diet, the beef diet, but hadn't lost a single ounce.

This family believed in monogamy, father knows best, corporal punishment, capital punishment but not abortion, alcohol but not drugs, mothers at home, voting Conservative, law and order, wage parity but not feminism, marrying White. They did not credit depression or mental illness, immigration or welfare, divorce or fooling around, racial intermarriage, midwives, social assistance, political correctness, female ambition. Women's Lib was a threat to family stability. In this clan, you had to marry someone everyone liked, produce no more and no less than two children, attend church collectively at Christmas and Easter. You could not move out of town. You had to remain within the fortress, powerfully locked together, bound up by the struggle of will between Clive and Dixie.

Hilda had had to escape this cult, this fierce, retributive family, it's primal beliefs. When she was an adolescent, they'd disapproved of her short skirts, her straight-D report cards, her boyfriends, her smoking. There had never been anything pretty about her. Her hair was straight and thin, her teeth crooked and yellow. She was the ugly duckling of the family. No one knew where she got her face. They asked why she didn't look like them. They'd nicknamed her *Albino* because of her pallor, her white lashes, her pink-rimmed eyes.

None of them had ever gone to the coast to visit her because, when she hitch-hiked out there the day she turned sixteen, she'd slept with someone called Mahmood, never set eyes on him again, delivered his child in a tent, (what's wrong with that? she'd asked them. Jesus was born in a manger, wasn't he?), raised this dark-skinned child alone, lived on mother's allowance, drew welfare, always worked under the counter, never held down a fulltime job. She named the son Herod. You are kidding, the family thought. What on *earth*? They were reluctant to call him that. After all, wasn't Herod the king who'd slaughtered the innocents? They were certain she'd chosen the name to provoke them, asked if she could not come up with something better, sent her a list of alternatives. How about Jim, Bob, Dave? They hardly knew this Herod. He'd flown here from BC with her only twice in twenty years, always on money she'd borrowed from friends and apparently never repaid. She owned a lot of money to a lot of people, some of them living clear across the country, some she'd known right here in high school, for heaven's sake. These lenders no longer answered their phones when she called. Herod had disliked this family. He said they were racists, they had a superiority complex. After the second visit, he'd written them a letter saying so. They saw Hilda's hand in it. A slap in their faces. Now Herod had gone missing. Nobody knew if he was alive or dead. You had to point a finger at Hilda for that.

Just as Dixie was slicing the pumpkin pie, Hilda announced she was thinking of moving back to Ontario. Yes, she'd had her fill of island life. She could move in with Clive and Dixie.

She had experience caring for seniors and she thought they could use her help.

"Is this because you're broke?" Miranda, who fancied herself the family gatekeeper, asked, her eyes fiery, her red hair blazing, her freckles popping. She had her mother's Irish temper plus her father's Scottish stubbornness. She had tanned limbs, a ropy neck. She came back early this morning with grey dust half way up her calves after a ten-K run through the labyrinth of tracks in the woods bordering the lake.

"Shouldn't it be up to Mom and Dad to decide on this?" suggested Eve, always the peacemaker.

"Not when it will have repercussions for all of us," Miranda said.

Eve's husband, Wyatt, rolled his eyes. He was suave and handsome, a Sean Connery type, his black hair slick and his big dark eyes quietly observant. He did not find this family's crude jokes funny or laugh at the way they ridiculed weakness and chipped away at the chinks in people's armour. To his face, they'd called him a pretty boy, a wet blanket, a killjoy, a snob, a drip, a suck, a big-shot, a nose-in-the-air. They'd said he was humourless, an outlier, a poor sport, full of himself, a cry-baby. All in jest of course. Sure.

("Don't take them seriously," Eve had often pleaded with him.

"This is a terrible family," he replied.

"Don't give them power over you."

"Let's divorce them.")

"Don't you think you should have the decency to stay out there in case Herod shows up? In case he -- I don't know – he's found in a shallow grave or washes up on a beach?" Miranda asked Hilda.

"Miranda?" said Eve patiently, trying to rein her in with a gentle raise of her eyebrows.

Miranda glanced at her husband, Gil, for support. He reached over and rubbed her back soothingly. He'd been in a near-fatal car crash when he was twenty-two. He'd required a tracheotomy on the spot. He'd had a serrated spleen, broken ribs, a collapsed lung, trauma to his liver, a crushed knee. He should have died. Miranda was his nurse in intensive care. He believed he owed every minute of his life since then to her. Helping him get dressed the day he was discharged, she said, "Let's get married." He was without relatives. She'd brought him into this house. He had fit in better than Hilda. He'd known from the beginning that this family's laws were not to be challenged. He'd spent his life fetching and carrying for Miranda. Hilda had once asked him, "Don't you ever get tired of servitude?"

Now Hilda left the supper table to smoke her cigarette. "How many times is she going to fail that kid?" Miranda asked the others while she was gone.

"I thought you didn't even approve of Herod," Wyatt pointed out.

On the islands off the BC coast, Hilda had milked cows, worked on a garlic farm, in a fish processing plant, on the general store cash register, dog-sat, house-sat, elder-sat, cleaned motel rooms, waitressed, pumped gas, painted houses, sanded and painted boats, cleaned beaches, read tarot cards, read palms, tended goats, kept bees, shorn sheep, picked berries, picked apples, been a carpenter's assistant, a fisherman's helper. A physical survival. She believed that Miranda, Dixie, Chip secretly envied her freedom, her experimental life, her self-realization, her escape. At the same time, she knew they liked to believe those islands were populated by misfits, recluses, petty criminals, gays, tree huggers, potheads, welfare bums, pseudo-artists, weirdos.

"She's come back here to upset the applecart," Miranda told Eve over the supper dishes.

"Why do we have an applecart at all?" said Eve. "That's what Wyatt wants to know."

"Oh! *Wyatt!*" Miranda said dismissively. "If she sends me one more of her so-called poems to read, I'll scream."

"I thought there were some good lines."

"Terrible stuff."

"But what do any of us really know about poetry?" said Eve.

"She broke all the rules, walked out of this town, to become – what? A failed human being."

"I didn't know there was such a thing as a failed human being."

"I'm not sure about you but I could never forgive myself if I'd lost a child."

By three on Sunday, the water pipes had been pulled out of the lake, the beds stripped and laundered, the beer bottles packed into a car trunk, mousetraps set in the kitchen cupboards, the fridge emptied, the electrical cords unplugged, the garbage driven out to the highway, the deck chairs carried up the hill and tarped.

Clive stood down on the houseboat watching the lake. He reached down and felt his scrotum. There it was, the lump he'd discovered in May. He'd been in the shower in the city at the time. He'd got dressed and gone downstairs. The kitchen door stood open. He went outside but he couldn't see Dixie anywhere. He started breakfast, then, through the kitchen window, saw something pale stirring in the deciduous woods behind the house. It was Dixie, wandering stark-naked among the slender white birch. He grabbed his trench coat, hastened out to her, hung it round her shoulders. She looked up at him, confused. "Dixie, it's me. It's Clive," he told her softly. He put his arm across her shoulders and guided her back between the trees and through their gate and up the three fieldstone steps into the house. Later, testing her, he said, "I don't think you knew who I was out there in the woods." And she said, "Of course, I did. Don't be ridiculous."

They were having their ritual drink before dinner in the living room, where the gleaming baby grand stood, her pride and joy. Earlier, she'd poured honey all over its keys and closed the lid. "You weren't wearing anything," he said. "That's a lie," she snapped.

Now, Hilda joined Clive down on the deck.

"Mom's never really respected you," Hilda told him.

"Oh, she has," he answered quietly. "In her own way."

"Well, it's shocking to hear how she talks to you, once a person's been away for a while."

"I don't mind."

She turned and looked up at him. "But, Dad. *Why*?"

At four, Eve came out of the cottage and went in search of Wyatt. She found him sitting way at the top of the hill behind the abandoned shed on a torn web chair thrown back there years ago as trash, his feet buried in last autumn's dead leaves. An open pocket book lay in his lap, but she could tell that he was too preoccupied to read it. He looked like a homeless person. He'd lost weight recently. Eve thought he looked shockingly old.

"What are you doing up here? They'll say you're antisocial," she told him.

"I *am* antisocial."

(*Sulking*, she imagined Dixie saying. *Thinks we're morons*, from Chip.)

"They'll say you don't like them," Eve said.

"Well, I don't. That's no secret. Can't we just get out of here?"

"We only arrived yesterday. We'll leave tomorrow morning."

"We have a cottage of our own not an hour away. What are we doing here?" He looked at her beseechingly, like a child.

It was sheltered, windless and hot back here, pungent with the powdery disintegration of the fallen leaves and the dry autumn earth. They smelled the hot tar under the lifting and crumbling shingles on the sagging shed. The oblique angle of the afternoon sun turned the light hazy and for a moment Eve felt like she was in a dream.

Wyatt had been troubled for a year, well, all his life, actually, but now it was so much worse. There were tensions at work. People had to be laid off. It was his job to pick who should go. He'd become an outsider at the office, was dubbed *the grim reaper*. It was pushing him over the edge. Eve did not want to go with him. Now she said, "You've got to get a perspective on your job. Layoffs are happening everywhere. With this economy, people all over are being terminated. It's not your fault. Why do you feel this guilt? As though you were god and should be able to control it. That's ego, you know. And you're not supposed to care about those people. They're not your friends. You've got friends right here and you turn your back on them."

He levelled a look at her. "Your siblings have never been my friends."

The voices of the others bounced up to them now. Eve wanted to be down there with them.

"Come here," Wyatt pleaded. But she feared that if she touched him, she'd be swallowed up by his darkness.

She turned away, calling over her shoulder, "I'll come back later and see how you are. I'll tell them you're napping."

"Don't lie on my account. I don't care what they think."

Hilda had answered her cell phone on Sunday morning. She knew it was Baxter. He'd been phoning her for days. Why hadn't she answered? he asked her. She told him she was in Ontario. There was a stunned silence at his end. "Why?" he finally asked. She wouldn't say how long she'd be gone. He said he wished she'd told him she was going away.

"Well, I wish you'd told me you'd closed the case," she rejoined.

He'd been the investigating officer when Herod disappeared. He was the only policeman on the island, which had a population of just four hundred, spread over three hamlets and a dozen farms. He was the perfect community cop, friendly and well liked, making it his business to know everybody. More of a social worker than a law enforcement officer, people agreed.

"Instead of me having to read it in the paper," Hilda said.

"The decision came from the mainland office. It wasn't up to me."

"It's not even a year."

"The trail went cold. There were no more clues to go on."

She pictured him pulled over to the side of the road in his cruiser to make this call. She saw the grey ocean, the wet, dark rocks, the flight of white gulls, she smelled the redwoods and felt a wave of longing.

"Isn't it time to close the door?" he said. "I've seen hope tear a person apart."

The day after Herod's disappearance, Baxter had sat for the second time with Hilda at a small wooden kitchen table in the place she was house-sitting for a woman named Everelda. Hilda was surviving on welfare cheques and watching over people's places, feeding their pets while they were away, keeping their gardens. The hard physical labour of her younger days there on the island was over now.

Baxter made careful notes about Herod's disappearance. Hilda didn't understand why he'd returned to talk to her again. They'd been through all these same questions before. He seemed to be double-checking her story. When he stood up to leave, she said, "Am I a suspect?" He smiled kindly, stepped toward her, took her easily in his arms, murmured, "No, you're not a suspect," and kissed her. She knew he cared about the islanders but she didn't know he cared this much.

People on the island had been upset by the case, by the unwelcome publicity, the crowds of reporters. Soon, they were pointing fingers at Hilda, at her lax parenting practices, at the fact that Herod, like her, was a loner and a high school dropout, a nomad. Why, they asked each other, had she never bothered to find a partner, a stand-in father for him? Not to mention that Herod's skin was darker than anyone else's on the island, that he'd grown a bushy black beard, wore some kind of ethnic-looking hat, a fez, it was called. Herod's disappearance was the only nefarious thing that had ever happened here. There was a tacit competition in this archipelago for the most crime-free island. Hilda had gone and ruined their record. She'd naively thought that communities such as this pulled together in times of crisis, but it looked like she was wrong. She saw its true character emerge. One scratch and out it came. Jealousies, grudges, blame, judgements, small-mindedness bubbling just under the surface.

Baxter was married to her friend, Regis, who ran the island's daycare. She was a hardnosed business woman, a busybody, and her bullying nature had garnered Baxter a good deal of sympathy in the community. Three months after Herod vanished, Regis told Hilda, "Herod was dealing drugs."

"That's not true," Hilda replied.

"Working for some drug kingpin in Vancouver, no doubt," said Regis.

"You don't know that." Hilda was over at the daycare at the time, mopping the floors, cleaning the toilets. Regis had asked her this favour when her custodian came down sick, even though she knew Hilda no longer did this kind of labour. Regis said, "We don't need shiftless people like him contaminating our island. We've all come here for a clean life."

Hilda had been a safe haven for many men, like a harbour reached after a long swim to shore. She'd absorbed their weariness, their fears, their doubts, their frailties, asked for no explanations or promises. She'd worked on the whale-watching boats, on the deep-sea fishing boats, served drinks and snacks to the customers, collected their tickets. She'd made the acquaintance of many men while doing this, tourists, islanders, boat operators. Some had slept with her the day they got engaged to another woman. Some the night before their wedding. She'd become an alternative to the alternative life here.

"I did my best to find Herod," Baxter told her on the phone, his voice breaking.

"I know you did."

"Sometimes you just hit a wall."

She paused. "Alright."

He cleared his throat, collecting himself. "Don't you have unfinished business out here?" he said. "There could be some kind of memorial for Herod. Even if it was just you and me attending, you'd have closure. You could read out one of your poems."

She wavered. How could she return? She knew she was not welcome there. If she carried on with the affair and was found out, she'd be run off the island. Of course, there were other islands to which she could flee, but gossip travelled faster out there than any boat could take her to one of them. Baxter seemed to read her mind.

"I have no trouble leaving these islands for you. My kids are launched. There's nothing holding me here. We could go to the mainland, up the coast or into the interior, wherever you want. There are plenty of police forces looking for officers. You're a west-coaster now. Your family never loved you. You told me that. You're a persona non-grata there. You don't need them. You have me." He was the first man who'd ever proposed such a thing to her.

After all the work was done, Chip had decided to take the Sunfish out for one last sail. Clive, observing from the boathouse as Chip unfurled the sail, called down, "You're in no shape to go out on those whitecaps," but Dixie snapped at him, "Butt out, know-it-all." Chip had five beers under his belt. ("If Chip wants a beer, he can *have* a beer!" Dixie had declared.)

Chip had ignored his chest pains for a year, but just last week, Kitty had made him go to a doctor. That very Friday, the day before they came up here, a cardiologist had told him that he had so many blockages in his heart that there was nothing they could do for him. Surgery would kill him. "Quit drinking. Stop eating sugar and starch. That might buy you a year," he'd said.

Walking out of the hospital, Chip told Kitty, "I'm not worried. These doctors exaggerate, just to scare you. I'm fit as a fiddle."

"Well, you look like shit," Kitty said. She was a foot shorter than he, she had a tiny doll's body and face. They'd been high school sweethearts. He'd married her because her petite figure reminded him of the young Dixie.

In the Sunfish, she told him, "I swear to god if you don't stop drinking, like the doctor said, I'll leave you." Of course, they both knew this was an empty threat, that he was not leave-able, for she was quiet, shy, compliant, had willingly stood in the wings of his life, a member of his audience, the lucky woman he picked, he the shining star of this close, destructive family, his mother's favoured child and, like Dixie, a showboat. Kitty had seen the way the family mood soared when he swaggered into the room, how they always counted on him to crack a joke or perform a pantomime, to act out their contempt for fear, weakness, doubt, unhappiness. And Kitty had always known she was an outsider, that no one could climb over the walls of this family.

"I'm going to stop. I'm going to get on the wagon," he assured her in the boat.

"Well, you seem to be doing the exact opposite."

"I just decided to tie one on this weekend, for old time's sake. Monday, I'll be dry."

Then he confessed suddenly, "I'm afraid I won't be myself anymore if I don't drink."

"Maybe you've *never* been yourself."

"I'm afraid I won't be funny any longer."

Chip had hold of the tiller. Kitty sat starboard, ducking again and again as they tacked and the boom swung from side to side. She looked across the water and saw Clive's solid figure watching them from the boathouse. Finally, they slid behind the island, and Clive disappeared from sight. This sent a strange chill over Kitty and she wanted to tell Chip, "It's too windy. Let's turn around. I don't like this speed," though she knew she was powerless against his will, and always had been. Seeming to read her mind, Chip cried, "Smile, Honey! Life is good!"

At that moment, his sunglasses flew off his face and sank into the water, and then Kitty saw a sudden look in his exposed eyes of fear and reckoning. After that, everything seemed both to slow down and to speed up. Chip's movements became leaden and he turned and looked at her, his expression deep with some final knowledge. His face froze and his body went rigid. Kitty watched him shrink into himself, as though he'd been punched in the chest. Then, he fell forward and she knew he was dead. Still, she leapt at him, the boat rocking dangerously, water sucking the hull and slopping over the side. She seized him by the shoulders but of course he was too heavy to budge, and anyway, she knew a resuscitation attempt would be a waste of time.

The boat slowed, it drifted, turned and rocked playfully, the tiller bobbing, the waves lapping at its sides, the sail empty and luffing in the wind with a smart, snapping beat. Overhead, gulls circled silently, searching for carrion. Kitty saw their white wings flash in the sun, their soft grey bellies, their yellow beaks as they peered down at her. She pressed her cheek to Chip's back, which was still warm from the sun. The boat had turned so many times that she didn't know which direction was which. She didn't know how to sail. And they'd come out here unprotected. Clive had called down to Chip, "Don't go out there without life vests. You know the rules." And Chip had waved and shouted back, "Ok, Buster!" with a wide grin, but he hadn't let Kitty return to the boathouse to get them, murmuring, "Don't pay any attention to the old goat. Let's get going. We don't have time for that."

In high rubber boots, Hilda waded into the cold, shallow water to where the motorboat bobbed on the waves. She swung it to the boathouse door, where Gil was waiting to grasp the rope from her and pull it in and tie it to a hook. Hilda got out of the water and joined him. Together, they stored the paddles, the gasoline cans, the seat cushions, the boarding ladder, the inflatable dinghy, the fishing rods. They coiled the ropes and hung the fenders in place. When they'd nearly finished all this, Gil said to Hilda, "I have fourth-stage cancer."

She stopped and turned to him. "What?"

"Pancreatic. I'll be dead before the new year. I can't tell Miranda. It won't fit into her plans. She's already bought my Christmas present, for Chris'sake."

"Jesus, Gil!" Hilda exclaimed, and that was when he moved solemnly toward her, took her by the shoulders, stepped her into the boat. She went willingly. He guided her down onto the carpeted hull. This motorboat, in which Clive had crossed the lake nearly every summer weekend to the little store that sold bread and peanut butter and beer, cornflakes, hot dogs, milk, all the things they'd forgotten to bring out from the city. Dixie would shout after Clive, "See if you can buy yourself a good mood, while you're over there!" Sometimes this was after her rum and coke. "Your father is a mope. Your father is too silent. Your father is so serious it's *killing* me." And someone would say, "Mom, you can't hold your liquor." She'd turn and moon Clive from the boathouse. He'd just laugh, scandalized, adoring.

Now, outside the boathouse, the lake sparkled with sunlight, the white caps lapped steadily. Inside, the smell of gasoline, of the fishy lake water, the damp life vests hanging on a row of wooden dowels. A motorboat roared by, setting their own rocking, so that Gil and Hilda clung to each other, buoyant, beyond the pull of gravity, beyond the power of reason, in a mystical space. Hilda was familiar with men like Gil. What was she to him? Happenstance, chaos, self-discovery. Overhead, they heard Clive's footsteps scrape across the boathouse roof.

Eve spotted Wyatt at the top of the hill, sitting behind the wheel of their car. With the glare on the windshield, the reflections of the sky and the trees, she could just make out his figure, but she saw that he was sleeping, his head tilted back against the seat. She felt a swell of hot anger. She climbed the slope, closing the distance quickly, and tore the driver's door open. The intense heat inside rolled over her, for the car was parked in full sun, all the windows closed. "Jesus! Could you not get up off your ass and lift a finger to help?" The sentence was out before she smelled the gas. She fell back, coughing. *Oh, god. Oh, god.* She stood there trembling, her breath coming in shudders.

His face was turned toward her, as though he'd anticipated her arrival, as though to say goodbye. Knowing it would be she who would discover him. Only she would care where he was. And later, she did wonder if this pose was a reproof, a statement of how she'd failed him. His eyes were wide open, as though astonished, and in them she saw everything she knew about him and everything she had never known. At the same time, she noticed his face had softened, it was more relaxed than she'd seen it in a very long time, even in sleep. Heat poured off the car hood. She smelled the rubber of the hot tires.

At one point that afternoon, the sun was so intense, a white-hot hole burning in the deep blue sky, the air so still and warm and flowery, that for a moment, they all paused and looked around, thinking they'd made a mistake, that it was still summer, not mid-October, and they had a simultaneous moment of confusion and doubt and hope. This collective feeling happened just at the moment before Chip died, before Wyatt turned the key in the ignition, before Gil and Hilda stepped into the boat, when Miranda was saying to Eve in one of the dark bedrooms, "Let's not kid ourselves. Choices. The choices we make lead us to where we are in life, not life itself. Life is an abstract idea. Life is just a medium, a conduit. It has no energy, no power over us. We create our own existence," and Dixie, in the living room, turned to Clive and said, "Where's Chip? Chip will make me laugh."

One ambulance came at 5:45, another at 6:30, after they'd finally brought the motorboat out again and gone looking for Kitty and Chip, still drifting behind the islands as the sun sank behind the pines. After the first ambulance departed, Eve told Miranda, "Wyatt wanted to leave as soon as we got here. He begged me to go. Maybe if I'd agreed, he'd still be alive."

"So, you're saying it's us who killed him? This family killed him?"

"Maybe."

On Sunday night, in the bedroom Hilda shared with Gil and Miranda, darkness hung thick as matter, it weighed so heavily on Hilda that she could not seem to fill her lungs with air. Then Gil reached his long arm across the narrow space, between the upper bunks, where the two of them lay and touched her shoulder, rested his fingers lightly there. She did not know if by this he meant love or gratitude or apology or fear or goodbye. She had received the sperm of this dying man. She had seen a lot of death on the west coast island, she had partaken in it. The slaughtering of lambs, the wrenching end of wildlife in iron traps. She had accompanied duck hunters, fox hunters, deer hunters on their expeditions. She had watched fishermen club a shimmering salmon to death with a mallet. She had done it herself, when it was what she was being paid for. She was not afraid of endings.

She heard Dixie creep down the hallway, feeling her way in the dark, sliding her dry hands over the log walls, her slippers whispering on the rough floor boards. In the kitchen, Dixie opened the big chest freezer and began the habit she'd developed as an insomniac, moving the frozen packages around like game pieces, muttering to herself. They knocked against each other, loud and dense as rocks. Then Clive padded by, in the hall, his steps longer and more urgent. He joined her there before the freezer, his arm across her shoulders. She called him, *Fuck-face. Fart-face.* "Now, now, Dixie," he said kindly. "Now, now."

Pseudo

WHEN HENK CYCLES home in the evenings, all the old men on the street rush forth, stumbling on thick legs, their curved bellies in dark wool coats pressed against the white iron fences that enclose their tiny front yards. Silver hair curls out like bright lichen from beneath their flat old-world caps. They wait all afternoon for his appearance, even now in late-fall, when the street lamps have blinked on and their breath is frozen in the air. They came here to Canada in their senior years, on the heels of their new-world children. At night, green or pink spotlights flood their tin-roofed porches, which are strung with Christmas bulbs year-round. In their yards, upended bathtubs shelter statues of the Virgin Mary and parades of Gnomes march between the tomato vines and the cabbage plants. Henk is like a son to these old men. They've taught him words of Portuguese, Greek, Ukrainian. "Henk! Henk!" they call imploringly as he cycles by, their thick, scarred hands clutching the air, their faces washed with love.

From her studio, Chandler observes this. She sees Henk return their waves, his fine profile, his optimism, his kind smile. When he enters the house, she asks him, "Why do they speak to you and not to me?" and he replies with a sage wag of his head, "Because we are of the *earth*." These men have brought Henk their homemade wine, they've exchanged seeds and cuttings with him, news about coming rain or frost, because Henk tore up the Indian grass and bull thistle on the three-foot-wide strip of land between the house and the street. He attacked the ground with a hoe, ardent as a lover, flung the soil about passionately, as though he owned an acreage and not a few square feet of urban clay. He will pull up a carrot, beaming as though it were made of gold, brush it carelessly on his shirt, eat it on the spot, dirt and all.

"Do they ever inquire about me, those old men?" Chandler asks Henk.

"No."

"What I do? Why I'm sitting at this window?"

"To them, your work wouldn't make sense. It wouldn't be worth talking about."

Henk runs a small make-believe farm for the school board. Troubled and disadvantaged children whose parents are alcoholics, drug pushers, murderers are bussed out there. Teaching middle-class kids has never interested Henk. He's looking for the ones who have nothing to hold onto. He hands them a shovel and tells them that if they make it their best friend, it will lead them back to themselves. Physical labour, he assures them, connection with the energy of the earth, bestows life. To these children, he is *Farmer Henk*. He uses the lessons of germination and growth to fill them with intention and wonder.

They have a log cabin out there with a wood stove, a cast iron water pump. As well as a couple of sheep, a few pigs, chickens, rabbits, goats. They grow and harvest hay and corn, spread their own manure, cultivate market vegetables, make soft cheese, tap the maple trees, bake corn bread, collect the eggs, whip up omelettes, produce soap, candles and wool. This labour keeps Henk lean but muscular, tanned, veins popping on his arms, the hairs there golden, his face burnished. Chandler calls him a *pseudo farmer* because there is no risk attached to his job, he is not truly at the mercy of nature's whim. If the crops fail or the animals get sick and die, he still brings home a paycheck from the board. He's been written up in pedagogical magazines. For these articles, he poses as a country bumpkin in suspenders, a piece of straw hanging from his teeth, his plaid shirt deliberately buttoned wrong, one pant leg in his boot, the other out. He uses words like *varmint, tater, uppity*. He has made himself into this folk figure.

He's lived in Toronto for twenty years, but he is not, as he says, *of the city*. He's never owned a car. In winter, he mounts his bike, dressed in snow boots, heavy gloves, a fur-lined aviator hat, layered up bulky as a grizzly bear. Rather than choosing a sheltered route to the farm, he cycles ten miles along the exposed shore, lashed by sleet and gales. He says he likes to have the Great Lakes wind slicing away at him, just to show it who's boss.

Henk's parents were Dutch immigrants, their English rough as bark. The family of twelve slept three to a bed. They drank directly from a pitcher of milk, passing it round amongst themselves at the supper table. They tore apart the roast chicken with their bare hands, ate it with their fingers, shared one family towel, bathed once a week from the same rapidly cooling water in a deep tin tub in the frigid kitchen. It was a lucky life, he claims, driven by imagination. He's never been better off than that. There is nothing to rival poverty, he says, when you're not aware you're poor.

One December, his parents piled all ten kids into the pickup truck and headed to Toronto in a holiday mood, to see the Christmas parade, the coloured lights. But on the way, they lost their nerve. They began to recall the stories they'd heard about mazes of one-way streets, gridlock, moving staircases, ticketing, and they turned around and fled back to the farm. "Did you cry?" Chandler asked. "Naw!" Henk dismissed the idea with a wave of his hand. "We sang all the way home." She did not know if she should believe this.

Once, Henk rented a car and drove Chandler past the homestead. The raw, unpainted house, leaning classically in the wind, was boarded up. Long ago, people had stopped trying to make a living off starved land like this. To Chandler, it seemed a harsh and primal place. Henk said, "Of course, it looked better back then."

"How much better?"

He laughed ruefully. "Actually, not that much. But I wouldn't have had it different for all the world." Chandler felt envious of what he seemed to have experienced there that had made him so unshakeably happy, so that he could now skip across life as though it were a playground. She turned and observed his profile, saw his lively eyes, a smile twitching at the corners of his mouth, his square chin, flinty as the rocks pushing through the infertile soil.

They live in a twelve-foot-wide house at the end of a cheap forties row. Most of the people on this street cannot speak English and many are on some form of social assistance. It is why Henk bought this place. He is at home with hand-to-mouth. The struggle to survive is what he knows. Their front door opens off the street, right into the living room, then comes a narrow passage where they eat and at the back a dark kitchen with fake panelling, open shelves, peeling linoleum, an antique fridge that trembles and groans like an old man. A stair goes up, with a crude banister. Henk knows Chandler is embarrassed to invite people here and she feels ashamed of her shame. When she moved in with him, he gave his study, upstairs at the front, with the bay window, to her for a studio, because it was the sunniest room and he said he wanted her to be happy. Now, ten years later, less entertained by her mercurial nature, he tries to tell her that sunshine originates inside a person, not outside.

She complains about the Korean neighbours' cooking smells in the adjacent unit, their family fights penetrating the paper-thin walls, their teenagers loitering outside, smoking hard against the living room window, beyond which glimmer the cold curbs and dusty gutters and simple wooden houses all stuck together on this junky, treeless street. Winter is coming and once again cold drafts sweep through the warped aluminum window frames of their townhouse and off the end wall of raw brick, never insulated because Henk likes its rustic appeal. Chandler's breath freezes in the air, she must wear gloves in her studio, a down vest.

When she steps outside to fetch the mail, she looks north to Bloor Street. She listens to the constant flow of traffic, smells the emissions, sees the clusters of homeless under the hard blue lights and her head spins because this is a long way from the forests and ravines and the quiet country-like winding roads of the neighbourhood of her youth, lying only a few miles from here.

Under her window idles a parade of trucks, waiting to pull up to a warehouse on the corner, a distribution centre for fruit and vegetables. Chandler chokes on the trucks' poisonous emissions. Henk tells her to toughen up, to get real. She had too easy a childhood, he says, over there in Rosedale with the pool, the teak furniture, the grand piano, the private schools and tennis lessons and ski trips and European vacations and sojourns in the Philippines, where her father was posted and they had six servants. "You've got to throw that away," he says. "The past will kill you if you let it."

Chandler can't sell her work. All her images are drawn from a file of nude photos of herself. "Aren't these a bit self-referential?" Henk has asked her. "Is it possible that people don't want pictures of you in the buff?" She lectures him that the nudity is irrelevant, that her paintings are actually about colour, texture, light. He shrugs. "They look like naked women to me." He likes to play the philistine. You can tell he thinks art frivolous, bourgeois, wasteful. He does not see it as vital to existence, essential, say, as carbohydrates, soil, sunsets, sleep. She looks at his contented, peaceful face and thinks that he has it easy, compared to her. It is not so hard to be a fake farmer. "Why don't you go up to Bloor Street and paint the addicts and the drunks who hang out there?" he asks her. "The man on the street might surprise you. The man on the street might turn out to be the most interesting subject around." He can say these murderous things and then in bed make such tender, such wholesale love to her, implying that he is capable of all forgiveness, all understanding.

Early December and her sister, Fontaine, drops by on the way home from work. Fontaine does not even glance at the paintings Chandler has laid out on the dining room table, hoping she'll buy one. When they were teenagers, Fontaine cautioned Chandler not to go to art school. "Art is the last thing you need. Art will only make you crazier than you already are," she said. Fontaine is a solid, practical girl, a problem solver. She runs a women's shelter up on Bloor. She has a husband and two children who adore her. In motherhood, she has become more beautiful than Chandler ever remembered her. Unfair. Her mahogany hair, pulled up in a bouncy, youthful ponytail, shines, her skin is smooth as ivory, her white teeth dazzling. She and Chandler sit drinking tea. Henk lounges nearby on the sagging couch, watching television. Fontaine says to Chandler, "If you can't sell your work, wouldn't it be logical to do something more practical with your life?" Chandler sees a look of commiseration pass between her sister and Henk.

"If you hadn't wasted all those years running off to Ecuador again and again," Fontaine reminds her. In Ecuador, Chandler slept with shrimp farmers, with the husbands of friends, with fishermen, con men, with a long-haired motorcycle bum who lived in a sort of cave. A poor little rich girl, says Fontaine, seeking squalor, looking to escape what many people in this world would have given their eye teeth to be handed – a middle-class life. Chandler never paid rent down there in South America, people took her in, like a refugee. In exchange, she painted portraits of their children, or murals on their walls or fences or floors, weeded their gardens, worked on the shrimp farm, in motels, on a cruise ship once, sold her sketches sitting on the sidewalks of Quito, pretending to be homeless and poor and not a successful banker's daughter who could fly home to Canada any time she got hungry.

After Fontaine leaves, Chandler says to Henk, "You seem happy when she's here."

"Don't you want me to get along with your family?"

"Not *that* well."

"She makes me believe something sane could come out of your home."

At three in the morning, Chandler, often unable to sleep, will sit up and shake Henk's shoulder. "Wake up! You have to talk to me! I'm failing at my work. I don't know what to do!" she'll cry. Then he'll press her back down on her pillow and stroke her hair, murmuring, *There, there. There, there.* It's what he does with the disturbed children when they flip out. *Farmer Henk.*

Chandler does not understand how she came to this place, though she lived every moment and made every decision that brought her here. What led to what led to what. She had never envisaged herself car-less, living in an icebox, inhaling diesel fumes all day, wrestling in the kitchen with root vegetables, like a peasant woman, foods Henk favours because they grow right in the earth, or fast upon it. Beets, radishes, carrots, turnip, parsnip, yucca. Her shoulders, her wrists ache from peeling and carving these dense, soapy, uncooperative, yokel foods. The house fills with their offensive smells.

It's the twenty-third of December and Henk is embarking on a two-week cycling trip. The past few summers, he's taken long bike pilgrimages to visit friends in Chicago, Edmonton, Boston. He sleeps in open fields, bathes in creeks, survives on wild berries, mushrooms, *grubs*, for all Chandler knows, returning gaunt, bronzed, bearded, savage-looking. Chandler would have liked to accompany him but she knows she couldn't keep up with him on a bike, let alone endure the primal life. "You've never done this at Christmas before," she tells him resentfully. "Christmas is supposed to be a time of celebration."

"All of life is to be celebrated," he replies in his cheerful, infuriating way, intransigent as a Buddhist monk. "All of life is a special occasion." He knows such statements enrage her.

All morning, she paces restlessly along the narrow, dark hallway between her studio and the bedroom, where Henk bends over, shoving things into a great backpack. How much stuff he is assembling for this trip, she can't believe.

"You could freeze out there," she frets. "How will you keep clean?"

"I'll wash myself with snow."

"What will you survive on? Everything out there is *dead*."

"I'll eat bark. I'll ice fish. I'll snare myself a white rabbit." And he's just the man to do it. As the eldest boy, he trapped pheasant, groundhog, wild turkey, fox, when, if he was unsuccessful, the family might go hungry. He is clever with traps, he knows the habits of wild creatures. He explains to her now, patient, soft-voiced, "I'm fifty, Chan. Life is short. I don't want to miss out on anything. I have to seize the day." Recently, he's been playing basketball in the evenings with a bunch of men, down at the local school, he's spent weekends at the library doing research. "On what?" Chandler has asked him, but he just smiles and shakes his head, as though, if he told her, she wouldn't understand. "Chandler, Chandler," he says quietly, pityingly. He's also learning Cambodian.

"What for?" Chandler asked.

"Just to exercise my brain."

Now, on the twenty-third day of December, while Henk is organizing his things, a large van pulls up beneath Chandler's studio window. "Another goddamned truck!" she cries, outraged. "Right before Christmas!" She threatens to go down there and blast the driver. Henk tells her to leave him alone. The poor bastard spends his life in a truck, he says. And no one wants to feel unwelcome around Christmas. The fumes are part of the beauty, the texture of the neighbourhood, he reminds her.

"Beauty!" Chandler spits out. Down and outside, she goes, coatless, a pair of thick socks and sandals on her feet. She reaches up and raps on the driver's window. He lowers it, spilling warm air down on her. She asks him to park elsewhere and to turn off his engine, to stop polluting the environment.

"I'm sorry, Ma'am," he says. He has a quiet, fatalistic face, fine rimless glasses, smooth cheeks, eyes pale as the winter sky. "This is the spot zoned for idling. I'm legal. See the sign?

I got to listen to my walkie-talkie telling me when to pull up to the dock. I got to be ready soon as dispatch calls. I'm not ready, I lose my place and I get hell. And these here engines, once you turn 'em off, they don't start up again too good. I got to keep it running. Thing is, you live in the city, Ma'am, you got to expect noise. You got to live with emissions. You want peace and quiet and clean air, you hafta' move to the country."

She sees the burden in his eyes, the powerlessness, but she doesn't care. She threatens to complain, to report him. When she turns back to the house, he scrambles down from the cab and calls after her, "Ma'am? Please. I'm sorry. Honest. But I'm just doing my job, see? You complain – these companies, they're always lookin' for a way t' get rid of drivers, t' shaft a guy. You call someone, you complain, I get fired. I need this job. I'm asking you."

When Chandler goes inside, Henk is leaning over the banister, looking down at her.

"Well, I can't believe you actually did that," he says with disgust.

"I can't believe you're walking out at Christmas."

"After I explained to you."

"I'm tired of your sociology lessons."

"What did you say to him?"

"I just politely asked."

"Oh, sure. And how did he react to that?"

"He said I was perfectly right."

"Like fun he did."

Half an hour later, she is in her studio when Henk passes by, carrying his backpack. He pauses at her door, murmurs something.

"What did you say?"

"Nothing."

She thinks he said *pseudo.* That she is a pseudo artist. She never completes anything, he has lately pointed out. All around her are unfinished drawings and paintings. He has called her, *a rolling stone*, incapable of sticking to anything, lacking conviction and follow-through, a spoiled person. She pursues him downstairs to the back door, stands there in the kitchen while he pulls on his heavy boots, his fur hat, gloves.

"I'm going to call you every night while you're gone," she warns him.

"Fine, fine," he shakes his head tiredly.

"Will you answer?"

"Well, why wouldn't I?"

"I don't want you to go away mad."

"I'm not mad."

"I have a bad feeling."

"Too much emotion, Chan," he says, detached. "Too much emotion."

She throws her arms around him and holds on. He stands there, trapped and wooden.

"Master of your own ship, Chandler," he says, not for the first time. "You've got to be master of your own ship."

He opens the door and steps outside, wheels his bike out of the shed. The gears and spokes are so rusty that Chandler says, "Lucky if that piece of junk makes it to the end of the street."

Henk pats the torn saddle fondly. "Good old Blackie."

On the thirty-first of December, Henk answers his phone for the first time since he left.

"What is going on?" Chandler demands wildly, looking out the kitchen window at a purple sky. "I've called you every single day, like I said I would. You haven't picked up once. I've been worried sick. I thought you were dead. I almost notified the police."

"I had no cell reception," he says. She hears the lie in his voice. For a moment, she is paralyzed. She pictures his rugged, windburned face, his big reddened ears, his lively blue eyes.

"You could have called me from some town hall. I expected you home yesterday or at the latest early today. It's goddamned New Year's Eve, you know."

"Calm down," he says.

She's got a lamb roasting in the oven, sweet potatoes, a pumpkin pie cooling on the counter, she tells him. "This line is terrible. You're breaking up. How much longer? We're in for a serious storm. You need to get home pronto. How far away are you?"

"A thousand miles," he says. His voice crackles, swells, wavers, fades.

"What?"

"Two thousand miles away, actually," he shouts across the line. "I'm going to level with you, Chan. I haven't been on my bike. I got on a plane on Boxing Day. I'm up North. I'm with a woman I met eighteen months ago. Someone I love." Chandler feels a tremor, thinks it's the ancient furnace shaking the floor, but, no, it's her trembling legs.

"What are you talking about!" she shouts.

Fontaine appears at Chandler's door the next afternoon. "Are you OK?" she asks, looking guilty. So. She knew.

"It's not my fault he left," Fontaine defends herself. "It's not my fault he told me." She had not even asked Chandler to join them for Christmas. Her husband, Chris, had said they should. But Fontaine had asked her, "If I do, will you mope? Will you wreck the day?"

Now, Fontaine pulls her phone out of her pocket. "You may as well know the whole truth," she says, and holds up a photo for Chandler to see. It's a picture of Henk beside a petite, brown-skinned woman. He carries an infant dressed in a tiny parka made of sealskin, a hood trimmed with fox fur. He displays the child to the camera while drawing the woman close. His face is proud, happy. He looks young, fulfilled. The child has dark skin and Henk's startling blue eyes.

Behind the three figures sweeps a vast, treeless landscape, windswept tundra, ice and snow, a grey ocean, infinity.

"What *is* this place?" demands Chandler, peering at the photo.

"The end," says Fontaine. The end of the world. Henk had said he needed to go to the end of the world so Chandler couldn't follow him. The baby was born in Toronto on Christmas Eve. He and the woman are now in northern Labrador. They're living in an A-frame built for their arrival, paid for by the community. It has brand new appliances, new floors, tight-fitting windows, heat.

Chandler absorbs the woman's high cheekbones, black hair, dark East-Asian eyes. Her name is Makara, says Fontaine. She was teaching English to Cambodian immigrants in a room at the library branch near here. That is where Henk noticed her. Last spring, she went with him on his cycle trip to Virginia. She was young enough, tough enough to match his speed on a bike. She did not mind sleeping on the ground, foraging for food. So, all those evenings last April, when Chandler was calling Henk on his cell, asking him if he missed her, if he was safe, Makara was standing at his elbow, eavesdropping, waiting for him to crawl with her into a sleeping bag.

In the Khmer language, Makara means *January*. She apparently speaks English in a soft, charming way. She is a happy person, Fontaine reports, a resilient person. She feels lucky every day to be alive, mindful of where she came from. She was born on a bamboo raft in a floating village on the

Siem Reap River. Its citizens ate a diet mainly of raw fish, they drank the same river water into which they dumped their human waste. They had a floating church, floating hospital, floating school, though all the children dropped out as soon as they could read because there was no point to education. There were no jobs in the bamboo village and they would never have enough money to leave it, to move to town, pay for an apartment, for food.

Visitors came in long boats from Angkor Wat to photograph them like tourist attractions in their lean-tos on the bamboo rafts, and to disembark at the floating café where Makara's mother served beer and potato chips to them and tended a deep tank in which crocodiles, captured in infancy, crawled over each other in the cramped, watery silo until, as adults, they were slaughtered and skinned and dyed green or blue or pink and fashioned into handbags or wallets or belts for sale to these tourists. When she was eight, Makara was rescued from the floating village by an uncle, taken to live with his family in Siem Reap, where she completed high school. The uncle was a tour guide. Eventually, some Canadian tourists sponsored Makara's immigration here.

"The existence she had," says Fontaine, shaking her head in wonder. "The way she grew up."

"Well," says Chandler bitterly, "she's sitting pretty in a shiny new house, isn't she? She's pseudo-third-world now."

In the small, troubled Labrador community, Henk will manage a boys'-and-girls' club for Inuit children, deal with glue-sniffing, teen suicide, arson, truancy. Makara will stay home with the baby and cook Khmer food. Prahok, mam, curried caribou, rice, filling the A-frame with the perfumes of tamarind and cardamom. She will teach Khmer cooking at the youth club. But, how will Henk be able to grow anything up there? There is no soil in Labrador! He will no longer be a pseudo farmer. Instead, from the local cliffs, they will watch the passage of whales, of icebergs on the North Atlantic Ocean. They will kayak on the frigid waters, cross-country ski, sit before their gas fireplace when the wind chill is minus-twenty and there are six hundred centimeters of snow outside. Chandler pictures the white northern sun, the sky like hammered steel, the purple shadows in the wind-carved snow.

"You asked," says Fontaine. "You wanted to know."

"Why are you on his side?" Chandler asks. "My own sister."

"It's not that I'm on his side. It's just that Henk is easier to understand." She opens the front door to leave. "Happy New Year, Chandler," she says.

Winter no longer visits this lakeside city. Weather patterns have changed. No more are they afforded the gift of snow, the pure, transformative, dazzling miracle of it. Only these gritty streets and these dense low skies like grey wool that crush the spirit from November to April. A pseudo winter. For many weeks, Chandler, glancing up, out of habit, from her easel around four o'clock, expects to see Henk cycling down the street after school. She watches for his bulky figure, for his pumping yeoman's legs, the sheepskin hat with the furry ear flaps blowing back in the wind. Her mind playing tricks on her. She thinks jealously of the twelve-foot-high walls of snow lining the Labrador highways like some kind of fantasy land, the epic storms, the virgin panorama, the temperatures to make the lungs crackle, the air pure as ether, the profound silence.

She reads the grief of the old men on the street. They glance over at her house sadly. It seems they know. Henk must have told them, he must have said goodbye before he left. She does not have the vocabulary in Greek or Portuguese to ask them if this is so. When she goes out, they won't look her way. They blame her. Their frowns say: Why couldn't *you* have left, instead of Henk? Since it was *his* house in the first place? Bent mournfully over their dead January gardens, poking at the frozen soil, they look orphaned.

Often, in the middle of the night, Chandler awakes, gripped by a painful clarity. Henk is no longer at her side, to counsel and sooth her. She rises, makes a cup of tea, gets back in bed with a lined notebook, lists all the ways in which Henk duped and betrayed her, how she's been *wronged, wronged*! Writing so angrily that sometimes her pen tears holes in the paper.

She had held herself above others. Yes, she had. This is what Henk had often told her. She had considered herself superior to him because he was a mere farmer, because he drove his food onto his fork with the ball of his thumb, bathed only once a week, believed one thin towel should suffice for them both. *Pseudo-poor*, he'd called her, because she'd always believed she was too good to live here. You can take the girl out of the middle class, he said, but you can't take the middle class out of the girl.

She stops drawing. She no longer believes in it or in herself. For thirty years, she'd thought she was an artist, thought she was in the game. Only now to see that she was just kidding herself. In some ways this is a relief because faith is hard work. She sorts through the piles of unfinished efforts, through the cupboards and boxes and drawers in her studio, making stacks of things that might be discarded. Every day, her judgement becomes more acute, her selections more cold-hearted. Her face flushes, her movements grow feverish. But, day by day, her body lightens, her spirits float as she carries out this purge. She tears the works on paper to shreds, she carts the oil canvasses downstairs, fills the trash bins with them, drags them out to the curb on garbage day.

In time, she ceases to picture Henk and Makara skiing across a pristine field, the baby tied in the deep hood of Makara's *amauti*. She no longer wonders what they talk about, how they look at each other when they wake up in the morning. She'd never understood why Henk cared so much about those damaged children on the pseudo farm. What kind of miracle worker he thought he was, believing he could heal them. She'd never had any faith in what he did. "You think I'm just a hick," he'd tell her.

For some time, hadn't he been saying he wanted to pare his existence down to something more elemental, more authentic? So, this was what he was doing up there now, stripped down as raw as the landscape itself, scoured by the crises of others, carved right to the bone by snow and cold and wind, just to prove he could stand it. Primal man. Now he is living with a woman for whom a meal of plain rice is a blessing. Inhabiting a land as unfriendly as the one into which he was born, hardened off by the temperatures, like a winter bud on a branch, the elements tearing at him like claws. All of it beautiful. Only in this way would his spirit burn bright. Gradually, Chandler comes to an understanding of this, or at least an acceptance.

Spring arrives, the ground breaking open like an over-ripe fruit, the air pungent with the smell of soil, of life-giving minerals. One day, the doorbell rings. It is the truck driver, there on the concrete slab. Would she like to go for a walk some Saturday? He shifts nervously on his feet, his face shy, hopeful. He has noted, he says, the abandoned railway easement behind here, just beyond the warehouse. Would that, he asks, be a nice place to go?

Chandler is shaken to see him there. This act of courage and forgiveness. For a moment, she is speechless. Finally, she confesses, "My partner left." A regular visitor to the street, he does not seem surprised by this news, he has catalogued the comings and goings of the locals, the incomers and the ship-jumpers. "You still have a home," he says. "That's something."

His name is Fern. He arrives on Saturday, wearing an olive-green suede jacket, dress pants, new leather loafers. For a man who sits in a truck all day, he is slender enough. To her surprise he has a handsome head of thick white hair. Until now, she'd seen him only in a baseball cap and had assumed he was bald. "Yes," he says modestly, amused when he reads the confusion on her face. "It's me."

It is a path raw and wild, with weeds growing at its verges, and pampas grass, still bleached and winter-killed at the moment, brittle and broken in the gully. Snagged among the roots lie empty pop cans, candy wrappers, condoms, even the occasional syringe. Still, it is a place of silence and tranquillity. Fern says, "I always felt bad for you all by yourself up in that window."

"Artists work alone," she answers.

"You never smiled. I figured you were lonely."

"There is a difference between loneliness and solitude."

"Is there?"

They have not gone far, when she spots something down in the ditch. She utters a small cry, rushes down the bank, negotiating the wet, spongy slope, recovers something from the weeds. Fern has followed her. "What?" he asks, alarmed. "What is it?" Muddy water seeps over the soles of his brand-new shoes, sucks at the leather.

"It's Blackie," Chandler says, her voice aggrieved as she examines the bike's ripped saddle, the rusted-out spokes, the shredded handle grips.

They go to a coffee shop on Bloor. After some prodding, he tells her that he was a ward of the state, as a child. His father, who'd sexually abused him, ended up in prison for murder. Fern had a twin sister. His mother loved this twin sister but hated him. She beat him and burned him with cigarettes and starved him until he was taken into foster care. The first foster mother kept him home from school. He was nine. She made him scrape the wax off all the floors in the house with a razor blade. When her boyfriend came home after work, he'd find Fern bound and locked in the bathroom. This boyfriend would untie him and take him for a walk in the park, holding his hand. When he broke up with the woman, the boyfriend reported her to the Children's Aid. The second foster home was a good place, with two boys a little younger than Fern. The parents were teachers. He loved this family and they loved him and seemed ready to keep him. He lived with them for two years. He believed any day they would bring the adoption papers to him. But then, a social worker said that, given his history, there was a strong chance he'd molest the younger boys, the biological sons. So, they gave him back. He could not believe they would reject him this way. He was judged guilty of a crime he'd never have committed. For a long time, he did not want to live. He cannot look at Chandler when he tells her this story, but she sees his eyes darken with pain.

"No one ever thought of asking me what I felt or where I wanted to live," he tells her.

Every Saturday through April, Fern comes over to walk with Chandler in the easement. One time, coming downstairs, she finds him reading her tome of loss and rejection, what, to herself, she calls The Good Book. He reddens, gets up quickly, closes the notebook. "You were busy. I noticed this lying here. I'm sorry. I was just killing time. I was into it before I realized what it was." Then he says, "Do you think you still need this? I could throw it away for you."

They go to his bachelor apartment, which overlooks a recycle depot, train tracks, a bus yard. There on a wall hangs one of the canvases Chandler threw in the trash. He'd salvaged it from the curb when she wasn't looking. "Snuck it into the back of my truck," he tells her, smiling, bashful, apologetic.

"I'd never met a real artist before you," he says.

They are at his kitchen table. She sits there contemplating his face. She pictures her charcoals and conte crayons at home, her heavy papers. "Will you sit for me next time you come over?" she asks. "I think I'd like to do your portrait."

The End of Autumn is Always Yellow

OF COURSE, IT wasn't just him. Half the town had been laid off. In the beer store, the dollar store, at the lottery counter and the gas station, Swatty ran into other men from the plant, his former brethren. But they did not hail each other. It was as though they'd become complete strangers, though in their labour they'd been intimate. The sight of each other was salt in the wound. A reminder of their mutual suffering, their deep loss, happier times. They were bound up with shame, the stripping of their manhood, the ignominy of the frog-march out of the plant. They'd been disenfranchised. They had loved the company and they'd believed it had loved them. It was their father and they were its sons. Now they were orphans. Once, they'd been a family but it was clear now that their kinship had been a fragile and ingenuous and delusional one. They blamed each other for their unpreparedness, their naiveté, their blind trust. For hadn't there been pay cuts to warn them, management shakeups, re-orgs, strikes, picket lines?

The day he was fired, Swatty arrived home at eleven in the morning. He parked in the driveway and quietly entered the house through the dark mudroom, passing the washer and dryer, to the kitchen. There, looking out the window over the sink, stood Opal, still in her cotton nightgown, her fingers curled around a tumbler of gin. You could not find the counters for the heaps of dirty dishes, stacks of magazines, piles of newspapers and old mail, armies of pill bottles. Opal seemed to know without asking why he was home at this unusual hour. She turned to him, a look of prophecy on her face.

He tried to make a joke out of it. "They gave me a gift of this cardboard box," he said, cradling it in his arms, like a baby. It contained the few personal items he'd hurriedly snatched from his station – baseball magazines, skin magazines, transistor radio, safety glasses, chewing gum, jelly beans, his bag lunch -- before they drove him from the plant like a criminal. In the parking lot, he'd looked around, dizzied. "I don't remember where I left my car," he told the two thugs in uniform, who stood on either side of him, a vice-like grip on his arms. It was true. There were thousands of vehicles before them, glinting in the sun.

They shook him like a rag doll. "Are you shitting us?" they barked.

In the kitchen, Opal regarded the cardboard box. She took a deep drag on her cigarette and exhaled. "Maybe you can have it bronzed," she said through the cloud of smoke. Three times in the past year, Swatty had come home with papers offering him a buy-out. He and Opal had bent over the documents at the kitchen table, considering the terms. Opal wrung her thin hands. "Take it," she pleaded with him, each time more urgently. "The writing is on the wall."

"There *is* no writing," he answered.

"This will be their final offer. Three strikes and you're out." In her face he read fear, judgement, helplessness.

"I can't leave the plant," he told her. "It's my home." It was where he went to partner with men. Here, in this house, he was a persona non grata. A man in a house of women is nothing but a weed in a garden. "They can't get rid of everyone," he told Opal. "Let someone else go. I'm staying."

"What do you think is so special about *you*?" she demanded.

"They need me."

"Nobody needs anybody."

"I got an award of excellence," he reminded her. How could she have forgotten?

"Piece of tin. Made in China. Probably cost them ten cents."

He blinked at her and reddened. Wounded, he slipped the papers back into the envelope, tucked it under his arm and, chastened, went down to their bedroom at the end of the narrow dark hallway. He slid open his underwear drawer and dug down deep, brought out the badge. He turned it over. Sure enough, there it was, stamped on the back. *Made in China.*

"It's the new protocol," Beauty told them at supper the night of the lay-off. "We took it in social studies. They don't fire people on Fridays anymore. Too many people committed suicide when they did that because you can't look for a new job on the weekend. People despaired. They slashed their wrists. So, you can forget any idea of killing yourself because of this, Dad. They did you a favour. They fired you on a Monday. That gives you four whole days to get busy and find other work." They were sitting at the kitchen table, Opal with her back to the window, Swatty facing her, the girls at the sides. In the room there was a nihilistic mood.

"You are a speck of rust in the rust belt," Beauty went on. "You are what they call the terminally redundant. *Redundant* is the catch word of the era. Worker subsumed by robot. I will never do what you did. I will never become a widget. I will not hold a job where I can be replaced by a machine." Beauty was sixteen and torn between her ambition to become a famous chef, a famous fashion designer or a famous photographer.

"So, how will you do that?" asked Honey.

"I will be a creator. A machine can't imitate creativity."

"It's happening already," Honey said. "A machine can bake a cake. A machine can take a photograph. A machine can design a dress."

"Not *my* cake," Beauty drew herself up regally. "Not *my* photograph. Not *my* dress."

She had a small, fine body. The divine brow of a Greek Venus, delicate temples, pretty ears, thick blonde hair plaited in a crown, a marvellous white sternum, a sculptural curve of waist and hip. She strove for artifice: nail polish, false eyelashes, lipstick, plucked brows, eye shadow, foundation and powder, pierced nose and lip. Honey, on the other hand, did not embellish herself. Her olive skin shone with health. She had a broader face, a softer, rounder, more generous body, loose and forgiving, a robust beauty. She was the easier-going of the two, the happier one. Beauty had the brains in the family, while Honey had struggled at school. At the local college, Honey had chosen to study marine biology. "I don't see a lot of fish here in the mid-West," Swatty had remarked at the time. Naturally, nobody listened.

"The death of blue collar, the rise of the computer," Beauty continued enthusiastically that night at supper. "Computers will move in with us. Someday, people won't even have human partners. They will marry robots. Marriages will be happier then. Robots don't criticize you or fight back. They will have sex whenever you want. Divorce will be obsolete. It will benefit women especially. Jilted men will no longer murder their estranged wives or girlfriends. They will love their robot partners."

"That sounds horrible," said Honey.

"There will be no more Ron Rashes," said Beauty, raising one eyebrow meaningfully at Honey.

"Who is Ron Rash?" asked Swatty.

"You could have walked away from that job with a pot of gold," Opal told him from her end of the table.

"I thought they were bluffing," he answered feebly. Past Opal's shoulder, Swatty saw the yellowed lawn choked with crabgrass, Opal's once-beloved garden, hewn out of the ugly patio stones, forsaken, the portulaca, snapdragons, petunias withering in the powdery earth and strangled by weeds. Alarmed, Swatty glanced around at the chaos in the house. Systematic neglect. Opal was sabotaging their lives!

"We have nothing now. Nothing," Opal said.

"They have to pay for retraining. It's in the union contract," Swatty said.

"What could you learn? You're fifty. Who would hire you?" she demanded.

The girls turned and looked at him in all their innocence and penetration. They were so powerful in their black and white judgements, their ignorance, their immortality. It occurred to Swatty that he didn't know his daughters. But it was too late. They were teenagers now and teenagers will not be known.

"Dad can retool himself," said Honey optimistically, her voice a purr. "He could become a paramedic. Or a personal trainer."

Beauty snorted. "An astronaut. A chemical engineer. A life-coach."

"We could lose this house," said Opal.

"I'll be long gone before that happens," Beauty said. "It won't make any difference to me."

After supper, Swatty padded down the hallway in his stocking feet. His knees had gone rubbery, he needed to lie down. Beauty stopped him as he passed her room. He stood there, gripping the door jamb. She sat at her desk, surrounded by text books. She loved school, she adored studying. A scholarship would be her ticket out of this family. "You can't be here in the afternoons," she told him.

"What?"

"The house has always been empty when I get home from school. That can't change. I need to be alone. I need Beauty time. My time alone here after school is critical for my spirituality."

"Where'm I supposed to go?" Swatty asked her.

"I don't know. That's *your* problem. Anywhere but here. You'll think of something." She bent over her studies with a fierce hunger.

He picked up one of her texts, fingered the pages. "Can I ask you something?" he said, timid, apologetic.

She took the book from him, smoothed the cover as though he might have damaged it. "What?" she demanded.

"What is spirituality?"

They'd moved as newlyweds to this horizontal neighbourhood, into this long yellow bungalow set prettily on a curve of the street, with deep lawns sweeping away in two directions, the house commanding sublime cross-breezes that guaranteed oxygen, life. But it was too good to be true. Soon, all of this promise had broken down, it had deteriorated along with their feelings for each other. Gradually, all of it had crumbled, ruptured, like their lives. Time had taken it away from them. Time had become not something benign and transparent as air, through which they guilelessly passed, but a corrosive force. Seams and fittings loosened, rusted, the elements encroached, invading around the windows and doors – rain, wind, dust, insects. The roof leaked, the kitchen cupboards swung by one hinge, the cheap linoleum flooring lifted, faucets came off in the hand, mould grew like a geometric garden in the shower tile grout, the sun-eaten window curtains hung in shreds, just as their feelings for each other were now in tatters. Beneath their feet, the cellar became an archaeological site, where over the years, from the top of the stairs, they wantonly pitched everything they could neither abide nor relinquish. Strata of sorrow, impotence and havoc rising beneath them, a complex history. A place unfit for human entry, a no-man's land.

All his life, Swatty had felt a stranger in this house, his very physicality an offence.

"It's gross, the way you look," Beauty would tell him after his shower.

"What do you mean?"

"Disgusting."

"How?"

"In that housecoat. It's too small. The belt barely reaches. I can see your chest hairs, your moist *skin*.'" She shivered, shielding her eyes with her hand, spreading her short fingers like a screen, purple nail polish flashing. "I – I can't look!"

Swatty had not wanted children, while they were the only thing Opal had desired. From the day they were born, the girls were in Opal's thrall, captives of her punishing love. She'd cleaved them to her like a second skin. The three of them moved in a private orbit. Swatty was not of their universe. He'd assumed that Opal's stripe of mothering was normal because he had no reference point. If you cannot even remember your own mother's face, you have no compass. Opal told the girls that Swatty had never dealt with his feelings about what his father had done. So, Swatty's loss was turned into a weapon to be used against him. He was seen as handicapped by his father's tragedy, maybe even deserving of abandonment. For years, Opal had been telling him he was depressed.

"I'm not depressed," he protested impatiently.

"The problem with you is that you won't go back. Everyone has to go back."

Swatty was fourteen when his mother disappeared while he was at school. His grandmother, Dallas, started coming over in the afternoons to do for them, clean and launder and prepare supper and such. His father had called her for backup, but he got more than he'd bargained for. The first night, before returning to her apartment, she waved a butcher knife in his face. "If I see one mark on these boys when I come back tomorrow, I swear, I'll slit your throat." Each day after school, Swatty crept softly through the upstairs rooms hoping to come upon his mother folding laundry or sitting in a chair reading a library book under a lamp. Sometimes he thought he saw the hem of her dress flutter past a doorway like a butterfly. For months, he trembled with fear and doubt and the world seemed very black. Then one day he stopped looking for her. He couldn't remember when. He had thought his quest a private one, but Dallas, without raising her eyes from the TV, said with a smirk, "You didn't find her, did you?"

One day, he came home to find police cruisers at their place. The house was full of the smell of exhaust. In the kitchen, stood two officers, trying to question Dallas. Their bulky figures crowded the small room, their blue uniforms darkened it like thunderclouds. "You seem very calm," they were saying to her. "You don't appear upset. You were here. The smell alone was a dead giveaway. You knew he went down to the garage. But you didn't follow. You didn't try to stop him. Your own son." She told them she was watching *The Smothers Brothers* on TV. She stood at the kitchen sink, cleaning carrots. The rasp of the peeler sent shivers down Swatty's spine. "Maybe you could have saved his life," they insisted, shuffling awkwardly on their feet, the two of them together no match for her. She answered, "I didn't see that as my job." The ambulance had come and gone. His father's body was on the way to the morgue.

They sat down that night to eat, Swatty, Dallas and his older brother Zane. It was a narrow pebble dash free stander on a street of six houses squeezed between a noisy commercial road and the overground tracks, not what you could call a neighbourhood by any definition, not a place where anybody should ever have lived, a wasteland.

"Are you glad?" Swatty asked Dallas at supper. The overground approached, its wheels, crying on the tracks, tearing at his ears, nearly drowning out his words. What he'd asked was of the moment and unrepeatable. He could not pull it out of himself again. He didn't know what his question meant, what he needed her to say, how it would help him or what he himself felt, for he had feared and hated his father but he had also, equally and against all reason, needed and loved him, and for this he felt both confoundment and shame.

"Your grandfather was a boozer," Dallas answered, "so your father came by it honestly. But my sympathy for drunks wore out a long time ago. All you get from a drunk is excuses and denial. In the end, you have to draw the line. And by that time, you're made of iron."

The next day, she came with her suitcases, moved into the master bedroom. Now, she was living rent-free.

Zane's sixteenth birthday arrived. Swatty went to the grocery store after school and spent all the money he had on a cake. His steps joyous, he carried it home in its square white box fastened with string. He had not believed he'd ever feel this happy again. He was proud of the way the table looked with the candles and coloured serviettes, and he hoped that this night would be a turning point for them all, it would somehow unify them, signal a new beginning as a family. He and Dallas sat in the kitchen, waiting for Zane to come down and see the surprise. Finally, they heard him descending the narrow stairs, encumbered by something bulky. He paused in the kitchen doorway. Swatty gestured excitedly to the middle of the table where the cake blazed with its candles. "Sit down," he urged, and then, noticing a large duffel bag in Zane's hand, his face fell. Zane told them he was leaving. He was moving in with his girlfriend, Cindy, and her folks. He stood there, tall and slender and dark, the very image of their mother.

Swatty's face crumpled and he began to cry. "Why?" he choked out.

"Because they're normal and we aren't," said Zane. Cindy's father was a firefighter, her mother a kindergarten teacher, decent folks living a decent life on a decent middleclass street. He turned toward the front door.

"Don't you want your birthday cake?" Swatty called after him, his voice cracking.

The door slammed and Dallas said, "We don't need that little bastard."

"But I love him," Swatty protested, his body convulsed with sobs.

"Best to throw that love away."

Throw it away? Zane was all he had, all he had! His grandmother placed her hand on his back. It felt like fire! An old woman's heat. They were burning up inside, these old women, their organs turning to ash. Everyone, everyone was gone now. He had nobody, nobody left. Only his grandmother, only her, and she did not even seem like his kin. She was old and she would die. He didn't love her and he knew she didn't love him.

Honey had graduated and of course been unable to find a job in marine biology. She was working at a nearby pub. "You can do better than that with a college diploma," Swatty told her.

"I like it there," she answered. "The patrons are happy. I find it refreshing."

"Maybe I should drop in."

"That would be embarrassing, Dad."

One evening, Swatty picked her up after work. He waited in the dark parking lot, the warm night flooding in through the car windows. Finally, Honey appeared. The pub had closed but in the brightly lit doorway lounged the owner, a skinny, pock-marked, pony-tailed man, tracking Honey indecently with his eyes as she passed under the high blue parking lot lights on her way to the car. Something clicked in Swatty's head: Ron Rash. When she got in, he noticed the soft, carnal look on her face. "What's he like?" Swatty scrutinized her closely.

"Nice."

"*How* nice?" he said, but she just smiled secretively and turned away to look out her window.

The next morning, Swatty went to Opal. She was under the pine tree, smoking a cigarette. "Is she sleeping with that louse?" he demanded.

She shrugged. "He's paying her more than minimum," she said. "Tit for tat."

"He's married and he's older than I am!" shouted Swatty. "I'd like to break his goddamned neck!"

He sought out Beauty, holed up in her room, her texts piled around her higher than ever, a fortress.

"Did you know about that pervert too?" he demanded. "Why am I always the last person in this house to hear about anything?"

"Believe me," she told him, "the less you know about what goes on around here, the better."

Swatty felt wretched about it, torn up. He retreated to the back patio, sat in Opal's torn web smoking chair. His feet rested on a stinking bed of cigarette butts. The air was corrupted with a sour brew of ash, tobacco, saliva. His eyes roved the miserable yard, the dandelions, the broken fence, the healthy Scots pine, which for years Opal had been nagging him to cut down because it cast too much shade. In the flesh of its magnificent trunk, she'd buried the blade of an axe.

Now that he was jobless and at home, Swatty began to pick up on the changes in Opal's appearance. The alarming weight loss, the rounded shoulders, the stick arms, the unwashed hair, the grey complexion. Why had he not noticed this before? She'd go out in the car for hours and come back empty-handed. "I thought you were headed for the grocery store," he'd say.

"I was followed," she told him. "I had to take a lot of detours to lose them."

"Who? Who followed you?"

"It took a long time to shake them. Then I forgot about the food."

Soon she was telling him that her computer had been hacked. Her credit card was breached, her identity stolen. She said someone had poisoned their drinking water. Someone had broken into the house, planted cameras. They were filming the girls naked and putting the videos on the internet. They'd been through her dresser drawers, stolen her bras. They'd hypnotized the dog. She'd ruled this house so absolutely that at first Swatty almost believed her. He examined the door locks for signs of forced entry. He ran the taps, took samples of water to a city lab for testing. With a flashlight, he searched for cameras in closets, under furniture, in the corners of all the rooms. In the process, he came upon two dozen empty gin bottles stashed beneath their bed and under the sofa.

In July, Honey was fired from the pub. It seemed the owner's wife had got wind of the affair. Swatty knocked on Honey's door, went in and found her face-down on her bed, sobbing. He sat beside her, shyly touched her shoulder. "I know you don't understand this now," he said as wisely as he could, "but some day you'll see this was the best thing that could have happened. You'll be happy it ended."

"Dad!" she wailed into her pillow, "what would you know about happiness?"

Finally, Swatty went to the girls. "Something's gone haywire in your mother's head," he told them.

"Are you saying this is the first you noticed?" asked Beauty.

"She's coming unhinged," he said.

They did not look as scared as he felt. They would be leaving, they had other irons in the fire, they were on their way out. They had their eyes fixed on the exit. It was August. Beauty had combed through the university catalogues in the spring, she'd filled out applications, shot them out in the mail. Now the scholarship offers were pouring in. Honey had bounced back from Ron Rash. She'd flung a suitcase open on her bed, was pitching her clothes into it. She had enough money saved, she said, to make it to California. She'd find a job in an aquarium. She'd be a dolphin trainer. She'd feed the Magellan penguins. The simple hope in her eyes destroyed Swatty.

He went to Opal. "I'd like to take you to the doctor," he told her.

"What for?"

"I'm worried about you. You're saying things that make no sense. No one has poisoned our drinking water. Strangers haven't been in this house."

"Just because you're too blind to notice what they're doing doesn't mean they weren't here."

"We are all on the brink of this," Opal's doctor told Swatty when he went alone, to ask him what to do. "Of madness. All of us. We are all on the precipice. Some people go over the edge, they fall off the cliff, and some don't. We have no idea why. We have no explanations for these things, no answers. Who is chosen. A switch gets tripped somewhere in the brain, a circuit breaks, and we don't even know which one. I realize this isn't helpful. But one thing I must caution you about. You will not get anywhere trying to help Opal. Trying to change the thinking of someone like this will only make things worse for her and for you. Unfortunately, paranoia is untreatable. The paranoid patient distrusts everyone, even her doctor. To her, we are all dangerous, out to get her. Everyone is a threat, the enemy. That includes you. And this condition causes such mental anguish, such fear that usually these patients will turn to drink or drugs to calm themselves. It's only natural. They have to, in order to survive. It's very sad."

"My father was a drinker," Swatty confided.

"Then, regrettably, you've come full circle."

In the kitchen one evening, Opal showed Swatty a set of shiny new knives. "See this?" she said, holding one up. "This is called the *Honesuki* knife." She touched its fine tip delicately with her finger, bent it and let it go with a *ping*. "It's ideal for working around bones and joints." Her eyes blazed with intent. Her breath reeked of gin, cigarettes, coffee, unhappiness. That night, Swatty pictured the knives in bed with them, concealed under Opal's pillow, ready to perform their butchering and trimming. Again, and again, he awoke, startled in a dream by a *ping*. It seemed like he was awake all night from this *ping ping ping*. Beside him, beneath the blanket, Opal lay like a pile of dry twigs. In her breathing he detected menace, homicide. Finally, he lay there in high alert. The minutes ticked by. He prayed for sunrise. A soft rain fell beyond the open window. There was no light in the sky until nearly seven. September had come.

Swatty drove Honey to the bus depot and stood beside her at the wicket, weeping shamelessly. Glancing over at him, the agent behind the glass bent his head toward the little speaker hole and asked Honey, "Is this person getting on the bus?"

"No," answered Honey.

"Because he can't get on the bus in that condition."

They went outside and stood together on the concrete platform. All around them, the trees had turned colour, the air shimmered with red and orange. Honey held Swatty's hand while he strove to keep the tears at bay. His knees shook, he feared he was near collapse. Finally, the driver came along and swung open the storage compartment of the bus. Honey handed him her suitcase. Before climbing aboard, she turned to Swatty, "You can always come out west and live near me, you know, Dad. I mean it. It's not your job to stay here. Staying here with Mom could kill you. That's why I'm leaving. I want to live." He watched her climb the steps, saw himself in her figure – the thick back, the broad hips, the heavy legs, the clumsiness, the durability.

When he got home, Swatty went into the bathroom to pull himself together. A cold light fell through the frosted window, the air bloomed with the fruity smell of mould. There on the counter sat one of Honey's old teddy bears, propped against the mirror. A knife had been driven through its throat. At the sight of it, Swatty went cold. Opal appeared in the doorway. "Who would *do* that?" she asked, exasperated. "Who would stab a teddy bear with a knife?" He turned and looked at her. He didn't know if she was trying to bate him or play him for a fool. Her eyes shone with a crazy foresight. He had met Opal at a Royal Oak. At the time, Dallas had said, "No good ever came from marrying a girl from a pub."

The next morning, Saturday, Swatty drove through showers of falling leaves to Zane's house. Though it was not far, it had always seemed a world away – a fake suburb of New England houses plunked down here in the Midwest like a Hollywood film set. A steep drive climbed to the front door. Cindy had decorated the house so authentically, with the most perfect choice of wooden decoys, needlepoint throw cushions, Currier and Ives prints, colonial quilt patterns, that it had been featured in a national decorator magazine. Zane opened the door and let Swatty step into the foyer but did not admit him further or invite him to take off his coat. Cindy didn't appear. They heard her light, swift, dancer-like footsteps overhead. She was a petite, pretty, stylish woman whose short skirts showed off her shapely legs. Swatty tried not to be jealous of what Zane had, but he did envy him. He'd never been invited to Zane's Florida condo. He'd never set foot on his cabin cruiser on Lake Michigan.

"Opal isn't well," Swatty told Zane.

Zane's lip curled. "She never liked us."

"That's not true," answered Swatty pacifically.

"She always thought she was better than we were," said Zane.

Swatty believed it was actually the other way around. "We had you over once and you never had us back," he told Zane.

Zane still had his job at the car plant. When Swatty started there, straight out of grade eleven, Zane had already been on the assembly line for two years. He took little notice of

Swatty, but Swatty was just happy to be near his brother. He felt like he'd come home. Soon, though, Zane had moved up to foreman, striding around importantly in a crisp shirt, plaid tie, chinos and shiny leather shoes, making notes on a clipboard. Then one day he stopped at Swatty's station. "I'm going up," he boasted.

"Take me with you," Swatty begged.

"Not everyone can go up," Zane said. "You're an assembly-line man. It suits you."

Thereafter, from his post, Swatty would look up at the office, a glass box hanging out over the plant floor like a temple, and he'd see Zane floating up there, his white shirt shining like an acolyte's raiment. Sometime after this, the robots started to appear, confined at first to an experimental corner of the plant floor. Their swiftness, their precision, their productivity chilled Swatty. He caught up with Zane in the parking lot. "Where's this going?" he asked, and Zane reassured him. "Don't worry. I've got your back."

After Swatty was laid off, Zane had warned him, "Don't walk in that picket line. Don't carry a sign. Don't embarrass me. You wouldn't even have worked there if I hadn't vouched for you." It was the first Swatty had ever heard *that*. He felt humiliated. A few weeks later, Swatty, driving nostalgically past the plant, saw new workers going in. Union-busters, minimum-wagers, twenty-year-old nothings. He called Zane and said, "They told us the plant was being computerized. Now they're bringing in new employees."

"Temporary hires. Tear-down crews," Zane assured him. "Year from now, be lucky if you can find a human being down on that floor." Swatty didn't know whether to believe him.

Now, at Zane's place, he screwed up his courage. "I don't feel safe around Opal," he confessed. "She's not well. Things could get physical. I'm afraid to go home. I wondered if I could crash here. Just for a few days, until I find a place to rent."

"There are hotels for this sort of thing," Zane said.

"I'm flat broke or I'd do that. I've been out of work for four months." *In case you hadn't noticed*, he was tempted to add.

"I don't want to get involved," said Zane, shaking his head. "I don't want to get caught between you and Opal. If she's dangerous…"

"She wouldn't even know where to look for me."

"You made your bed when you married her," Zane said and swept the front door open, inviting Swatty to leave. In rushed the cold autumn wind.

Red-faced, Swatty hurried down the sloped driveway to his car. He swung the door open. Before he was able to get in, Zane called out something. Swatty swung round to look at him, up there on the porch.

"What makes you think Mom loved you?" Zane called down the driveway.

"What?"

"What makes you think *anyone* loved you?"

Zane committed suicide. Nobody notified Swatty. The obituary was published in the local paper but he did not subscribe. So, Swatty missed the funeral. He found out only when Cindy came to their door one day. He was surprised to see her. She hadn't been near their place in twenty years. Up close, he could see that she'd had a lot of work done on her face over time. She looked both stretched and padded, her natural beauty destroyed. Fine silver scars glimmered on her jaw line and eyelids. She didn't say that Zane *killed himself.* Not those words exactly. She said, *He took his own life,* as though that was a less damning act, gentler, nobler, more sane. Cindy held something out to Swatty, a white envelope. On it was handwriting that stirred something buried deep in his memory. He stared at it.

She said, "Zane has kept this for thirty years. Your grandmother knew about it. She opened it when it came in the mail, even though it was addressed to you and Zane. In time, he found it accidentally and confronted her. She told him not to tell you. She said she didn't trust your mother not to walk out on you a second time. But of course, she was just being selfish. She wanted a free roof over her head. That was when Zane washed his hands of both of them, Dallas and your mother."

Swatty took the envelope from her.

Cindy hesitated before turning away. "Zane was a drinker. You didn't know that, did you?"

"No."

"I thought I should to tell you. Not that it excuses him, but the truth about illness can explain behaviour. He hid his drinking well. But he went down his father's path. He always knew they were two of a kind. At the same time, I think he saw your mother in you and he was jealous. He wasn't easy to live with, your brother. No. He was an angry person. I told him long ago that he needed to give this letter to you, but he refused."

Swatty looked at her and saw her differently. The hair spray, the Botox, the cosmetic surgery. A protection, a mask to disguise her suffering. Until now, he'd thought her a vain and shallow and materialistic woman.

Swatty folded the envelope and slipped it into his trouser pocket. He put on a jacket and walked through the neighbourhood. He breathed deeply, dizzy with oxygen. Zane was gone. The news had brought him a strange, an unexpected relief. Now there were no blood kin left to reject him. Washed with gratitude, released, he passed houses he'd never noticed before, made one turn after another, coming finally to a small park, with no idea where he was. He went and stood in the middle of the grass and, his hands shaking, he pulled out the envelope.

Dear Boys,

I did not abandon you. I went away only to prepare a place for us. I've settled in a city a safe distance from

your father. I want you to come now and live with me.
I've found a good job and I've rented an apartment,
a nice home for us. Don't tell your father or Dallas or
anyone else. Here is a money order made out to you.
Cash it right away. You don't even need to pack a bag.
Get on the Greyhound bus to this city. Then take a
taxi to the address above. We will have a happy life
here together, I promise, just the three of us. Hurry. I'm
waiting for you. All my love, Mom.

He looked across the park at a yellow tree. He'd been fired in June and here it was November and he hadn't even noticed the coming and going of autumn. All the red and orange trees were stripped, all their red and orange leaves, curled up like seashells, thickly blanketing the ground now, but here before him stood this miraculous chestnut, steadfast, holding forth its glory, like a blazing sun. Its constancy, its brilliance filled him with hope. He'd forgotten. He'd forgotten that in this part of the country, in this part of the country, the end of autumn was always yellow. He took in the vivid tree. It was a clear message, he thought. His mother was still waiting. He gripped the letter, its paper brittle, brown and curled at the edges as a dying leaf. He lifted it, pressed it to his cheek, held it there, as though to staunch a wound. He closed his eyes and pictured his mother watching at a window for his appearance. He would go now and search for her, at this address. She might still be there. If not there, in another place. Expecting him. There would be a way to track her down.

That night, Swatty had a dream, and in this dream, he showed his mother the one and only photograph he had of her, a cracked black-and-white snapshot with an old-fashioned scalloped border. In the dream, he asked her, *"Who are these friends you are with? These two women with the big noses and bulgy eyes and frizzy hair, who are not in the same league as you, not pretty at all? What are the three of you laughing about? How old are you here? Was this during the war? Is this the way you always curled your hair, with these waves and rolls? Why do you look out of the corner of your eye that way at the camera, with your chin down? Were you shy? Were you embarrassed to be so happy? Is this your coat, hanging so loosely on you, with the sleeves long and sliding down over your wrists and the shoulder pads sticking way out? Is this your coat, is it the coat of a man? What colour was your lipstick? Because of course here it looks black. Why does your mouth seem so large and so striking in this dark shade, your lips so shapely, your teeth so square and dazzlingly white and perfect? Were you considered very beautiful at the time, with your high, bare forehead and your broad features and your thick, sculpted hair? Were you ever this happy after I was born? Do you have friends now as good as these? Do you ever think of me?"*

Some Temporary Thing

WHENEVER I TOLD Otis we had to get out of Reprieve, he'd answer that he couldn't leave because the school was his *child*. "What do you think is out there, anyway," he'd ask me maddeningly, "that's different from this town? People are the same everywhere. *Life* is the same. If you're searching for happiness, I'll tell you where to look. In *there*," he'd say, tapping my sternum. "Happiness is an interior thing. It's not outside you." I'd tell him to stop acting like he was my guidance counsellor.

Otis teaches design at a high school that was built when we were in grade thirteen. It was intended for students who were weak at academics. When it went up, we laughed and called it The School for Dummies. Welding, auto mechanics, hair dressing, typing were what it initially offered. But when Otis went on staff, he pushed for bigger things. Industrial design, urban planning, photography, animation, broadcasting, fashion, printmaking, computer programming, glassblowing, ceramics, film production came onto the curriculum. Soon, gifted teachers flocked to Reprieve, lured by the opportunity to be creative, the quiet life, the leafy streets, the cheap studio space, the affordable housing. Despite this influx of talent, every year Otis is voted top teacher. The students go to him even for personal advice, though the school board pays good money for a guidance counsellor to do that very thing. Otis tells me, "I've never met a student I didn't like," and, depending on my frame of mind, I can find this attitude obnoxious, enraging, facile.

The other day, I was standing at the store window, when a clutch of students ran by, long-legged girls, their pretty faces glowing with athleticism, their chests bouncing, their blonde ponytails swinging, their smooth limbs sculpted in bright Lycra costumes, and there in the centre of them, like a high-priest initiating a college of vestal virgins, jogged Otis, looking as youthful as they, his feet flying high, the soles of his running shoes flashing, his body flowing along, powerful as a river. They splashed through the winter slush, happy as if they were running on a hot beach. Then, Otis glanced my way and our eyes locked, but when I waved, he passed on without acknowledging me.

Wounded, I went to the little glassed-in office at the back and closed the door. "I think Otis is ashamed that I work in this place," I told Milt.

He looked up from his magazine, personally affronted. "Why *would* he be?" he demanded, raising a jelly-filled donut to his powdery lips. A tray of them lay at his elbow. He is our chief shop lifter. Every morning he pilfers goods from our bakery, whole boxes of Danish, hot cross buns, brownies. "You didn't see that," he'll tell me, sliding them into his drawer. His body flows down like a mountain from his ears to his mushroom-shaped backside, a man imprisoned by his own addiction, by some emptiness. I do not know where he was born, if he is gay or straight, if he gorges himself because he suffered child abuse, if he has friends. Though there is a desk for me in this very office, I don't linger because Milt swallows the space, and because the trapped air smells sickeningly of sugar and sweat.

Milt is the titular store manager but I am the de facto one. I hire and fire, manage staff, take care of payroll and customer relations, troubleshoot, do the bookkeeping, the ordering, the inventory. Milt has no intercourse with the staff. He comes in the back door, then fritters the day away, flipping through magazines off our own racks, on the subjects of food, astrology, mysticism.

"I'm selling elbow pasta," I explained to Milt, "while Otis enriches the youth of Reliance."

He frowned. "You do just as good work here as he does in that school," he said, licking his chubby fingers, caked with icing sugar. "Maybe better."

"Those kids worship him."

"Well, everybody here thinks you walk on water. In case you haven't noticed. This is a good place. An important one. Don't ever forget that," he said, eyeing me severely, his eyes magnified behind thick glasses, his skin, ravaged by sugar, pitted and mottled with purple shadows, as though he'd been through a war. "Our customers are just as important as his students. Maybe *more* important. And besides, do you think Otis might be a bit of a snob?"

This is the store that time forgot. Because our linoleum floors curl up, our fluorescent lights flicker, our antique cash registers shudder and groan, our old metal shelves sway like drunks, the wheels on our carts wobble and lock, we are able to keep our prices low. In the canned goods aisle, I was cornered that morning by Mrs. Likely, a regular customer from the assisted housing that surrounds us, along with pawn shops, beer parlours, strip clubs, a soup kitchen, a food bank, a methadone clinic, the Salvation Army store. Harsh floodlights, shadowy doorways, boarded up windows, trash blowing down the curbs, this is our neighbourhood. We see a lot of police cars out here, where Main Street becomes the highway, we hear continual sirens, red lights flash across our front windows.

The day Otis jogged by was the busiest of the month because in the mail had arrived the welfare checks, the disability cheques, the unemployment cheques, the mothers' allowance cheques. It's why we jokingly call ourselves Welfare Foods. Spaghetti, tomato sauce, soft drinks, frozen pizza, dried cereal, potato chips are our most popular items. Mrs. Likely squeezed my elbow so hard that an electrical charge shot up my arm. For her, the scavenging of food is a life-or-death affair. Her son, she's told me, is serving eight years in prison for second degree murder, her daughter is a prostitute. That morning, her alcoholic husband had forged his signature on her old age cheque. She opened her palm and showed me three toonies, all he left her. In her other hand she held, as though gripping a flotation device, a can of Chef Boyardee. I fetched a basket, led her round the store, picked two dozen items off the shelves, took her up front to our head cashier, Myrna, and made it a no-charge.

Myrna had shown up that morning with a shiner. "I know," she told me, "it's a beauty." This isn't an embarrassment to the store, or anything new. In this neighbourhood, a black eye is considered normal. Other cashiers will call in sick because their wrist was broken by their husband, they've been in a bar brawl, they've pulled an all-nighter, they are down at the police station scraping bail together for someone. I can't fire them because there's nobody different from them to hire. The most steadfast is Myrna, a lifelong employee who is sixty but looks eighty. Over the years, I have watched her shrink to skin and bones, like a wind-scoured landscape, carved away by the powerful weathers raking her life. Her husband has not held down a job in two decades, he is addicted to gambling. Her grandson, Mo, stocks shelves for us, a cumbersome, slow-moving, listless high school dropout. Like others we've employed, he's already had a brush with the law. He has a learning disability but is strong enough to toss around boxes of tinned goods as though they contain feathers. I find these boys enigmatic, grave, already numbed by life. None of them lasts very long.

I was scrubbing potatoes at the kitchen sink that night when Otis got home. He stepped up behind me, smelling of perspiration, the cold and slush of the jogging trail.

"Milt says you're a snob," I told him.

He laughed, entertained. "He does, does he?"

"You didn't wave when you ran past the store today. I was at the window."

"I didn't see you."

"Yes, you did. You ignored me."

"No."

"But I am, after all, a mere store clerk."

He applied his hands to my shoulders, like a healer. "*Nobody* is a *mere anything*. Besides, you aren't just a clerk. You run that place and everybody knows it."

"I don't exist outside that store."

"You exist for me," he says, wrapping his arms around my waist.

"I have no friends."

"You have Milt."

"Milt is not my *friend*," I said, insulted.

Otis bent and pressed his cold cheek to my neck, a pure and simple gift. I felt his vigour, his buoyancy, the happiness radiating from him as naturally as heat from the sun. He is like a thin electrical wire buzzing with energy. Looking up,

I observed his reflection in the darkened window. His eyes shone with contentment. The balder he got and the more pared down his features, the handsomer he became and the wiser looking, like some Old Testament prophet. There were moments when I felt betrayed by his unexpected attractiveness and authority. Back in high school, he was nothing to look at. He wasn't even someone I was proud to go out with. He was merely the best I could get at the time. I thought he was just some temporary thing.

No longer is he the person I dated as a teen and got tied down to this town because of. He's become an entirely different man, highly regarded, a mover, well connected, with his own world around him that I'll never be part of. You could call him *important*. Not in a city fashion, more in a town kind of way. He sits on the library board, the hospital board, The United Way, and other bodies that help the indigent, unwed mothers, runaway youth. With his input, Reprieve has been built into a model town, written up in newspapers. Nobody ever asked *me* to join these kinds of committees, nobody thought of a grocery store clerk for that.

When I met him, Otis was not popular. He was not a boy anyone would have looked at once, let alone twice. So, how had he turned into this star? In high school, he was quiet, awkward, invisible, living on some cloud. I dated him only because of his shameless desire for me. There would be, I was certain, a worthier prospect down the road. He did not seem aware of the important people at school. If I mentioned them, he'd say, "Who? Is that his name? Oh, I didn't know that." Now he seems to have become one of those very people he ignored, that shine brighter than anyone else.

The summer I was eighteen, I had a job at the hospital as a ward clerk. Leaving my shift every afternoon, I'd find Otis waiting for me outside in the shadow of the hospital, his bicycle leaning against its red brick wall. He'd cycled in from the golf course, where he drove the refreshment cart, polished the members' clubs, raked the sand pits, groomed the greens. Climbing up onto his handlebars, I smelled on him the sweat of his labours in the sun, the pesticides and detergents and gasoline he handled. He'd pump us effortlessly up the steep hill to my house. Then, upstairs, he'd unzip the front of my blue polyester uniform, ease me down onto my bed. My room was stuffy and dazzling from the sunlight reflected off the garage roof, the air potent with the smell of melted tar beneath its hot shingles. Against the steady *whoosh* of traffic passing below on the busy road, Otis panted, moaned, sighed with anguish and delight.

What were those afternoons to me? I recall the searing summer winds, the pavement heat rising before us in waves as we crested the hill, the window sheers softly luffing, dream-like, into the room, the explosive laughter of passersby on the sidewalk below my window, the musical jingling of the milkman's glass bottles as he went round to the kitchen door, carrying his broad, flat iron basket, the *slap* of the rolled up

evening paper tossed onto the front porch, the bumpy landscape of the chenille bedspread against my skin, the steep
slope of the ceiling turning from yellow to pink to blue in the
fading light. We took those hours for granted, we squandered
them. Or, at least, I did: disdainful, heartless, grudging.

His lovemaking was sweet, bashful, tormented, implor-
ing. He showed the same amazement every time, as though
he'd never seen my nakedness before, and this should have
signalled to me the childlike, wondrous manner in which
he'd forever approach quotidian life. Nothing I felt for Otis
matched his authenticity, his depth of emotion. I do not
remember feeling any tenderness for him at all. I liked the
idea of a boyfriend more than the *fact* of one. He was a tool,
a means for me to acquire sexual experience before going
off to university. Mainly, I felt a mixture of boredom, mild
curiosity, vexation. All the while daydreaming: What more
constructive thing could I be doing at this moment? How
could I be improving myself? Surely there was some way in
which I could be flowering.

Like many teen girls, I did not see what all the fuss was
about, I believed sex ridiculous but mandatory. It had
become an obligation, I couldn't think how to get out of it.
While Otis fumbled away, I closed my eyes and waited for it
to end, pining instead for Storey Toogood, blue-eyed, sandy-
haired, the handsomest and richest boy in our school, student
council president, football captain, head prefect. Much later,
I did not like to think I'd been (or still was) a callous person

unmoved by Otis' pathetic display of need, his indignity and his greed and apologies and shy supplications and generosity. How had I become this judgemental, stingy person? It troubled me now to consider this.

When I found out in October of that year that I was pregnant, Otis said, "We would have wanted a child anyway."

"I never said I'd marry you!" I cried.

He smiled, stood before me and rubbed my arms as if to warm me. "Don't be that way," he chided softly, his eyes hurt. The following day, he knelt before me with a tin ring from Woolworths, which would soon turn my finger green. "I'm so happy," he said, like a puppy looking up into my eyes. "This is the luckiest day of my life." I was like a goddess to him, he professed. I was all he'd ever want in life.

But after that, he seemed to forget I existed. He turned his passions public, developing a high profile that final year in high school, somehow blossoming once I was officially his. He pulled ahead, perhaps propelled by the responsibilities of fatherhood. He dressed smarter, ran for things, was recruited for causes. Wasn't this what I'd thought I wanted in a boy? Yes, but not this boy. I did not want it in *him*. Out of our accidental sacrament, out of our mutual blunder, he began to forge such baffling ease with the world, such a fluid passage in life, such reward. He never even warned me he was going there.

No one knows what it is like to have a stillborn child. *Placental insufficiency.* Most likely, they said. A plunge in nutrients and oxygen to the fetus. *There is no life force.* At seven months this is what they said. I couldn't take in the doctors' words. They fell against a wall that had gone up around me. After all the fighting in my heart against the idea of motherhood, of a child, now these were being taken from me, these things would not be mine. At first, I refused to believe it. Otis sat on the edge of my hospital bed and took my hand and softly beseeched me, "Hazel. Hazel." I couldn't make up my mind how soon to have the labour induced. I knew once it was induced, I would have to face the truth. Finally, Otis had to decide. The chill in the delivery room, the thin sheet covering me like a cold skin, the icy table, the uncomfortable stirrups, the harsh lights. A cruel place to hatch a child, alive or dead.

The nurses asked me if I wanted to hold the baby, a girl. They would bundle her in a tiny blanket for me. But I was afraid that the weight of the child on my chest would crush me. That I would feel its shape in my arms forever. And, deep down, I believed I was not worthy of holding her, I had caused her death, I was to blame. My anger about the pregnancy had killed the child. She had sensed she was unwanted. I could not even look at her, for fear of seeing betrayal in her face. The nurses asked: Did I want them to take a picture of her that I could look at later? Did I want a lock of her hair as a keepsake? I shook my head vehemently. No. No. No. Now, of course, I realize that was a mistake.

"Where is my husband?" I asked when they wheeled me out of surgery. "He's with the baby," they answered, avoiding my eyes. They'd guided him to a bereavement room reserved for this kind of thing. "Why did you to do that?" I later asked him.

"Just to send her off," he answered. "She knew me. I felt it. She understood what I was telling her." He had known the right thing to do. Why had I not? Couldn't I at least have held the child? Could I not have given her something? Was I that selfish? Yes, yes, I was.

Later I told him, "You abandoned me right at the moment I needed you most," which was not really true. He rocked the baby for two hours, in that mourning room, paying homage, singing to her, channelling, believing the child to be in some way still spiritually present. It was to be his life practice: to stick with the people everyone else had forsaken, the untouchable, the discarded, the failing. All his life, he took the time necessary to complete every act, never leaving an effort half-finished, honourably bringing things full-circle, like some kind of shaman or healer. Belief was what motivated him. Unfathomable to me. He said the baby was perfect to all appearances, nothing at all wrong with her. "Why are you telling me this?" I shouted. She was tiny, he'd said, light as a feather, really, only a couple of pounds. Her nails were so beautiful, so perfectly formed, her fingers and toes pink and tightly curled, as though she were alive and grasping something.

I felt he should have asked me first if it was alright with me if he held her. I believed the baby was more mine than his, for hadn't I been the soil, the garden, the medium, the sustenance, while he was merely the seed? He read it in my face and reminded me: "You never wanted her in the first place. I did." Out of compassion, they moved me off the maternity ward but I said I could still hear the babies crying. "That's not possible," Otis, sitting close, said patiently, stroking my hair as one would a child. "They're two floors away. You're imagining it."

I'd dropped out of school in October. There was a lot of shame back then, about teen pregnancies. At the school, I was labelled cheap, a pick-up, while Otis was seen as cool, a real man. "You'll be able to go back and finish grade thirteen now," he told me after I was discharged from the hospital. "Start with summer classes. Get your diploma."

"I wasn't good enough for them when I was pregnant," I said bitterly. "Why would I be worthy now? I will never walk past that school again, let alone go in. And don't give me that sad look."

It was April. Otis dove into his studies. He was in final exams. He'd been accepted at teacher's college. He was on his way. At first, I thought I'd leave him then and there, go off someplace, never come back to Reprieve, but I put it off month after month, thinking I needed a foolproof plan, a guarantee of happiness. The more remarkable a person Otis became, the less I seemed to know myself. About that time, I read or heard about a bird called the Swift. The Swift stays in the air for up to two and a half years at a time, never landing. While aloft, it feeds on flying insects and airborne spiders, drinks raindrops, turns off half its brain in order to sleep in flight, returning to earth only to mate. If only I could be a Swift, I thought, and depart the earth altogether, for there was nothing worth staying here for, even Otis.

I started working at the store, more as a joke than anything. Something to tide me over until I made up my mind what I was destined to do with my life. Then it became easy to go in there day after day and gradually take it over, organize things better, help the customers, hire and train, since Milt wasn't doing it, and in time it looked like I was getting someplace.

I do not get my groceries at Welfare Foods, even though I could have a discount. I don't want my cashiers looking over what I buy. The items I put in my cart are my business. Instead, I drive over to a small store in a pleasant residential district, not rightly my neighbourhood at all, where I pay full price, just to feel like I belong there. It has a parking lot surrounded by a tall palisade of beautiful black pines, like something from a cottage town. Nobody there knows me, or so I think. One winter Saturday, I fill my cart and proceed to checkout. My groceries are rung in and when I'm paying, the cashier asks, "See that girl three tills down?"

Reluctantly, I look. "I see her," I say with reserve. I keep my distance from the local adolescents. I don't want them to confuse Otis's conviviality with any friendliness on my part. I don't afford them the slightest opening.

"She slept with your husband."

"I beg your pardon?"

"She had his baby."

"That's not funny."

"Who said it was a joke?"

"I don't think so."

"No? Don't believe me, then," the girl shrugs, smirking.

"Well, I don't."

"Suit yourself. But for your information, her name is Sapphire. She's taking hairdressing now. Not at his school. No, he put her someplace else. I'm doing you a favour, telling you this, in case you didn't know."

I cannot stop myself from looking again. The cashier she means is short and plump, swarthy-looking, with a shock of bright pink hair falling on her forehead, black nail polish, a ring in her nose, a stud in her lip, tattoos on her neck. A puffy face I judge has to do with alcohol. Her eyes are heavily lined all around with kohl, making them look hard, small and cunning, like a squirrel or some other rodent. The very thought of Otis fraternizing with this girl is absurd.

"He paid for them studs and them tattoos. He pays for anything she wants. He don't have much choice. Her cigs and her cell phone. He's paying her fees at the hair school. He's feeding that kid. Your husband sneaks around with it. Mr.

Upstanding Citizen. Mr. Saviour of All Things. Do you get it now?"

I turn and hasten outside.

"Hey!" the girl calls after me, laughing. "You forgot your stuff!"

There are only a dozen cars in the parking lot. Still, I can't find mine. I roam blindly up and down the rows, pushing my grocery cart through the snow, like a homeless woman, the plastic bags in it snapping in the wind. Somehow, I drive out of there. It is January. The trees look like they are made of glass, for we have had a freezing rain. I hear the industrious sound of people chipping ice from their porch steps, their car windshields. Children slide, shouting happily, along the sidewalks, trying to skate in their rubber boots, adults pick their way carefully, crouched over, clutching at telephone posts, fences.

I have put the groceries away by the time Otis comes in from the gym. I am trimming beans at the sink, my back turned to him, when he enters the kitchen. He sets his hands gently on my hips like a dance instructor inviting me to tango. He is like a magician, I think. No, like an acrobat who flies through the air weightless as a bird, saves himself at the last moment by catching the slenderest of bars suspended by invisible ropes, gravity-defying. If I were to throw him out, I know he'd land on his feet, nimble as a cat. He touches his chin to the top of my head.

"There's a girl you like," I say without turning around.

I feel him stiffen almost imperceptibly. "Oh?"

"Somebody named Sapphire."

A heavy pause. A slight trembling of his hands, a tired sagging of his body. "I don't like her," he says. "That's finished. You're the one I love."

"She drinks too much."

"Well, I don't know."

"A slut."

"That's not a nice word to put on anyone."

"Don't get moral with *me*," I tell him. "And there's a child. What about *her*?"

"I'm not involved with the mother anymore but I can't abandon the child."

I would like to ask: For how long? How many times? Where and how? Why? I pick his hands off my hips and turn to face him. I say only, "Was she even on the pill?"

He is embarrassed. "We used condoms." I wait for more. "But then one time we didn't."

"Because you wanted a baby?"

Maybe. Maybe, his face says. For, being forty-five, being, despite all outward appearances – deep down inside, on the brink of – nothingness? – he'd decided?

"I couldn't tolerate the vacuum in our lives anymore," he says, honestly, leaving me nothing to argue with. In the grey evening light, falling obliquely through the kitchen window, his face has a sculptural look, a troubling nobility.

The best teacher in town, so many students had come up to me to say. *And the most fun. Very hands-on. We all love him. Like a father or a brother. Like family. Truly.*

Lying awake in bed, I picture the girl, her crass looks, her cheapness, and I cannot match these with the man I'd believed until now I knew, so good, so clean-cut, a model of propriety. Why he would choose someone so low, the most abject and shoddy of students, as I see her? This nothing tart, this blue-collar girl, to create a child with? Why? Not one of those blonde goddesses so handy to him, with the toned bodies and the prizes for jumping, running, shot-putting, a scholarship student. Instead, this girl bussed in to school from a trailer park on the edge of Reprieve, this fringe person, this throw-away? It was a slap in my face, a humiliation, in my mind. Had he instead chosen someone attractive, intelligent, accomplished, I might have felt less insulted, could have understood, maybe. Maybe. This is crazy thinking, I know.

Sometimes in the mornings – for a long time now – in the mornings when the alarm clock goes off, Otis will reach across the mattress, rest his hand cautiously, almost apologetically on mine, as he would with a mother or a sister or a friend. We have nearly stopped being intimate. Otis claims that, with his demanding schedule, his early-morning coaching and his late-afternoon counselling and his board meetings and networking and advocacy and report-reading, he is just too tired. Then, for a while, we had sex on Sunday mornings. Instead of going to church, I joked. Now it has tapered off to once a month, like a housekeeping chore, like changing the filter on the furnace.

No light touch on my hand today. By the time I am awake, Otis has left for school. On the kitchen table, I discover a note, written in his handsome, fluid teacher's penmanship. *I know about the tubal ligation. I know why we never had a child. Dr. Fear told me years ago when I went to ask him why we couldn't conceive. He could see I wanted a family in the worst way. He saw how I was suffering. I know you are going to say it was your private business, a breach of trust on his part. But I believe I had a right to know.* I stand there in my housecoat, looking dumbly at the piece of paper, which quivers in my hand. He could have told me in person, but he decided to leave this memo for me to read alone, probably out of kindness, to spare me embarrassment, to let me save face.

Because: the very first day Otis went off to teacher's college, I'd gone straight to my obstetrician, the same doctor who'd delivered our stillborn child, and asked for a tubal ligation. "You're still grieving the loss of your baby," he told me gently. "You're in shock. You're fragile right now. This is not a good time to make such a big decision. I could refuse to do this, for your own good. I don't mean to be patriarchal, but you might regret it."

"I won't regret it."

"What are you? Nineteen? We don't usually perform this operation on women your age. Because there is no undoing this, you understand? Maybe you'll change your mind. When you get a better perspective. People do. Women do," he said. "You're in a state. An emotional state. Why don't you go home and think about this for a while?"

It was only day surgery. When Otis got home after work, I was in bed, sleepy from the anaesthetic. I told him it was just the twenty-four-hour-flu. We continued to try for another pregnancy. I saw such hope in his face when we made love, such trust, such need, but I was unmoved. "Don't worry, I know we'll have another child," he'd soothe me, thinking I must want it just as much as he. "We're going to have a family. This is the year it'll happen." But gradually, that expression he had went away. Gradually, I ceased to hold promise for him. Finally, I told him my doctor said I would never conceive again. There was something wrong with my uterus. The wall of my uterus was too thin to hold onto an egg.

I wouldn't have admitted it then, but I do now. Now I do. I was trying to punish Otis for getting off Scott-free, as I saw it. Yes, I would have to concede that. There he was with his high school diploma and his teacher's certificate and his developing career and his sudden growing connections in Reprieve, and I was left with nothing. At the time, I told myself I feared another stillbirth, I could not suffer such a loss again. But in truth I know I was trying to even the score. I didn't recover from the stillbirth as I should have. Maybe I *chose* not to recover. I was too full of anger, resentment. Bent on blaming him. And I was jealous of the opportunities I began to see raining into his lap like a shower of gold coins. I held that against him. Yes, I did. A child was the one thing I could deny him. This, at least, he would not get.

Eventually, he told me it was alright that we were barren, he had plenty of kids at school to keep him busy. I'd blamed him for my pregnancy, though I never said it. Wasn't it his reckless seed, after all, his selfish desire? I held him responsible for the way my life went off the rails. He knew it and seemed at peace with my feelings. We never spoke about the stillbirth, never worked through it together, though he wanted to. I would not discuss it, so he nursed his grief on his own. He began to bury himself in extracurricular activities, taking on the track team, the basketball team (a sport he never once played in high school), branching off soon into community work. Still, at night in bed, he'd hold me and caress my hair, selfless, fatherly, attentions for which I never thanked him. I would pretend to sleep. Now, I think: all that tenderness unacknowledged, all that feeling thrown away. Those priceless moments. Waste.

Thinking back on those afternoons with Otis thirty years ago, in my adolescent bedroom, I try, out of regret and loss, to embellish them with splendour, passion, unbridled lust. But we were neophytes, too young and ignorant and callow to achieve anything like ecstasy or even to know such a thing existed. Was that what Otis had been looking for in this sullen girl, this cashier, this would-be hair cutter? Sin, eroticism, the sensation of jumping off a cliff? I could not live up, back then, to the person he adored. I could not credit who he thought he was looking at. Was that my fault? Now, I see how careless we were, profligate, naïve. I realize very clearly that it was I who was the ordinary one, not Otis. And I had crushed his offerings under my foot.

Suddenly I am swept with fear: that Otis might run out of goodwill for me, run out of love and forgiveness. Perhaps he already has. In his eyes, I've at times read something – puzzlement, impatience, disappointment? -- about my failure to be happy. "What is it you want," he once gently asked me, as though I were one of his students, "from life? What is it you think life has to give? Life doesn't give to you. *You* give to *life*." When he made love to me in high school, I never believed he'd know anything more than I did, I never thought he'd try someday to act like my life coach.

"I don't know who I am," I've said to him. "I have lost my voice."

"Dig down deep. It's there. You'll find it. You have to believe that."

"So, is she related to you, then?" Milt asks me at the store, all innocence.

"Of course not."

"I thought you'd be her step-mother or something."

Because: now the cat is out of the bag and it seems all of Reprieve knows, or maybe always knew, about this secret child. Everyone knew, while I walked around in some mindless dream. There are no professional repercussions for Otis. He will never have to account for his indiscretion. He's too important to the school, to the town. He's too loved.

"I guess he never stopped needing a child," says Milt mystically. "I guess some men never stop wanting that," and I see a dark cloud pass over his face. His eyelids flicker in my direction and I wonder for the first time if he has had a longstanding crush on me.

"What about you?" I say.

"Me?"

"Did you ever want one?" I say, ashamed that I've never asked him this.

He swallows, looks away. "It's a regret I live with," he admits quietly.

They called her Autumn. It seems that, once it was clear we would not conceive, Otis secretly took the crib and playpen and baby clothes and stuffed animals we'd bought and he put them into storage, eventually bringing them out for Autumn. This deception wounds me but maybe I have it coming. Sapphire works weekends at the grocery store and, weekdays, learns to cut hair. The child is watched in the trailer home by Sapphire's mother. Otis takes Autumn, now two, out on Saturday afternoons, when I'd always thought he was at the gym. He takes her to the playgrounds, to story time at the library, puts her in swim classes, music classes, art programs, gymnastics. Trying to turn her from a trailer park kid into a middleclass child. A silk purse out of a sow's ear, I think – unkindly, I realize. What business is it of mine? And why do I suddenly want it to be my business?

One day, Milt screws up his courage to ask me pointedly, "You've got a big house, don't you? What's the use of all those empty rooms? Couldn't that kid sleep over sometimes?" Then he says, "People think forgiveness is a favour to the offender. But really, it's mostly a benefit to the forgiver. It's the only way to heal." How does he know this, I wonder? This friendless, interior, sugary man? I'd underestimated him, I'd dismissed him, I can see. He looks at me and it is obvious he knows this. Still, he cares. He pardons me. I feel ashamed of what I said about him not being my friend. I am amazed at his importance to me, how much I rely on him as a sounding board. The tenderness and gratitude I feel at this moment. His look – both injured and merciful.

I don't reply. But, one Saturday in early March, I drive over to Southside Park, where I suspect I'll find Otis pushing a stroller along the quiet roads that wind through the baseball diamonds and soccer fields and picnic tables and dormant gardens and tobogganing hills growing bare of their snow, all deserted now, it being the shoulder season. I park the car and sit for a moment, reflecting. I'd always thought Otis a simple and superficial person because of his happiness, his resilience, the way he bounded along in life, experiencing bliss in the most trivial things. But now I see that he has a quiet and brilliant understanding of life. I see his depths and the need I denied him. He'd been yearning for a child all this

time and if I'd bothered to consider him, I'd have seen it. And
he did wait. He did wait more than twenty years before he
gave into that craving, before he strayed.

Looking across the park, I now see him walking close to
the river, the silver ribbon of water shining behind him like
some supernatural, some life-giving force. He seems taller to
me now, than when he was as a teen, his head rounder, he
walks with the lightness and grace of a dancer, joy in every
step, just as slender and reedy as he was in high school but
now not so awkward or comical.

I get out of the car and walk over to get a look at the
child. Otis is bent over, reaching into the stroller. In his face,
the same earnestness and faith and longing I saw all those
married years when he made love to me. His devotion makes
me think I should start to consider change.

"I forgot to do something with my life," I have told Otis
repeatedly over the years. How many times has he urged me,
"Go and get a degree. Study something. Commute to the
college, like I did. It's not hard. You can do anything you set
your mind to."

Or: "Switch to a different store. Apply. With your experience, they'll want you. Go upscale, rub your elbows with the
rich people, if it will make you feel better about yourself." But
I stick stubbornly with what I have. At least the customers
aren't rushing up to me, saying, "Your husband is a god. He's

enriched our family. He's transformed our children. He loves everyone. My fifteen-year-old daughter adores him."

I work at not hating this nothing town. I try to smooth the bitterness out of my mind, like ironing a nice dress. But I also ask myself: Was all this really destined to happen? Was I supposed to be attached to this man, both self-effacing and a prodigy? Or was there some other path I could have taken, blossomed on my own, been happy? If I hadn't mounted that bicycle at the end of my hospital shift? Would I have been a different person than I am now? Did I make choices or did I, like a passive object, just allow life to wash over me? Why did I, drugged by the smell of tar off the garage roof, permit Otis to slide the zipper of my baby-blue uniform down like a surgeon cutting me open, while the milk man passed below the window, whistling some silly tune? *When the red, red robin comes bob, bob, bobbin' along, along...* Why did I do it? Why?

Snow is falling heavily. I look out the front window and see clouds of white powder flying through the air, Otis madly shovelling our path. I set Autumn down on the carpet and go out onto the porch, hugging myself against the winter cold.

"Why don't you wait until the storm's over?" I call to him.

"I love it out here!" he shouts back, above the wind. "It's magnificent! The sky is stunning!"

I look upward, baffled. "Where?" I ask. "Where is it stunning?"

Vagabond

I HEAR HILARY upstairs on the phone, conducting her interviews all day long. She works at a small desk pushed to the window in the spare bedroom, now adapted as her office. The bed is covered with neat stacks of articles and reports and drafts pertaining to her current project. Hilary is a thorough, canny woman and her soft-voiced informality on the phone sufficiently disarms her interviewees that they unwittingly surrender all the information she is seeking. When she completes fifty of these conversations, she will write an analysis of the government program she's been engaged to evaluate. She retired from a top-level job a year ago but has signed onto these contracts as a result of recent events. She is not happy about this because she is sixty-five and believes she has a right now to rest and enjoy life.

Her current assignment will consume two months and yield her thirty thousand dollars. I didn't ask her to farm herself out and I have argued that we've no need of the money. I don't give a fig about the five-star resorts in Thailand and Sicily and Costa Rica that she so passionately believes we require in order to escape the eastern Canadian winter. Just as I did not want to move at our age to this exclusive neighbourhood cut off from the rest of the city by rivers and bridges and parkways and fenced estates, nor do I understand why she thought we needed so many rooms crowded with so many expensive couches and chairs and tables, so many objects of no utility, vases, baskets, bowls, trinkets to clutter the tables.

Our house is a split-level. Hilary's voice drifts down the four steps to where I stand barefoot in the living room on a luxurious Chinese carpet. I close my eyes and long for the feel of the cool, packed mud floors of my African schools. If I question Hilary's values, she will not answer me. Very well. We have come to a point in our marriage where it is best not to talk about important things. Who, at our age, wants to justify their life choices?

It is October and I escape to the back yard to lose myself in the raking of leaves. Up flies the smell of minerals and worms. Soon I am sweating pleasantly beneath my cotton shirt. I pause and regard the soil entrenched in the dry cracks of my fingers and palms, and I remember how I loved pitching in to build the mud schools in Africa, though, as project manager, I was supposed to stand back and direct, like a concert conductor. I gaze up at the bare branches of our magnificent elms and my mind craves the sight of the plane trees and the baobab trees and I feel the heat and the dry winds of that continent and I picture the bending yellow grasses and the dry soil lifting in the wind like red sails. I miss the bright cotton clothes and the tightly curled or plaited hair of the African children and their simple happiness. I hum one of the songs they taught me and sometimes I release my rake and clap to the rhythm, as they did.

"I saw you out there," Hilary said to me one day. "What were you doing?"

"Just singing to myself."

"You have to stop that."

"Why?"

"It's embarrassing. The neighbours are going to think you're crazy."

"Who cares about the neighbours? They're not our friends."

I have been home from Africa for over a month. When I stepped in the front door with a split lip and a black bruise on my cheekbone, Hilary rushed at me with ointment, Band Aids, cotton wool, rubbing alcohol. We ended up squeezed together in the small bathroom, between sink and tub, and Hilary's agitation and the heat and bulk and putty-like softness of her body made me claustrophobic. I lost patience and finally, I snapped, "Stop fussing. I can do it myself. "

"What happened?"

"I just tripped at the airport."

"But why are you home three weeks early?"

"Here. Give that to me. Leave me alone. Stop. Will you just *stop*!"

"There's no need to be unkind," she said, leaving the room in a huff.

Later that day, missing the African heat, I said to her, "I'm cold."

"It's summer," she answered. "Don't be silly."

The fact is that, one dark evening in Niger, on my way back to my room, I was knocked down on the road, beaten and kicked, my wallet and watch stolen and even my shoes. I had to walk into the hotel lobby barefoot, my clothes torn and dirty, my face bloodied. The humiliation. This was in a small village where for years I'd been known to everyone and – I'd thought – loved. I'd believed myself a valued friend, an honorary citizen. The attack made me question my entire life's work in Africa, if I belonged there at all, of how much arrogance and paternalism I'd unconsciously been guilty.

A doctor was summoned to the small hotel, the lesions on my arms and legs treated, my sprained wrist bound up, a pair of old shoes found for me. I lay down on my bed in the dark and I could not stop shaking and weeping. I panicked and decided to go home. For a few weeks I went into the headquarters of my NGO, here in this city. Finally, they told me that they wanted me to leave. I am seventy-seven and I have more experience than all the other consultants there put together. But they said they could see that my trauma had caused me to lose conviction, and that, clearly, I was not able to concentrate. In truth, I didn't seem to know anymore who I was.

"What's the matter with you?" Hilary began to ask me.

"What do you mean?"

"You look – altered. I thought I saw you shaking in the bedroom."

"It was the light tricking you. The afternoon sun will do that."

I never told her about the attack or that I'd been terminated. I couldn't share with her my defeat because I feared that she would think some weakness of mine had invited the assault. Instead, I told her I'd taken retirement. So, now she is angry with me because suddenly I am no longer bringing in a salary. She has a handsome government pension but still this is not enough. I ask her how many holidays we really need. I'm tired, I tell her. I've travelled all my life. I don't want to get on another plane.

What she and I seem to talk about most now is the dollar value of our house and the state of our bank accounts and of our investment portfolio. She maintains that we'd have decent savings if I'd charged more over the years for my services. She says that I was never able to shake off the niggardliness of the New Brunswick mining town that was my home. But when it comes to the deprivations of the third world, how can you stand in a classroom before children sitting in rows on a mud floor, their stomachs empty, and tell them you're worth five hundred dollars a day? They will never see a bank account or live in anything but a worthless hut made of earth or of salvaged materials, tin or cardboard or plywood. I have tried to explain this to Hilary but she will not understand.

Hilary pursued me to Africa. It had been her department that gave my NGO the grants. I did not know her at all. I'd noticed her only once in a large board room. So, I was astonished to see her walk onto one of my building sites, a school for a hundred girls. I asked her why she'd come. She said her division had a big budget and she loved to travel and would write up some bogus report afterward. I thought she was joking but she was not. We got in a jeep and I took her on a tour of our projects and she pretended to scribble notes but I could see she hadn't the slightest interest in what we were doing. She wanted to go on a safari. What she'd really come to Africa for was to see the elephants and zebras and giraffes. She asked me to go with her. I obliged, only because I thought it would strengthen our chances of more funding. We booked separate tents but somehow ended up in the same bed.

I must have thought at the time that she was beautiful but I do not see that anymore. Maybe it is my failing eyesight. But it seems to me now that her nose is very sharp and her chin flinty and her lips thin and hard. On that African safari, she seemed to love me more than did my wife, who was bipolar and for my long absences punished me with the torture of silence. I was distracted by the urgency of my projects and allowed one thing to lead to another. That's what I remember if memory can be credited. A convenient abdication. Before I knew it, Hilary and I had rented a house together in Canada. The day I went to my old place to pick up my belongings, I found my wife dead. She'd committed suicide. She knew I was coming. She made sure I was the one to find her.

Hilary loves her body and loves to spoil it. She goes weekly for massages, facials. She is a very sexual woman, though you would not guess it from her appearance, for she is overweight and still gaining, her small head seeming to shrink while her body expands, like a marble atop a basketball. She is not fat, no. She is just large and fleshy everywhere, disguised by flowing garments piled on in many layers. The bigger she's gotten, the more expensive her clothes, cashmere, bespoke blouses in Japanese silk at five hundred dollars a pop. Sometimes for lunch, she devours a large plate of bacon, waffles drowning in syrup, whipped cream, sugary strawberry sauce. I sit in the kitchen eating a single piece of buttered toast. She tells me I cannot survive on this. But the more she consumes, the less appetite I have. Her office smells of ice cream, chocolate, the carpet is littered with cellophane candy wrappers. In bed, when she insists on intimacy, her weight on top of me makes my pelvis ache, my ribs feel about to snap, I cannot breathe.

Hilary came from what sounds very much to me like a middleclass family but she complains that she did not have what she wanted. However, I have never heard her mention hunger or thin winter coats or shoes with the soles worn through or drafty windows and cold rooms, nothing that has persuaded me she lacked for comfort. I do not understand this greed and self-pity. She talks of the insult and indignity of sharing a bedroom with her sister but she did not, like I did, sleep in a room with five other people, two of whom were her parents, in a bed with three across and one along the bottom.

I had wanted a child after Hilary and I married. We tried for years, without luck. Then one day, searching innocently for something in one of her dresser drawers, I came upon a disc of birth control pills. It was marked Monday, Tuesday, Wednesday, and so forth, and the empty foil pouches were up to date and the prescription was current and it was clear that Hilary had been on a contraceptive all the time I was zealously making love to her, driven by hope for a son or daughter. Of course, I felt utterly duped and betrayed. If she hadn't wanted a child, she could have simply said so. But I never spoke to her of my discovery. I was too proud to admit I'd been fool enough to trust her and I couldn't bear the clever excuses she was bound to offer or argue with the blame she would no doubt heap on me.

Instead, I told myself it wasn't important and I poured my energies even more ardently into my work in Congo, Togo, Malawi, Sierra Leone, and I began to think of the children there, who ran to me so eagerly in the mornings outside the schools, as my own. Those stretches in Africa were the happiest of my life. Even now I sometimes wonder how things would have been different had we had a child or if I had not divorced or if I had remarried to a different woman. But what is the point of such musings? They only lead one round and round in painful circles. And now is not the age for me to question the past or the future or to make great upheavals or demand the right to choose.

I try to tiptoe unnoticed along the upper hallway, past Hilary's office, treading silently on the Persian carpets, intending to watch TV, with the sound turned very low. In the corner of my eye, I see her hunched at her desk in her hot, heavy wools, like a big hairy ball of yarn, her body tensed, waves of resentment rolling toward me. Her hair is pure white and grown thin and cut short as a man's and on her crown has developed a bare pink patch, bright and tender as an ulcer. Beyond her lie the soulless street, the cemetery across the way, stretching up a wooded hill. She calls out grudgingly, her voice shredding the air, "It must be nice to be able to put your feet up and watch television in the middle of the afternoon!" I feel the great existential gulf between us, wide as the ocean that separated Africa from North America, and I wonder why we are trying to pretend that we honour each other.

Some days, I escape the back yard to walk our unfamiliar, deserted, hilly streets, which are like a country village, without sidewalks, winding prettily, up and down hills, and in and out among pockets of forest, past mansions with pools, stone walls, iron gates, embassy flags, past the tennis club, the rowing club, the sailing club, past the windy lookout high above the turbulent black river. I am passed by one limousine after another, by many Mercedes with darkened windows, their passengers invisible. There are two private schools here, set on immense, rolling properties, with handsome brick buildings, fine libraries and gyms, soccer fields, picnic grounds, dark thickets of pine trees. I stand outside their fences, bewildered, trying to comprehend this privilege until, out of their doors, students spill, yanking off their striped ties, hiking up the pleated plaid skirts of their hated uniforms. I think of the African children, many of them in English uniforms, the grey skirts and shorts, the threadbare white blouses, always grimy, unwashed for weeks, passed on from child to child, family to family. How proud they were to wear them, to belong to something, to be allowed to learn. Then I feel like I'm living in an alternate universe and that Africa was the real world.

At times, I walk so long that my legs weaken and tremble and I become short of breath. One day, I see the city bus rumble along the street toward me and I throw up my hand to hail it, welcoming the opportunity to sit down and rest. The bus wheezes to a stop and slowly I climb the steps. I draw out my wallet to pay the fare but the driver waves my money aside, saying, "Seniors ride free, Sir."

"Really?"

"Every day of the week."

That first time, I just go downtown to the bank and the public library. But the next week, I think: Why get off? Why not keep going? The miner's son in me cannot pass up this adventure that costs nary a cent. I start to ride the bus for hours each day, along the swift freeway, on the parkways, beside the rivers, over the bridges, into neighbourhoods I didn't know existed, way out into the suburbs, then through farmland and into bedroom communities and small villages. Seeing all these unfamiliar landscapes excites me, I have entered virgin country, a child again, not a care in the world, a spectator of life. Like a newborn, I drink in the beauty, the wonder of every tree, every garden. I turn my head and see the silver river, a ribbon of mercury, I watch the black forests slide past dreamily, like a scene in a moving picture. In my head, I write the script.

Hilary doesn't complain about my daily absences and in fact she seems to welcome them, but she does not turn down the opportunity to make a joke of my new hobby, endlessly amused by what she calls my love affair with public transport. A bus bum, she calls me. Too cheap to buy a ticket.

"Is that what you're going to do with the rest of your life?" she mocks me.

"Maybe."

"Ride that smelly bus?"

"I have a window on the world. I meet people."

"It would be nice if you let me know what time you're coming home."

"What difference does it make?"

"When you were in Africa, I had the house all to myself. Now, my privacy is gone."

"That must be really terrible for you."

Gradually, the drivers come to know my face, they nod when I get on and wave me past. To be sure, there are other seniors aboard but they don't travel so frequently or so far. I like to study the different kinds of people who get on and off, muse about what their stories are, if they are happy or not, the things they desire most in life. I try to catch their eye and many of them smile at me and I come to think of them as my community. People acknowledge me on the bus who, on the street, would have regarded me as just another old man. A few seem to consider me some kind of official rider, that is, an authority on routes. They will say: Do you know which stop is closest to the shopping mall, the hospital, the movie theatre, the museum, city hall, the con-ed school? What is the best transfer point for such and such? They could go up to the front and inquire with the driver but the drivers change and I do not. They would prefer to ask someone they recognize. They know they are safe with me. Also, the drivers, on the whole, do not seem to like passengers.

I am a small man and that appears to be an advantage. I am under five feet and slow-moving and my hair is white now and my eye brows and eye lashes are also white and my skin is pale as flour, so that I have become a colourless person, wearing a pale buff jacket and a khaki safari shirt, and beige chino trousers. I am like a harmless ghost, a threat to no one.

Autumn unfolds. With the shedding of leaves, the river day by day becomes more visible, more dark and powerful, the wind chopping its surface. Out in the country, the chocolate soil, deeply scored by the plough, lies in voluptuous furrows, spread with manure, its fragrance flooding the bus each time the doors snap open. Along the parkway, the grassy boulevards turn gold, the pavements darken in the muted light, night arrives earlier, so that often I make my way home from the bus stop under the glimmering street lights, a diminutive man, shuffling reluctantly along the road's verges, a stranger in my own neighbourhood.

Most people boarding the bus keep to themselves, choosing the empty seats when they can, happy to stare privately out the window, lost in their thoughts as we weave along. I like to park myself at the back, where I can see everyone come and go. But one time, when we pass the university, a young man climbs aboard, shrugs off an enormous backpack, drops it onto the floor, and swings in beside me, the only empty seat left. He is a sturdy boy in his twenties, thick in the limbs and chest, quite the opposite of me, and I am happy to squeeze over to the window to make room for him. We ride along as one, our bodies falling together, this way and that, as we sway with the rhythm of the bus. I feel the strength and warmth of his shoulder against mine. He says he's noticed me before, that it's nice to see a familiar face and asks me where I'm going.

"Round and round in circles," I answer, "which seems to describe my present life." Shifting in his seat, he turns to me, intrigued, his face so open and sympathetic that my story suddenly pours out, the first time I've spoken of it. I tell him about the attack in Africa and the sense of failure it has brought me and the realization that I am no longer needed by anyone.

"I don't know why I ever went to Africa in the first place," I confess.

"Because you couldn't stay here," he says firmly.

"I'm afraid I led a false life over there. I failed to be loved."

"Maybe it's not there that you see failure," he suggests. "Maybe it's here."

He is very tall and, as I speak, I am like a child craning my neck to look up into his big, friendly face, his ruddy cheeks and red lips and square yellow teeth and bright blue eyes. His bushy red beard and thick red hair make me think of a Viking. All that is missing is the fabled horned iron helmet. He asks me if I am widowed.

"Why do you ask?"

"You look alone."

I tell him that my wife and I live on separate planets. "I'm wondering if it's possible for two people to share the same truth," I tell him.

His name is Brian and he comes from northern Ontario, where his family has been shaft-miners for generations. Since he was fourteen, he's worked in the mines for a summer job. His father died of emphysema and his mother managed the mine canteen. He's studying psychology and criminology. He wants to work with addictions in the penitentiary system back up north, in Sudbury or Kenora or North Bay, where there is great poverty, great anguish, especially among the indigenous population. We ride along contentedly. I ask him where he lives and he says, "Nowhere, happily." He explains that he's in second year and all his money has run out. He has a map of the city's homeless shelters and if he can reach one by six o'clock, he usually manages to secure a place. The shelter staffs know him, they give him space in broom closets, basements, furnace rooms, to do his studies. It is all working out better than he ever dreamed, and why would he complain about a free bed?

He says he feels at home in the shelters. He meets a real cross-section of men there, many of whom have done time. He talks to them and later makes notes. He is getting more of an education there than in his classes. Their stories may become his thesis when he goes on to do his MA. When he can't snag a shelter bed, he sleeps in doorways, alleys, on park benches. I ask him what he'll do when winter comes. He smiles. "I'll cross that bridge when I come to it. Well, here's my stop," he says, reaching up to pull the cord. He rises, picks up his backpack. "How far are you going today?" he asks.

"No rush to get home. I'm a persona non grata there."

He smiles. "Then, you're like me. A vagabond."

Vagabond. I like the sound of that.

A few days later, again near the university, I see him get on and he is about to take an empty seat further up, when he spots me, checks himself, and sways down the aisle, grinning, seizing the leather straps for stability as the bus shudders and rumbles off. He slides in beside me. This becomes our habit. I watch for him and I see that he is watching for me. We ride together three, four times a week, bouncing along on the worn and torn vinyl seats, our bodies at one on the turns, our feet scraping the gritty floor, our reflections paired in the darkening windows, blasts of cold air washing over us as the doors fly open and closed. We talk about his classes and his profs and about my years in Africa. I always schedule my route, my transfers, so that I am passing the university about five o'clock, and I do not mind admitting that I sometimes fantasize that I am going to meet my son. I see no harm in this.

Now, I awake every morning, my heart bursting with an old joy that is at first inexplicable, for I don't sense through the open window the heat and dust and smell of Africa or hear the clatter of crude wheels on packed earth or the music of children's cries or see an equatorial sun sliding across the bedroom walls like a ball of fire. I lie there for a moment, confused, and then with a flood that buoys me up, I remember Brian

"You're acting weird," Hilary says to me more than once. "Don't tell me you aren't. You're hiding something from me. I know it."

"What do you mean?"

"You're walking around on some kind of cloud."

"There's no law against that, is there?"

One evening when we are eating dinner, I suddenly can't get out a word I was about to say, an inconsequential word, such as *like* or *care*. I feel one side of my face drop. Food falls from my mouth. The rest I can't swallow. I cough and the fragments tumble from my lips, bouncing off my chest, grey, masticated. One eye blurs, while in the other, colours shout, shapes leap out at me. My arm goes heavy. I watch it drop to my side as though it isn't mine. My fork falls from my fingers and clatters to the floor.

There is a cry from Hilary, I see her mouth twist, I hear sounds but can't understand the words. I try to reply, I know not what, but my syllables are garbled, for my tongue has turned thick and dead, a piece of foreign flesh. My head swims. I begin to fall sideways, but slowly, as though I am floating in water. The pictures on the walls rotate, the table tilts and yet, strangely, the cutlery stays put, the goblets, shining with pink wine, do not spill. Hilary arrives beside me, forcing me back into my chair. She picks up the useless arm and places it on my knee. Bending, she thrusts her face close to mine. Later, she will say: *You should have seen how you looked. Horrible. Horrible.* She hangs over me, clumsy, powerful in ways offensive and frightening. Panicked, weeping, she makes for the kitchen, where the phone hangs on the wall. In a moment of clairvoyance, I sense that her tears are not for me but for herself. She seems to move in slow motion, every gesture malevolent, dangerous, a sinister force, ready to undermine and diminish me. At another time, I might not have given room to these harsh thoughts but, in this moment, I am entitled to every protection, for I cannot fend for myself except with my mind, I must draw on all my resources.

I am both completely aware of what's happening and completely without agency, my body disarmed but my mind charged with a mighty clarity. Cast into a kind of existential state, frozen in time, trembling with prophecy. I see Hilary and myself dissociated, the room, the furniture around me alien as she, unconnected to myself. Hilary presses the phone to her ear and suddenly the paralysis I'd felt entirely dissolves, as though my body has exerted a herculean effort to shake off this attack, sensing that her call will put me in grave jeopardy. My body thaws out, as it were, I can move again. I cross the room toward her, pry the phone from her hand, hang it up. She is shaking, perspiring, while I feel cool and calm.

"I'm fine, I'm fine," I insist. "It was nothing. A small spasm. Look at me. See? There's nothing wrong. Get a hold of yourself. Stop making such a scene. It's over. I'm ok. I'm not hungry. I'm going upstairs to rest."

But she will not relinquish her advantage. The following morning when I descend the four carpeted steps to get my breakfast, there she stands, blocking the hallway, holding out my jacket, my flat wool cap, the car keys jangling menacingly in her hand.

"I'm not sick," I try to tell her, "I have simply had a revelation," but she purrs firmly, "I'm taking you to the doctor." I have found that the angrier she is with me, the more velvet her voice grows and I have come to fear this softness, like a snake's hiss. Minutes later, we are weaving through the neighbourhood. I see the girls on the private school grounds, the wind snatching and lifting their short plaid skirts. They shout with ravished delight, with happy outrage, their knees red as apples in the cold, for November has descended upon us and, in the sky, snow falls weightlessly as soap flakes. Now, we sweep recklessly through the city while my mind spins with fear, confusion and resistance. Beside me, Hilary, her chin thrust toward the windshield, her head armoured in a tight wool helmet, spins the wheel. Perhaps I deserve this reckoning, I think, because suddenly, my past flies up in my face and I am washed with guilt and regret, for I slept with Hilary in Congo and betrayed my wife and drove her to suicide and I had not known that life would lead me to such knavery.

In Dr. Humble's examination room, Hilary draws from her purse a tattered slip of paper, reads from it a litany of my crimes. I am forgetful, sometimes walk with a shuffle, falter, show poor judgement, lose things, confuse the days, talk to myself, wander at night, and other offences, all of these things trumped up. They are not true or not true enough to expose. I open my mouth but she holds her hand up, silencing me. What does she know about my feelings? How long I want to live and in what manner?

Dr. Humble, a handsome and timid young man, turns to her. He listens solemnly, nods, seems to forget about me. She talks to him, lathering on the fake charm. Her lipstick is a crimson gash, its waxy substance clinging to her razor-sharp eye teeth, like flecks of blood. Her skin has been pummeled weekly by an aesthetician, shot with artificial collagen in the cheeks and the corners of her mouth, with Botox in the lip, the brow.

I sit uncomfortably on the brittle paper drawn over the examination table, shivering, my legs bare and blue in the cold room, my varicose veins leaping out like fat worms, my dangling feet filling with blood, throbbing as though they will explode, my toenails yellow and thickened. I am a mutable old man who will be dead in five years, statistics tell me. The room smells of my feet, of my groin, perhaps also of urine because my penis leaks, possibly staining the paper beneath me. But, also of the harsh detergent in the hospital gown, so meagre, thinner than skin itself, no protection. It is as though I am wearing nothing, shamefully naked. The throat of the gown rides down onto my hollow chest for my shoulder joints are stiff and painful and I was unable to reach up to fasten the grosgrain ribbons and too proud to ask the nurse for help. A wind sweeps over my exposed backside, pressed down on the crackling paper.

"Most likely a TIA," says Dr. Humble. A mini-stroke, as it's popularly called. He begins to write prescriptions for a battery of tests for veins and heart. One investigation at a time. I want to tell him that he is wrong. That it was not a stroke but a lightning bolt, an awakening, I am like St. Paul struck from his horse. At the window, the leafless branches batter the glass. This is how I feel: stripped, howling, excluded. I want to strike Hilary and the doctor. Hilary dabs at her eyes with a tissue drawn from her purse: "What will I do? What will I do if this happens again?" she sobs. "Here I am, barely over sixty, taking care of an octogenarian and when I'm eighty myself, there will be no one to take care of me." So. This is the real reason we've come here. Now I understand that what she saw at dinner the night before was not me, frozen like a dumb statue, but herself, alone in the house, a widow, a victim.

"If we had had a child," I blurt out, "you would have had someone then."

"That is just cruel," her voice shatters the air in this small room. "I couldn't have a child and you know it."

Dr. Humble shuffles his papers with embarrassment. I turn again to the trees for sympathy. Then I feel a breeze, for now the door has swung open, the tails of Dr. Humble's white coat flutter out into the hallway like a gull in flight, he is gone without so much as a goodbye. I wonder: what comes next? In my chest I feel a flame of fear about the future. Now, I must get dressed. I am short and the step stool is too low. I try to climb down from the table, falter, Hilary grabs at my arm, steadies me, I reach with my toes until both feet touch the floor. She holds out my trousers, my shirt in the frigid space with the trees beating at the window glass. I take the garments from her. "Please go out," I tell her. "I am entitled to some privacy."

"Very well," she says testily. "But I hope you realize you'd be lost without me."

We drive home, silent most of the way. The houses, the streets slipping by are unrecognizable to me. I'm confused as to which route Hilary is taking. Finally, I blurt out, "You're glad, aren't you? That it happened. Now you think you've got the upper hand." She reddens and grips the steering wheel as though to break it in half and I assume she won't speak to me for days, but I am not troubled by this, knowing that she will eventually relent, because in the end we care less about what our spouses think of us than complete strangers who call us out in the grocery store line. When we arrive home, I do not go inside. I skirt the house to the back yard, where I seize the rake, cling to it as though it is my only friend. Its tines singing, its smooth wooden handle quivering like an excited partner in my hands. Craving connection, I tear at the thin, yellowed grass, at its dry, loose earth, at small fragments of leaf I've missed, the delicate ribbons. They leap and fly and twist in the wind, still alive.

That night I awake in the dark. The clock on my night table reads two. I roll seamlessly out of bed, grope my way through the darkened house, the rooms illuminated by street light washing in through the windows. So. It is true. I do get up in the small hours. I don't know how many times I've done it or if this evening I've risen just to spite Hilary. But it is not blind wandering, it is a thoughtful journey. I stand at the door of each room, contemplating the furniture, ghostly in the grey-blue light. Nothing here speaks to me. Then, into my mind flashes a sign that I have unconsciously seen over and over from the bus, placed in a window on the top floor of a red brick Victorian house. The words FOR RENT are etched in my vision. I have a glorious idea.

In the morning, while Hilary is soaking for her hour in the tub, I dress quickly and pack a duffle bag, throwing in one spare trouser, one shirt, one sweater, a single pair of underwear, of socks, a razor and toothbrush, the bare essentials. I scribble a note to Hilary, saying that the house and its contents are hers, I want none of it. I hurry along the street to the bus stop. Soon, I am in the centre of the city, where I disembark at a bridge and walk along a wide, quiet road to the big red house I remember. Large snowflakes are falling. There is bite in the air. I am wearing a wool coat and scarf, leather gloves. A slight, energetic woman with fine, white hair falling in a curve to her chin, leads me up two flights of narrow, creaky stairs. I follow her slowly, gripping the banister. At the top, we enter a tiny flat. She switches on a few table lamps. There are two small bedrooms, a kitchen in a corner with hot plate, toaster oven, microwave, kettle, half-fridge. A bathroom with an old chipped tub on claw legs, a tiny bowl sink, a toilet with a ring of rust in it. The furniture is old and bashed, the rag rug and the bedding threadbare. I like the look of it. "I'm afraid everything is original," explains the woman.

"Yes, it's very authentic," I say appreciatively. Three white radiators under the windows throw off plenty of heat.

"Long ago, it was servants' quarters," she explains. This thought pleases me. Still out of breath, I pause at the bay window, warmed by the sun pouring in. There is a wide bench there, cushions to lean against. With relief, I sit down on it.

"There are a lot of stairs," the woman says, her eyes kind. Already I feel a connection between us.

"I can manage them."

"I could put a chair on each landing, so you could rest on the way up."

The walls are curved because we are in the top of a turret, with a fine vaulted ceiling in wood, painted forest-green.

I feel like I'm in a bird house. I look down through magnificent Norway Pines planted in a column. Their dark green branches are wide and strong and horizontal. Beyond them, far below, lie a grassy median, a parkway, the canal.

"You'd be able to watch the skaters pass by, come January," says the woman. "It's a beautiful sight." Her eyes are grey, her face is pale, with very fine lines.

"I would like that."

"Do you skate?"

"I know how. I'd like to take it up again." I set my bag down beside me on the window seat. "I'll take the place," I say.

"When would you like to move in?"

"Now. Today."

At five o'clock, my bus approaches the university. There stands the library, silhouetted big as a factory against a sky streaked with purple and black, in its rows of bright windows, dark figures moving among the stacks. I wonder if I could obtain library privileges. I picture myself sitting in a small cubicle, reading books, as I did when I myself was a student. This is how I could pass the time, waiting until Brian's classes are finished. I search frantically for Brian, then I spot him running down the library's wide staircase, where the wind drives the new snow into the corners of each step. He is late. He has seen the bus. He is running, his back pack jouncing heavily, but I know he won't make it. The bus begins to pull away. I have an irrational fear that I might never see him again.

Half rising, I reach up and yank frantically on the yellow nylon cord, ringing it over and over. The driver slows, glances in his wide mirror at me, annoyed. I pull it six, eight times. "Please," I shout over the shoulders of the other passengers, who turn to look at me with frowns, wide eyes. I am surprised by my voice, high and thin as a child's. "Please. Please stop. My friend is coming. Please, driver. Wait for my friend." We slide to a halt in the greasy snow. Brian climbs on, moves toward the back while the bus groans, hisses, rocks. When he sits down beside me, I feel the cold coming off his nylon coat. He cups his reddened hands together, warms them with a puff of breath, gives a small shiver.

"You understand that I am just an old man," I begin.

He shifts in his seat, surprised, and grins. "Why do you think I like you so much?"

"I've rented a flat," I look up at him earnestly. "It's small but there's a table where one could study. Two bedrooms, an adequate kitchen. I was wondering. Would you take shelter with me?"

He places his big hand heavily on my shoulder. How long since I've been touched? I tremble.

"Campbell," he says matter-of-factly. "Of course."

Rhetoric

HE WAS AT the point of despair. In all their five years of coming up here from Phoenix to rent this old cottage in this raw countryside of lake after lake, it had never rained. Now and then, his grandmother, Honora, raised her eyes from her book to observe the downpour and said impassively, "This is not Canada." The screened porch ran the width of the cottage on the lake side. Tormented, Henry patrolled back and forth along the warped window screens, his hand skimming the dusty sills, his slender bare feet sliding over the floor planks, painted gunmetal grey. Far below, the black surface of the lake was dimpled with raindrops, beautiful and heartbreaking.

All year long in Phoenix they talk about coming up here and after they've gone home, they talk for weeks about how sublime it was and soon after that they start talking about coming again. Every week and every month they speak of this cottage as though it were a mythical place. They would leave the States in July and they would fly up here to Canada, a landscape of dark pine forests and diamond lakes and raw land everywhere you looked.

On the first day of rain, he'd carried out from the living room a stack of board games. Clue, Monopoly, Chinese Checkers, Snakes and Ladders. He set them down quietly on the coffee table beside where his younger sister, Eden, had draped herself on the wicker couch, her heels propped up on the arm. Next to her on the floor she'd piled the tattered cottage collection of Trixie Belden and Nancy Drew pocket novels. She intended to read every last one of them. "Oh, I hate those games," Eden said, though last summer they'd been an addiction. The look she threw him with eyes that bulged like conkers and that seemed to follow everyone these days with such derision, peeled his skin. She was a moody and absolute girl. She was a girl of extremes. She'd pulled her long brown hair up into the highest, most punishing pigtails possible. In Phoenix she'd secretly dumped the dresses Kitty had packed for her into the bottom of her closet and come up here carrying an empty suitcase. Now she wore a woman's sweatshirt she'd found in a cottage closet. It hung down to her thighs and looked like it was the only thing she had on. Honora thought it provocative. She said, "In Canada, eight-year-olds don't look like you," and Eden tossed her head with disdain and answered, "Well, I'm A-*mer*-ican."

In other chairs, Honora and his mother, Kitty, also bent over books. When the rain started and Henry saw them gravitate to the living room bookshelves and pull down these novels, a chill went through him, for now he would be on the outside. He was to turn ten here and to be unable to read at ten was humiliating. He feared books. What he saw on the printed page sickened him. The letters swept back and forth like flying kites, like flocks of maddening crows, like schools of swimming fish, like colonies of leaping rabbits.

In January, his teacher had sent him to the front of the class and commanded him to read. For fifteen minutes she trapped him there, sweating and shaking, until his head throbbed and he vomited on the floor and all the children laughed. It was for this reason that he had no friends. He was not worthy, he was a laughingstock. Finally, he was tested and found to be dyslexic, a word, in his mind, charged with negativity. *Dys. Dis.* Dysfunctional, disappointing, disabled, distorted, disagreeable, disloyal, disorder. The red strip of plastic they gave him to prevent the words from rolling like marbles off the page didn't work. Now, they'd begun to offer him graphic novels.

He moved close to Kitty, hung at her shoulder. "Are you going to read the whole time we're here? Is everybody going to be reading the whole time?" he asked her, anguished, pressing against her hot, fleshy shoulder. The sunporch lamps glowed like yellow moons in the gloomy morning. A Feather Duster moth beat its fragile wings madly, inside one of the translucent shades, and Henry felt his heart flutter against his ribs in reply. The rain drove down and everything swelled and drooped. His mother's long hair stuck to her temples and her t-shirt clung to her large breasts. They had Phoenix tans year-round. They never experienced winter down there. It was a privation. He had never felt the bliss of a snowfall, only the savage sun of the southwest, the torrid heat of the semi-desert.

"One book," Kitty told him, annoyed. "One book is all I get to read the entire year." With her thumb, she fanned the yellowed pages, sending a musty wind up into his face. "Two hundred and fifty pages. Am I not entitled to that little?"

Honora lowered her novel. "You are a picture book boy," she told him, "and there's no shame at all in that." But there *was* shame. "Poor Henry," he'd overheard people say about his handicap, "Poor Henry." He feared he would never grow up. He would not learn. He would always be this nine-year-old boy who could not read.

"The rain will stop," Kitty murmured, still reading, absently stroking the inside of his arm. "You'll be fine." He waited. Finally, she was obliged to tear her eyes from the page and look up at him. They regarded each other for a long moment. He could see that she did not believe her own words. Her job was to believe he would be fine and she did not. He saw deep into her but he knew she did not see into him. He wondered if she was a shallow person, an unintelligent person. The fact was that he required special teaching, a private tutor but it would have to wait because at the moment they hadn't the money for one and this catastrophe did not seem to trouble anyone but him. Both his parents had recently been fired.

He did not know what their jobs had been or why they'd been let go. "That tutoring is free here in Ontario," Honora had pointed out. He had come up here to Canada hoping to forget about his handicap but its strangling roots were seated deep within him like a cancer.

This was the third day and each day he'd felt less hope and less energy. Tonight, Kitty would again escape to the club, an old fish camp set up on the granite cliff at the apex of their cove. At bedtime, Henry would press his face to his bedroom screen and watch her flit like a deer through the woods, her bare legs glimmering in the dying light. Later, music, drunken cries would tumble down the rock face and spill through the cottage windows, making it hard to sleep. In his dreams, Henry would see Kitty dancing, pressed up against a strange man, wearing a short, strapless dress that Honora had told her was inappropriate.

Henry did not like her going there. "Grandma says there's too much alcohol up at the club," he'd told Kitty earlier.

"If you ask me, Grandma would be a lot happier if she had a drink every now and then," Kitty answered. "She had her wild days but she doesn't want me to have mine. There's nothing worse than a party animal turned teetotaler."

On the first morning here, before the skies opened, he had joined Honora down on the dock just as the sun rose. It had always been their practice, to spend an hour together down there while Eden and Kitty slept in and for Henry this was the most memorable part of the holiday. They sat with their shoulders touching, their feet dangling in the lake, and listened to the miraculous silence and watched the mist lift like feathers off the water and the sun gradually paint the pine trees on the far shore orange. Honora was still in her sour-smelling flannel nightgown. Her cheeks were dry and papery. She'd had her eyelids done twice, snipped and lifted, so now they did not crease naturally, they looked dead. That first morning, she told Henry that the cottage rental was costing two thousand dollars a week.

"Is that a lot?" he asked.

"Who do you think paid for this holiday?"

"I don't know," he said. She told him to guess. "Daddy?" he said.

"I paid. I paid for this rental and I paid for your airline tickets and I paid for everything you'll eat and do up here in Canada. Did your mother tell you that?"

No, he admitted.

"Of course, she didn't. Do you think that's honest? I think it's important for people to know who paid for what."

"Why?" he asked.

"It's not about the money, per se. It's how you value and thank people."

Honora was a penny pincher. She did not have internet in her house back in the city, she thought it a threat to the soul. She did not have a dishwasher or microwave. She still used a dial phone. She was living in the past. Almost all her friends had died but this did not faze her. She read all day long on her couch, under a wool blanket. "You're alone too much," Kitty had told her. "You're going to get weird."

"Maybe I *like* being weird."

"They will put you," Kitty predicted, "in a nuthouse."

The rising sun struck Henry's delicate ankles and wrists and collar bones and his long fine nose and almond-shaped eyes and his very wide mouth with its red, beautifully shaped lips, the middle of the upper lip, the cupid's bow, lifted as though he were always about to speak. The sun traced the deep cleft in his chin, his thick eyebrows, and these, together with his neatly and handsomely parted sandy hair, had caused his mother's friends to often cry, "Look! He's like a little man! How adult. How lady-killer!" He would always have this face. He had a man's face already. People mentioned certain movie actors, looking at him.

"Who is Cary Grant?" he asked Honora, down on the dock, his face smooth and serious. He was a boy who did not smile much.

"I had a crush on him years ago. Every woman did."

"So, he's old?"

"Dead," Honora said without regret.

Soon, she would climb up to the cottage and put on a too-short, girlishly-flowy sleeveless dress exposing her jiggly arms and her drapey knees. She would not wear a bra. She was seventy-eight and did not realize she was old and this was an embarrassing thing, he could now see. "I don't give a damn what people think about how I look," she'd say. "My fat ass," she'd declare, slapping her behind self-mockingly, "I can't get my fat ass into trousers anymore."

At lunch, they sat crowded together at a small table on the porch, from which they could look down on the steep wooden stairs zig-zagging like a waterfall to the lake, for this was the Precambrian Shield and here the shores were rocky and precipitous.

"Henry has twelve pubic hairs on his crotch," Eden announced.

Oh, why had he ever told her that? He felt a pain in his chest like a stab wound. The table fell silent and he reddened. He was learning that you couldn't trust a female with a secret. A secret in the hands of females became a weapon. They would crucify you with it. Once you'd revealed a secret to a female, you were seen as weak, and females could not abide weakness in a man. They sniffed it out, they hungered for it, they used it to destroy you.

"Are you putting all your money on Johnny Diamond?" Honora, flattening chicken breasts with a mallet, asked in the small, dark kitchen, before supper.

"Oh, I don't know," answered Kitty, conflicted. Henry, leaning in the doorway, could tell she wanted to talk to Honora about it but wasn't prepared for a fight. She tore and tore at a head of lettuce, dropping the miserable shreds into a salad bowl.

"Because, he's not going to be your prince charming."

"I know that," Kitty muttered impatiently.

"He is not going to whisk you up and carry you off on a white horse."

"Okay, okay."

"And anyway, I wouldn't trust a stock broker as far as I could throw one."

"Well, this stock broker happens to be loaded."

Kitty threw the knife at cucumbers, at tomatoes, and tossed them into the wretched salad. The mood in the room was homicidal. "I don't want to argue about it," she told Honora. "This is my happy place."

But, wondered Henry, if this was her happy place, why were they living in Phoenix? Why didn't they simply move up here to Canada? He was born in the U.S. but Kitty was Canadian and she'd told Henry she could get him in. He would be allowed.

"It's not off the table, moving up here," Kitty told Honora. "It's sitting there as plan B."

"Not with Duke in tow, I hope."

"He *is* my husband."

"He's your husband, *but.*"

"This is my life," Kitty pounded her fist on the counter, the knife flashing, "and maybe right now you should mind your own business."

"Say whatever you want to me," Honora answered lightly. "Go right ahead. I can't be insulted or hurt or disappointed, if that's what you're aiming for. Nothing affects me anymore. Nothing wounds."

"Maybe you're dead," Kitty said. She had an Arizona accent now. Honora had accused her of sounding like an American. A voice sharp enough to cut raw meat.

Following lunch that afternoon, Henry had pursued Kitty into her room. He sat on the edge of the bed and watched her pull a low tank top on over her push-up bra, and, over her thong, a pair of thin shorts that fluttered just below her buttocks. She applied more mascara to what was already heavy and flaking. She did not remove it from her lashes at night, but applied more coats when she rose, along with lipstick, blush. Henry found the effect gaudy. He had never seen her true face. Now, with a brush, she tore at her brittle, over-processed hair, shook it loose across her shoulders and cried, "Brassy!" laughing at herself. She was curvaceous and soft, with full hips, a meaty waist, heavy legs.

"I dated Johnny Diamond in high school. Did you know that?" Kitty asked. Of course, he knew it! She'd told them all a dozen times. "I don't know why I dumped him," she mused. "I don't remember what I saw wrong with him."

"Do you still love Dad?" Henry asked, aggrieved, his fine forehead creased.

"There is love and there is love. Of course, I still think Duke's a halfway decent person, don't get me wrong, but I'm not sure he's the one for me anymore, that's all."

Henry got up and went over and pressed his cheek between her shoulder blades, his thin arms reaching around her doughy waist. Her body felt like it was on fire. "Honey," she complained. "It's too hot. You're killing me."

"I'm depressed, Mom," he murmured into her back.

"What do you mean?"

"Depressed."

"Do you mean a little sad sometimes or very low all the time?"

"Very low," he answered. "And when I look at the world, things are all jumbled." His dyslexia was spilling over into his life.

"Are they?" said Kitty. "Are you sure or is it just your imagination?"

Of course, the world did not swirl around as the words did on the page, not physically, but maybe emotionally it did.

"Maybe you just need some vitamins," she said and these words were like a hook in his heart. Vitamins! "Listen," she said, "we can talk about this another…" but then her phone pinged and she snatched it up from the dresser and cried, "Johnny's here!" and dashed out of the room. He ran after her through the cottage and outside, the screen door snapping closed behind him. He leapt down the steps after her, watching her backside, her hips jiggle, her chest bounce and knowing that they would never speak of his feelings again. She clambered into the boat. He stood on the dock, waving and calling, "Bye! Bye!" over and over, but the engine roared and Johnny Diamond, barefoot, muscular, deeply tanned, with powerful thighs, golden hairs on his legs and arms and a million-dollar smile, was twisted round at the steering wheel, grinning at Kitty, and she did not even hear Henry, nor did she turn to wave goodbye.

Henry climbed back up to the cottage to join Honora and Eden in the screened porch. It was the seventh day and they were still reading, even though the rain had stopped and the sun pounded down hour after hour. They had double-crossed him. They read here in the porch or down in the Adirondack chairs at the water's edge and nobody but he, not even Eden, had swum enough to speak of or used the kayak or the paddle board. He sat down on a wooden chair, his long beautiful hands and his skinny arms hanging down between his smooth bronzed knees, and he asked, "Does Johnny Diamond love Mom?"

"Oh, I don't know," said Honora tiredly.

"He *does*," said Eden authoritatively, her sharp chin stabbing the air. She'd discarded the young adult novels and was attacking the old magazines she'd found in the living room. She lay on the wicker couch, ardently turning and turning their glossy pages. *Vanity Fair. Glamour. Tatler.* "Filling her head with trash," Honora had told Kitty. "That girl is heading down a bad path."

"Mother, she's only *eight*!" Kitty had protested.

At five o'clock, Henry ran down to meet the returning boat. He followed Kitty up the jaggedy stairs. "Did you stay in the boat the whole time?" he asked. "Did you go to Johnny Diamond's cottage? Did you stop anywhere for a walk?"

"Yes, we took a little walk."

"Where? Where did you walk? In the woods? Where?" But she did not answer him. She entered the kitchen and again picked up the long knife.

"Maybe we'll stay here in Canada after all," she told Honora. They were both chopping things, their backs to each other.

"Oh?" said Honora cautiously, and her head came up like an animal sniffing danger.

"You said that was ok. Remember? To live with you."

"For how long?"

"While I look for a job."

"How many months would that take? That might take quite a while," said Honora.

"Now, I suppose you're going to say you were speaking figuratively," said Kitty bitterly, gripping the knife like a dagger.

On his birthday, Henry rose very early and put on the shirt and cargo shorts he had brought for this day alone. Before the mirror, he combed his hair neatly in his smooth man-style and then he sat on the edge of his bed with his fingers laced between his knees, waiting for the others to get up. Honora did not rise, she had a migraine. Finally, at eight o'clock, he heard a stirring. He went downstairs and found Eden sitting at the small porch table with her bowl of cereal and a *Cosmopolitan* open before her. "It's my birthday," he told her. She turned to look at him. "Not the whole day," she said. "This whole day isn't about your birthday. Just the cake. Your birthday isn't everything." She appraised his green shirt, printed with yellow cacti – prickly pear, saguaro, jumping cholla. "You can't wear that up here in Canada," she told him. "It doesn't go."

Eventually, he entered Kitty's room and shook her awake. She looked up at him, confused and red-eyed. He'd heard her come in from the club at five in the morning. That was when he'd gotten up. Now it was eleven and nearly half of his birthday was already over. "Was Johnny Diamond at the club?" Henry asked her. "Was he?" When Kitty finally came into the kitchen, she leaned her elbows on the counter, her hair hanging over her face, and said, "I am a *mess*." She searched through the cupboards until she found a Betty Crocker mix, so old that the box was broken and stained and faded. He reminded her that she'd promised to make him a cake from scratch. "My head is *killing* me," she said. "I can't remember *anything*." He stood at her elbow and watched her pour water onto the pale powder. "Is it white?" he asked. "It's not a white cake, is it?" But it was. He dipped his finger in the batter. It had no taste or smell. What was it made of? Kitty rummaged through the drawers. "What kind of cottage is this? How can a cottage have no birthday candles?" she cried.

But then something catastrophic happened. After lunch, Duke suddenly appeared on the upper deck. They had not heard a car. Kitty leapt up from her Adirondack chair and bounded up the long steps. She wore a bikini and her generous brown curves glistened with tanning oil. She asked Duke what he thought he was doing there. He said he was lonely and he'd flown up and taken a cab out here. "Don't worry," he confided in a low tone, leaning toward her. "I used your mother's credit card number. We'll be long gone before she notices." That's when Kitty slapped him hard across the face. The *crack* rang out like a gunshot. Eden, reading down on the dock, jumped up to look. Honora, resting in her room, came out into the sunporch to investigate. Kitty threw her yellowed pocket novel down so hard that the spine broke and the pages began to blow across the deck. Henry ran after them while Kitty disappeared into the cottage.

"She's calling Johnny Diamond," predicted Eden, who'd come up the steps.

"Who?" asked Duke.

Sure enough, soon they heard the roar of an approaching boat. Minutes later, Kitty was aboard and it sped away. Henry stood on the dock beside Duke and watched the boat disappear through the cove neck, the strings of Kitty's bikini twisting gaily in the wind, her back arched fetchingly, her bare stomach offered up like a gift. Henry said sadly, "I wish they had asked me to go with them," and Duke said sharply, "Look, I didn't come all this way for you to go out on some boat." Henry turned toward the stairs. "Where do you think you're going?" said Duke. "Sit down here with me." Reluctantly, Henry remained. "Who is this Johnny Diamond?" Duke asked helplessly. "I never heard of him before." He held Kitty's flipflops carefully in his hands, as though safeguarding them for her, like a pair of glass slippers.

Henry looked up at him. He observed Duke's white hair, the constellation of broken veins on his nose, his big, hard gut, and he could see how much older and less attractive Duke was than Johnny Diamond. His father was older than Kitty and old people could become irrelevant. Just look what was happening to Honora. Duke was sixty and he'd lost his job and he was diminished, it was understood. No one would hire him, at this age. He lacked a future. Henry saw the torment on Duke's face and for a moment he felt sorry for him because he could see that Duke was at this moment like himself: on the outside. His parents were nothing more than children, Henry thought with disgust. They had been terminated. They had no prospects. They had no more control over their lives than he had over his own. Only Honora seemed to have control. It was because she did not care about anything. This was the only way.

"Did you bring me a gift?" Henry asked him softly.

"I didn't have time," Duke snapped. "Don't you think I had other things on my mind? And that is not the kind of question you ask a person." Henry blinked rapidly, stung. They sat and looked out at the water.

"Mom says we might not come back to Phoenix." Henry told him presently. He did not know why he said it. His loyalties were swinging wildly between his parents. He wanted to punish his father for coming to Canada but also to push Kitty into a corner. Only by pitting them against each other, he somehow knew, could he ensure a place for himself.

"Well, I hope you don't believe it," Duke said vehemently.

"She told Grandma. I heard her."

"That is just *rhetoric*," Duke snapped. Henry did not know what this word meant, but could not ask. He knew that you cannot get the truth from an angry person.

At supper, Honora handed Henry a card.

"He can't read," said Eden flatly.

"I'm quite certain that Henry can read a two-line card," Kitty rebuked her.

There was no gift from Kitty. "You need new running shoes for gym," she patted his wrist. "We'll get those for you in Phoenix." He sat there wondering how this could be considered a birthday gift. She was his mother and she was unprepared, Henry saw, she was incompetent.

"You were out long enough on that boat," Duke told Kitty. His face was flushed. He had brought vodka in his suitcase and when Henry passed Kitty's bedroom, he'd seen Duke gulping the clear liquid straight from the bottle. Now they were all squeezed together at the little table, the lake a shining disc below.

"Did you come up here just to spoil my happy time?" Kitty answered, narrowing her eyes at Duke over the rim of her wine glass.

"I had to be here for Henry's birthday," Duke explained. But, they all knew this was not the reason he'd come. He had snatched the spotlight from Henry. Duke had co-opted his birthday without asking. He had stolen it, employed it as a weapon in their marital war, destroyed his celebration. Henry looked from Kitty to Duke, saw the familiar daggers flying between them. He felt drained of hope. He rose woodenly from the table and went out through the screen door and ran down the long twisting steps, his sandals clattering. Kitty called after him but it was his turn not to look back.

He jumped into the water. His clothes dragging at him, he dove deep. He could hold his breath for two minutes but he intended to stay down longer, maybe forever. But soon he felt his heart begin to pound and his head to throb and his lungs threaten to tear his chest open and he could not master these forces. It was a bright evening. The sun shot through the lake, arrows of light turning the water gold, making the weeds, the rocks, his own limbs shine and flicker. The moment came for him to open his mouth, breathe water, fill his lungs with it and sink. But he found he couldn't. It was more frightening than he'd imagined. He hadn't the sheer suicidal will. He was only ten. Panicked, he struggled upward, kicking, reaching with his arms, exploding to the surface, gasping, flicking water out of his hair, his eyes, and there was Kitty's head bobbing in the water, over near the dock.

"Henry!" she shouted angrily. "You get over here!" He obeyed. Honora, Duke and Eden stood on the dock, watching him climb the ladder out of the water. He was humiliated. Kitty followed and stood beside him. She gripped his arm hard, her face thrust into his. "What were you trying to do? Scare the shit out of me? You are such a *baby*." She threw his arm at him.

"Yeah, a baby," Eden agreed. "No way he's ten." Honora had picked up a towel. "Poor Henry," she said, wrapping it around his small shoulders.

Kitty looked down at herself. "My dress!" she cried, dismayed. Duke saw his moment. He stepped toward her, enfolded her in his arms, pressing himself against her wet dress, stroking her stringy hair. Her body slackened. She leaned into him. She murmured in a conciliatory tone, "Let's go up to the club after supper." It was pathetic. Their love could not be trusted, Henry saw. Nor could their hatred. Nothing could be trusted.

Up in his room, Honora helped him peel off his wet clothes. He stood beside his bed in his dripping white briefs, water still running down his thin legs, forming a puddle on the wide floorboards. They heard the others downstairs, the pop of a champagne cork, the commencement of jollity. He turned and pulled his pajamas out from under his pillow. It was still bright outside. The lake reflections danced across the ceiling.

"Come down for your cake," Honora told him.

He shook his head. "It's not real," he said. And he did not go.

The morning they left the cottage, Henry, watching Kitty press her clothes into an open suitcase, felt a painful pressure in his chest. "So, we're really going back?" he said. "So, we're not staying here with Grandma?"

"She didn't mean it when she said we could live with her. I forgot she's never meant anything she says." Kitty had put on her airplane clothes, a cotton safari suit.

"What about Jack? What about Jack Diamond?" said Henry, confused.

"There are plenty of Jack Diamonds," she said but he could tell she didn't believe it.

"I could stay here," said Henry earnestly. "If I stayed here, they'd give me my own teacher to learn to read. Grandma said."

"You can't stay here. You'd miss us. Besides, you're my son, not hers. And your friends are in Phoenix." Friends. That was how much she knew.

"When you get a job, will I have a special teacher?"

"I hope so. Not right away, but later."

He struggled to believe her. "When? How long? How long will I have to wait?"

There would be no divorce, Henry saw. They would not carry through. Kitty and Duke would not save them all from this wasteland, this purgatory of not-love. Theirs was a fake melodrama, a false script. Kitty and Duke could not live with or without each other and this seemed true of many things. He himself was one with his dyslexia. He could not live with it or without it. His mother could not live with or without Honora. Every day after they got back to Phoenix, she would call Honora, sometimes twice daily, friends again, as if they had never fought here. Hypocrites. They would all remain in this state of limbo. More destructive than a breakup, the air in the house always like shattered glass, the joblessness, the drinking, the looming bankruptcy, the ennui. "We are flat broke," Kitty had told Henry the morning after his birthday. "I'm only telling you that because you're old enough now to know." So, that was what you got when you were ten.

Down on the dock, the morning of their departure, Honora had told Henry, "I can eliminate anyone I want from my life."

"But, why?" he'd asked, dismayed. "Why would you want to?"

She had cut off her two best friends and some other crazy ones and her ex-husband and a cousin and a boyfriend and a neighbour and a son and a former colleague. One by one, just like that.

"What about me?" he asked, worried. "Could you eliminate me?"

She turned and smiled at him wickedly. He saw madness in her eyes. "Depends on how you turn out."

He did not understand. Turn out? Hadn't he already turned out? Here he was, her flesh and blood, a full-grown boy, ten now.

Then she scanned the lake as though searching for something. "I am so jimjammed," she burst out, confused, "I have never felt so jimjammed in my life." He saw the speckled, destroyed skin on her chest crack and coil and funnel down horribly into the soiled edge of her white tank top, he saw the sagging curve of her unsupported breasts and the terrible flaked blue polish on her toenails and he heard her rocky old breathing.

They would drive into town and thence to the airport. Tonight, he would lie in his own bed in Phoenix, where he would dream of Canada, of the flickering reflections on his bedroom walls, the rich, buttery echo of his footsteps on the cottage floors, the hot boards of the dock burning the soles of his bare feet, the bright wind off the water, the powerful stink of weeds and fish in the lake, the pure and lonely song of a loon carrying across the transparent evenings. In this dream he would not suffer disappointment. All of these things he would picture and smell and feel vividly, he would dream this dream over and over again, for months, until it was time to come up here again.

At eleven o'clock, they filed through the cottage like a parade, one behind the other, bearing their suitcases, through the screened porch, where the games Henry had produced the first morning were still stacked, unopened, on the coffee table. Then through the spring door, their heels ringing on the deck boards, and then on the steps, descending to where the car stood on the soft, root-choked, powdery earth under a white pine, the trunk flung open and all the doors yawning to cool things off. Henry, following Honora, looked up at her white hair and suddenly he saw snowflakes flying off her head. Cold and wet, they struck his cheek and he grieved for the winter that she would enjoy here without him while he blistered in the southern sun. It destroyed him to leave the lake, which shimmered now below, miraculous, above it suspended the cottage that had always promised so much, if they would only believe. They piled their cases in the trunk but before they got in, Henry cleaved to Kitty, weeping. "Oh, Honey," she cooed, as though she were a real mother, "what's wrong?" but he knew she would not understand.

When We Were All Very Young

IT WAS A reckoning, to be back in Hamburg, the very city where we'd married and to which we'd now come to recover half the fruits of our union. The one mistake had led in time to the other. Though we should have come there as equals, I knew that accounts were bound to be settled and that, in the end, I'd come up in the red. I had no one to blame but myself. The joke was on me.

I'd booked us rooms right on the Elbe so that Anka would have the water and its reflections to look at. Not a cure for grief, by any means, but at least a solace. After checking in, I stepped out onto my balcony and I saw her out on hers, one floor below, and she noticed me up there, and turned a cold shoulder, retreating to her room, as though I were a stalker. The hotel tab was coming out of my pocket and it was I who'd booked and paid for our flights from Canada, just as I'd funded Uta's passage to Germany along with her tuition, but not a word of acknowledgement had I got, let alone thanks. I was of course still paying the mortgage on the family house, as well as Anka's living expenses and she had also billed me for the spontaneous Barbados vacation on which, in an act of revenge, she'd taken Ezra and Uta immediately after I moved out.

She'd told me back home that I could not come to Germany to retrieve the remains, that by leaving the family I'd forfeited my rights as a parent. If you'd asked me, I couldn't have told you exactly why I'd come, unless it was to stake a final claim on Uta.

Before we left Canada, Anka had gone to the airline desk and changed her seat so that we wouldn't be sitting together on the plane and, upon our arrival here, she'd moved far away from me at the baggage claim and she'd taken a separate cab, though we were destined for the same hotel. I thought it unkind and petulant of her to act this way but I could not accuse her of these things because when you leave a marriage and a family you are a scoundrel and not permitted to point a moral finger at anyone. You are a cad with no right to complain.

All her women friends had banded around her like an army, and I was the turncoat, the traitor now, the enemy. I do not know if this is what men do when a woman deserts her husband. I think not. I think they see the break as natural and inevitable and perhaps even as fortuitous. Possibly, they envy him. But they do not circle the wagons. No, they leave him dangling from a cliff.

Out there on the balcony, Anka's hair was bright and pretty in the sun and the wind and this surprised me. Somehow, she looked younger and lovelier than she had in a very long time, and I was washed with sudden doubt and remorse, unable for a moment to remember why I'd left her. But then, I realized my emotions were playing tricks on me, as though, if we could just turn back the clock, Uta would still be alive.

We'd lived all our married life in a pocket of a dozen streets, bordered on one side by the city's oldest cemetery, creeping up a wooded hill, and on another, vast parkland and the black river. On summer mornings, our children rode their bikes over to a grand old wooden boathouse to learn to sail. In the afternoons, they climbed up from the water to a dozen red clay courts for tennis lessons. Always, on our street, you could count on the smell of flowers or fresh-cut grass or fallen leaves or barbeques.

It was a simple neighbourhood of post-war housing, box-like homes, most of which were gradually done over in beautiful ways, with wings attached, sunrooms, fireplaces, dormers, garages, porches, pools and patios, iron fencing, until you could hardly make out the original structures. Admittedly, our own house had been renovated piecemeal, with awkward additions, a warren of hallways, illogical flights of stairs, the kitchen and bathrooms untouched, going back to the '40s. Still, it was where we'd raised the children and where their friends lived and it was debt-free. A flat, treed neighbourhood, quiet but alive with families and children, happy.

I was getting ahead and paying the bills and when I got off the city bus at six, in the shadow of the cemetery hill, and walked down the cooling, deeply shaded streets, where children skipped and cycled and safely played soccer right in the road, I saw the other fathers doing the same, marching homeward, brief cases in hand, all of us in our suits and ties, like a robotic army in uniform. I had loved Anka when I met her in Paris. Must I not love her still? But when I entered the house after work, I could see she took less and less notice of my arrival. She had the children and her many friends and her tennis all day, and art classes and a cycle group to distract her. The months passed, and the years.

But, one day something happened that set our lives on a new path. Anka had a bad fall on the tennis court and she was confined to her bed for six months with a serious concussion. During that time, I made dinner at night with Ezra and Uta and we watched television and eased up on the homework a little, and they seemed to me relaxed and happier, more like kids. But, finally, Anka's world stopped spinning and she was able to get up. And it was as though the blow to her head had provoked a revelation. She declared fervently that our little house had become a prison for her and she'd go mad if we didn't move. She dismissed my objections to a new mortgage and ignored the dismayed expressions of Ezra, now sixteen, and Uta, fifteen, who did not want to be torn from the only home they'd ever known. Somehow, Anka got it into her head that we had to live in the neighbourhood next door, which stood on top of a shale cliff, with embassies and grand houses and views of the turbulent river.

So, in no time at all, we were floating through the new place, like fish in a crystal-clear aquarium. To be honest, it was a beautiful house, a long, modern bungalow, a rectangular box, its rooms flowing, seamless as a river, one into the other. The whole back of it was a glass wall through which poured a wondrous light that nearly blinded us. We walked around, stunned by its clarity and by the view down the wide, steeply sloping lawn to a soft deciduous wood and, beyond the treetops, the miracle of a lake floating in the sky, shimmering like a sapphire.

But something was wrong. Right from the start, it seemed we didn't know who we were anymore. We'd undergone some kind of troubling transformation, strangers to each other and to our old selves. Ezra and Uta wandered the rooms, restless, disoriented by this transplantation, awkward and uncomfortable in the itchy wool uniforms of the nearby private school, where Anka had insisted on enrolling them in the international baccalaureate program, something they'd never even heard of before.

Again, and again, the day we moved in, I stepped through the sliding glass doors, onto the thirty-foot wooden porch, which was suspended high above the lawn and which spanned the entire back of the house. I was mesmerized by the sight of the lake, so close it seemed I could reach out and touch it. It stirred in me something ancient, buried. Feelings of discontent and longing came over me, because, at university, I'd been a star on the varsity team and later swam in a masters' group at a public pool, until Anka told me that my early morning absences were an unfair luxury that a father of two young children couldn't afford. In the warmth of the sun on the balcony, I felt something germinating within me. I stared at the blue disk of water. My heart lifted, I felt joy, thirst for its waters.

The following morning, I slipped out of the house at dawn, long before the family had even stirred. I made my way by instinct, south, along the winding, hilly streets, past dark forests, past small, unexpected meadows, walls of sheer rock, pockets of wildness scattered among stone mansions. Finally, I could smell the water and see it's luminosity in the sky. I located a narrow dirt path leading to a strip of dark sand and the lake. There were others there, all old men in baggy trunks, up at sunrise, out of a lifetime of habit, gathered like pilgrims for a dawn ritual, as though this were a sacred pool. They nodded to me as they dropped their towels on a log and eased their feet out of their sandals on the shore. No one spoke, as if a word would shatter the sanctity of the place.

I plunged into the lake and instantly felt like I'd had a transfusion, every one of my senses tingling, my heart pounding with both happiness and yearning for connection. The lake was half a mile long. With no trouble, I swam the distance eight times over. Out of the corner of my eye, I saw the old men's pale arms breaking the misty surface, their slow, weak strokes, each of us, seeking solitude, striking off in our own direction. Afterward, a wet towel draped round my neck, I weaved my way back home, the pavements growing hotter now, the crowns of tall maples turning orange in the rising sun, the world waking up. My mood both sublime and troubled: somehow, I realized, I'd lost myself a long time ago.

I entered the house through the side door, into a small vestibule where hooks bulged with coats, shoes formed messy heaps, recycling bins overflowed. I stepped into the kitchen, refreshed, cleansed, invigorated by the cold lake. At the table sat Anka and the children, eating breakfast, boxes of cereal before them on the table, a bottle of orange juice. All of them bent silently over their books. After the exhilaration of my swim, the banal domesticity of this scene deflated me. Anka, large, soft and shapeless in her pilled plaid housecoat, which smelled eternally of perspiration, looked up, at first surprised, for she hadn't even realized I'd left the house. She took note of my swim trunks, the towel hanging over my bare chest and she raised an eyebrow. "This should have been discussed," she said, her lips pursed, and I realized that, for a long time, I'd been expected to seek her permission to be happy.

Ezra and Uta didn't even glance up from their reading. I looked at them with the eyes of a stranger. Uta was physically like me, thin, nervous, with a pointed chin, a sharp nose, small eyes, her long hair, pulled back, exposing big ears. She was a serious, intense girl, often moody, and I had to ask myself if she'd absorbed this discontent from me. Was I this way? Had I always been? In contrast, Ezra, like Anka, was quiet, heavy, immovable as a mountain.

This was May.

·

I met Anka following university. I'd gone to Europe for the summer and in Paris, at the end of August, I spotted her on a bench in the Luxembourg Gardens, sitting with a man in a suit. He turned out to be a German diplomat learning conversational French from her. Her long blonde hair, her full red lips, her irrepressible laughter so turned my head that I couldn't pass by. I found a spot under a horse chestnut, and bided my time there, leaning against its trunk, until the lesson was over. As soon as the diplomat walked away, I strolled across the dusty ground, through sighing drifts of copper leaves, to where Anka still sat. Before I could even open my mouth, she smiled up at me expectantly and said, "Yes." She was a tall, sturdy, fair German girl who spoke five languages. For two years, she'd been travelling through Europe freelance teaching – French, German, Italian, Portuguese, English. Later that afternoon, on Rue Madame, where the Paris breezes sent the sheer curtains fluttering like clouds into my tiny hotel room, beneath my window, motorcycles screamed past, their tires chewing up the cobblestone pavement, I shook with wonder at the bold, free way that Anka gave herself to me. I'd never known a girl so cosmopolitan, so independent, self-assured, sexual, free.

I was twenty-three, unambitious and torn about my future. I had a degree in engineering but I hated the field and I wanted to get out. I thought Anka could help me find a new vocation. When she spotted me in the gardens, she claimed, she knew instantly that I was North American. She said she'd always wanted to see Canada, she had never heard anything bad about it. Days later, we were on our way to Hamburg, where I met her parents and we married at city hall, then headed for Ottawa. On the flight, we talked about how she'd continue teaching, maybe establish an international language school. I took her for a fearless, enterprising career woman, bound to go places. I didn't know she was already pregnant when we boarded the plane in Germany. Ezra arrived, then Uta a year later. Anka never worked again.

A year went by in the new house and it was summer again. I resumed my morning pilgrimage to the lake, passing over the hilly terrain, through envelopes of cool air. As I approached the water, the familiar figures emerged out of the morning mist and it occurred to me that, in time, I would become one of these stiff, feeble old men creeping toward the water, with rippling white thighs, sunken chests, drooping pectorals, and this thought filled me with despair. I pushed the feeling aside and dove in.

Then, one morning, a young woman appeared on the bank around six, peeled her sundress off over her head, flung it onto a tree branch and waded into the water in her bra and pants. She swam near me and lingered there, treading water. It seemed rude not to speak to her, so I remarked that she was up very early, for a young person. She laughed at my naivete and said she hadn't been to bed yet. I swam back to shore, went home and forgot all about her. But a few mornings later, she turned up and once more swam straight for me.

"Out all night again?" I asked.

"Why not? You should try it some time," she told me. She remarked that I swam like it was a job and that I didn't look like a person who knew what fun was. "You're married, aren't you?" she said. "It shows. Are you a rule man? Can you think outside the box? How's this for outside the box?" She swam close and kissed me. I thought she must be drunk.

"You know why I came back here," she said.

"No." We were treading water, face-to-face.

"Yes, you do." She reached under the water and touched my groin.

So. This was how it happened. How grown men fell into the arms of young women hardly older than their own children. I'd always thought it preposterous, but now it seemed like the only thing that would save me from drowning. "Come on," she said tauntingly. I swam after her and, on the shore, we collected our clothing, crept along the beach into a dark pine forest, where I spread my towel on the ground, hardly believing what I was doing but convinced that union with this girl would save my life.

The scent of sweet sap, the cool shade, the soft, spongy bed of red needles, the floating, stirring, fanning branches of the pines, like a low roof over our heads, the warmth and texture of her skin after the cool water, her breath and her hair against my face, her arms circling my neck, her slender legs wrapped round my waist like a spider. I was trapped – happily – in her embrace. Out in the clearing, in the rising sun, the old men gradually left. From the corner of my eye, I saw their dripping trunks and pale, boney knees. I didn't care what they thought.

Later, I walked home, feeling astonished, happy, reckless. Before entering the house, I tried to calm myself, concerned that my euphoria might show in my face. As usual, there sat the family, eating breakfast. Ezra, the spitting image of Anka, square-faced, heavy of tread, was hostile and morose that summer. He'd come home from first year university, where, released from Anka's overbearing academic supervision, he'd partied hard and ended up with an overall D. Uta, her nose stuck in a thick German language text, bit her nails. She had not been accepted into medical school in Canada and was headed for Hamburg in the fall – Anka's idea -- to study medicine there and live with Anka's cousin. I had not been in favour of this plan. "Why push her?" I'd asked Anka. "Maybe she should take a year off. Maybe she wasn't meant to be a doctor. Life gives us signals, you know. Life sets out a path for you."

"Does it?"

For years, I'd been saying to her, "Why are you always meddling in the kids' homework? It's theirs, not yours." And she'd answer, "I enjoy it." And I replied more than once, "If you're looking for stimulus, you could go out and get a job."

I must have been wearing a ridiculous expression of hope when I came in from the lake, because Anka asked me, "What the matter with *you*?" She glanced at the wall clock. "Why are you so late?"

"I did a few extra laps."

"You don't even look wet."

"The sun is hot. It dries me off on the way home."

Ezra and Uta took no notice of our exchange. It seemed to me that Anka's insistence on top marks had turned them into serious, burdened adults. I no longer recognized them. They were their mother's children, to be sure. For a year, I'd been putting in longer and longer hours at the office to pay for the mortgage, the new furniture, the private school, college tuition, and when I finally came home in the evenings around nine, I ate supper alone and the children had often already turned out their lights. When I did see them, they brushed past me in the halls as though they couldn't remember who I was, scarcely speaking.

In Hamburg, I'd arranged for a lawyer to meet us at the funeral home after we'd been to the morgue. He was tall, with a fine head of white hair, a kind, tired face. He opened the police report. The driver had been charged with reckless driving causing death. The lawyer pulled out a letter from this man, which respectfully requested that we meet with him. "A rather heartfelt and touching plea," said the lawyer, looking from Anka to me, his eyes solemn, inquiring, compassionate.

Anka dismissed the idea instantly. "It's out of the question," she said. She was wearing a straight skirt too tight in the hips, so that it buckled across her stomach, and an oatmeal sweater that clung to her heavy breasts, reminding me of the voluptuousness that had attracted me to her on that gold and bronze autumn in the Luxembourg Gardens. Now, she had a new hair style that, I had to admit, was quite becoming. Cut off blunt and falling in soft, loose curls to her jawline, it made her look younger, more current. That she was still beautiful pained me unexpectedly – the bright blue eyes, the fleshy cheeks and full mouth, the square white teeth.

"He would like to tell you how he feels," continued the lawyer patiently, "to convey to you directly his profound regret and apology. He is apparently quite shattered by the accident. Speaking from professional experience in similar situations, I feel I should point out that it could help not only him but the two of you. It might assist you with – with closure, you might say."

"I'd rather shoot him than meet him," said Anka, her jaw set. "Nothing he could ever say would make any difference to me. I won't absolve him of guilt. I want him to suffer, just as I am. I want him to think about what he did every day of his life. That's the only revenge I have now."

I said, more to the lawyer than to her, "Maybe it's the right thing to do."

Anka snickered. "I didn't know you knew right from wrong."

The lawyer glanced at me sympathetically and this was enough to open the floodgates. All my pride crumbling, I choked out, "Uta wasn't speaking to me before she left Canada. I never had a chance to explain anything. I never got to say goodbye." I felt Anka's body stiffen and recoil.

"I'm sorry," said the lawyer quietly, his grey eyes sad.

"I forbid you to speak to that man," Anka said. "You betrayed Uta the day you walked out on us. You're not going to betray her again. I hope you realize you're responsible for her death. Your desertion totally threw her off. She lost her equilibrium. She was still a mess when she left for Germany. If it weren't for you, she'd have seen that car. She'd be alive now. You don't deserve to be here. You are not her spokesperson or mine. You have no voice in this at all."

Maybe it was true. Maybe I was unworthy. I didn't know.

Just before Uta left for Hamburg, I'd driven over to the house and parked my car a few doors down, hoping to intercept her on the way to the yoga class I remembered she attended each morning. I hadn't been allowed to see her since I left Anka and I wanted to wish her well. Sure enough, she came walking along the street, one of those rubber yoga mats rolled under her arm. She looked to me fragile, lost. She didn't recognize my car. When she drew alongside, I swung the door open and stepped out quickly. "Uta," I said softly, smiling. But a wave of pain flashed across her face. Though she'd always been a high-strung girl, I had never seen her look so tortured and I knew I was the cause of her distress. She shrank away from me as though to ward off a blow and hurried away. I took a few steps in pursuit. Hearing me behind her, she swung round. "How dare you!" she shouted, her face crimson, the veins on her neck standing out like wires. "You killed our family!" she screamed, her anger so chilling that it froze me in my tracks. "You decided that stupid girl was more important than me and Ezra and Mom. You traded the three of us for some nobody. A person you don't even know!"

She did not always come to swim, the girl at the lake. I'd wait on the shore, consulting my watch every few minutes, and then, when time was running out, I'd plunge into the water and do a few laps, frustrated, disappointed. Some of the old men, emerging from the water, raised their eyebrows in my direction, curious and sardonic. I ignored them. For the rest of the day, I'd be distracted, worried that I'd never see her again. Her name was Suki. She'd finished her university degree and, living nearby with her parents, she was impatient to find a job and be out on her own. She was pretty, petite, olive-skinned. I found her heavy mascara and eye liner, her black lipstick and tattoos and piercings tantalizing as an exotic dancer. She had an ease about sex that reminded me of Anka in Paris. Eventually, she'd come strolling along the dusty path as though it were an accident that she was there at all and, noticing me waiting impatiently under the pines, would frown, puzzled, as though she couldn't remember who I was.

Several times, I asked if she'd go with me to a restaurant in the hills for dinner, but she said, "I like what we have. Don't you think it's lovely here under the trees? Why spoil it?" So, she kept me dangling and to be honest I found that exciting. But, over the weeks, she gave herself to me more and more tenderly under the trees and she was always reluctant to leave and I grew to hope that her feelings for me were deepening.

"I love you," I told her once. "Do you love me?

"I never thought about it," she said. "Why complicate things with big statements?"

I felt younger, happier, more optimistic than I had in twenty years. I sleepwalked through my home life and, when Anka and the children didn't even notice, I had to admit that I'd existed on the periphery of the family for a long time. By late-summer, the mornings were growing darker and the lake cooler and cloaked sometimes in thick fog. Lying back on my towel, Suki shivered and I saw that it wouldn't be possible to carry on this way much longer.

Toward the end of August, I told her, "I want to leave my wife. I've got my eye on an apartment for us. You'd be free from your parents and you wouldn't have to worry about rent. Please." And she put her arms around my neck and said, yes. Yes, this was what she wanted.

In my hotel room in Hamburg, I called Suki every evening and listened anxiously to her phone ringing, knowing that she was never without her cell. I left messages, trying not to sound like an anxious adolescent. *It would be great if you could call back.* Then, *Please, I just need to hear your voice.* And, finally, *I'll die if I can't talk to you today.* Finally, I'd been in Hamburg for four nights. We had to wait for a plane that had enough cargo room for Uta's casket. I'd contacted the lawyer to make sure I'd be informed when it was time to leave. I feared that Anka might try to take Uta back to Canada alone, leaving me high and dry in Hamburg. On the fifth afternoon, I received a text from Suki. *I've moved out of your apartment. It was never anything but a half-way house for me. I never said I loved you. I just thought of you as an adventure. You're old enough to have known that. And I'm not interested in your boring grief.*

Later that night, as I lay in the dark, reflections from the Elbe flickering over the ceiling of my room, Uta's words came back to me. *A person you don't even know!*

He was five feet tall and walked with a slow shuffle that made me wonder if he was ill. He had thin white hair, pale powdery skin, faded blue eyes distant with sorrow. I waited for him at a small table in a coffee shop several blocks from the hotel. I had wanted to ensure that Anka didn't see us together. Why did I decide to meet him? I cannot say. To share my shame, my culpability? That's what Anka would have said.

He sat down opposite me but was too flustered to decide what he wanted to drink. He thanked me for coming. "I am so ashamed of what I've done to you," the words came tumbling out, his voice shaky, "to you and your wife and your -- child. Your daughter. I don't expect you to ever forgive me or to understand. But I had to tell you how destroyed I am by what happened and it's only right that I should suffer, because I don't deserve to live. I wanted you to know that this terrible waste has not gone unpunished." He spoke a formal and perfect English. "I have two daughters and five grandchildren living right here in this city. Yes," he said sadly. "I am lucky to have this. But since the accident, they have not spoken to me. Since the accident I have not seen them. It was all in the papers, you see. So, there is embarrassment for them at the office, at school. There is shame." His green wool scarf, I noticed, was sprinkled with dandruff. There was a white crust in the corners of his mouth. "They are angry with me. They are angry that I am eighty years old and capable of this crime. What can I do? I am an old man. Now I wish I had died in the accident. I wish your daughter were sitting here with you and I were dead. I would be happy now to be dead. I am of no value to anyone anymore. I have become a pariah. I've never had a car accident. In all my lifetime. At my age, they do not test you unless you have an accident.

Now they will say I must be tested, but I do not think I will want to drive again. No."

"Did you see her face?" I blurted out, suddenly realizing that I was looking for connection with Uta, and this man was the last person on earth to see her alive. "Did your eyes meet? Did you see if she looked shocked? Frightened? Can you tell me her expression? What did you see?"

He had come here to beg and now I'd turned myself into the beggar.

How high up did she fly? How fast and how far? Can you give me a picture? What shape did her body take when she went through the air? An arc? An arrow? A jackknife? Was she looking down or up at the sky? How did she land? Do you think she knew what had happened? Did she know she was dying? How long was she alone, there on the ground? Did anyone go to help her?

"I don't know," he stammered. He looked horrified by my questions. "I realize it's terrible, but I don't know. I'm sorry. If only I could tell you something. But it all happened in an instant. And she landed – some distance from me, you understand? On a small knoll, a grassy rise. In the middle of a traffic circle. Hence, the confusion about right of way. That is all I can picture. Probably her neck was broken but I cannot say for sure. Probably she died instantly. I stopped my car. But I could not get out. I could not get out. I could not move. I am ashamed of that. Ashamed. It is the least I could have done, but I was frozen. The police didn't make me go over and look. Because I am old, they did not make me. I have nothing to tell you. I cannot help you. I am sorry."

I craved answers, to be there for her, in a way, at her death. But I did not know if I even had the right to pose these questions. If such questions were obscene. If they were an invasion of Uta's privacy, a violation of her dignity.

The man's eyes swam, his shoulders shook with weeping. I felt hot tears on my own cheeks. "My wife said I killed her," I explained, my voice trembling. "We'd separated, you see? Shortly before my daughter came over here, I had left the family. My wife says it was my fault that Uta died."

"No," he shook his head slowly, his voice suddenly steady, firm and fatherly, "you didn't. You didn't kill her. I killed her. It was me." His hands, on the table, were balled up in tight fists, like two speckled stones. I reached out and covered them with mine, holding tight. The dark clouds over the city suddenly opened. We turned, surprised and somehow relieved to watch the rain pouring down. Everything at that moment seemed right. The two of us sitting there and the rain washing down the windows, both a healing bath and an absolution.

At last, I brought out a small notepad shyly and requested his address. "Would you mind? In case I want to write to you some day? In case there is something more I need to ask or say. If that would be alright with you?"

My partners do not mention my divorce or, after the initial brief expressions of condolence, Uta. The emptiness in my life now. They do not know how to talk of these things or they do not care or, being men, they are not expected or obliged to. They cannot speak of emotions. Speaking of emotions in an engineering office is unseemly.

In my apartment building, I see men slipping through their doorways with young women. I don't know if they've found these girls on the web, in a bar or on a street corner. Does it matter? I have no desire now for a woman, permanent or temporary. This seems impossible, given how important Suki had, supposedly, been to me. I cannot bear to examine this contradiction. I have already made a big enough fool of myself.

Some of these men in the apartment building are my former neighbours. Yes, fathers on my old street. Once the children started college, the men on the street woke up, saw escape. It became an exodus. Now we are all living in this cold tower downtown, in identical, unlivable apartments with tiny rooms, galley kitchens, stark bedrooms with a suit or two and a couple of shirts hanging in the closet. If I spot one of these men waiting for the elevator in the morning, I quickly return to my apartment, pretending I've forgotten something. He silently thanks me for this. We want to forget the past, our old lives, how we know each other.

It is winter now and the canal has frozen over. Walking to work in the mornings, I stop on the bridge and look down at the dark figures of the skaters stroking smoothly below on the scarred ice. I must begin a new life, I think hopefully. Tonight, I will go to the sports store that I can see from my office window, I tell myself. I'll buy a pair of skates this very day, I will. But every night after work, I turn instead toward home, saying, tomorrow. Tomorrow I will begin afresh. I promise. Tomorrow.

"You understand there is no rational connection," the counsellor tells me. "You did not cause the accident."

"Maybe I did."

"That's an emotional thought, a superstitious thought, not a scientific one."

"Maybe that's actually the way life operates. Powerful connections we don't even know about. Invisible forces. Paths of energy."

"You believe that taking the blame will somehow heal you."

"I might."

"Have you let your wife's anger define you?"

"In the past, I suppose."

"And now?"

"Maybe still."

"Do you think she is the authority on morals?"

"I have trouble thinking about anything."

"Do you think you have morals?"

"Am I allowed to have both morals and needs?"

"Are you seeking forgiveness?"

"I don't know."

"Forgiveness, not necessarily from Anka and…" here, he pauses to consult his notes.

"Ezra and Uta," I fill in, not for the first time.

"Yes, from them but also from yourself?"

"I have not examined that."

"Do you still go over there?"

"Where?"

"To the old neighbourhood? Or the new?"

"Yes."

"Which?"

"Both."

"Why?"

"I don't know. I don't know anything you think I should know."

"Let's start with the old house. What do you hope to find?"

"Glimpses of the children? Me with them? Pictures of happiness we must have felt back then? When we were all very young?"

"And do you find that?"

"Memory can invent anything it wants."

"And the new house? Why? Do you want to see Anka?"

"No."

"To reconcile with her?"

"No."

"Are you sure?"

"Sometimes Ezra visits from school. I think I might catch sight of him."

"Would he talk to you?"

"Probably not."

"What then? Tell me the reason."

"Maybe I'm looking for – a feeling."

"What does that feeling have to do with?"

"I don't understand it."

"Loss? Sorrow? Acceptance?"

"I don't know."

"Justification for why you left? Redemption?"

"This is exhausting me."

"You are discouraged. You must keep your spirits up. You must control your self-talk. Control what comes into your mind. Any negative or destructive thought can be turned away, with practice. It is a useful survival skill."

A silence falls between us. This often happens. The counsellor has said that these uncomfortable pauses are necessary. My mind creating space for feelings to float up. Once again, I consider never returning. He reads my mind.

"Come back next week. You're not well enough yet to go it alone."

It is a large mall, where his offices are, on a busy road, with acres of parking and hundreds of vehicles. No matter how well I think I've memorized the spot I left it in, I can never find my car. I walk up and down the rows, reading licence plates dumbly. I feel like I am in a dream. I might be dreaming all of this.

Pre-existing Condition

LAST YEAR I had cancer and all winter I lay on the living room couch, covered by a plaid throw, fingering its rough wool fringe and looking out hour after hour at the squirrels leaping along the black branches of the maple tree in our yard. Then, in March, just when my hair had started to grow back, just when I was finally strong enough to sit up in an armchair for a couple of hours, Ansel perched on a footstool at my knee and took my hand expectantly. He'd grown thinner and his face was more lined and tired and his red hair now flashed with flecks of silver and his boyish freckles had faded, as though he'd been scorched by my cancer and aged by the demands of my care. He told me that he'd gone out and bought an apartment for us near the river. He explained that he could no longer cope with the demands of the house and he wanted to concentrate on his bridge club and his golf game and his cycling and his workouts in the apartment building's gym.

But I wondered if in fact he wanted to move because he thought my breast cancer was sure to return even though

I'd got the all-clear from my oncologist. When the cancer returned, he may have reasoned, it would be better not to have the house stairs to cope with or doorways too narrow for a wheelchair to fit through or bathrooms unsuited to the infirm. And I must say, I felt a little betrayed, despite all he'd done for me.

I agreed to go, though it grieved me to give up the house I loved. I gave in because I sensed that during my illness, I had lost agency, that my position in the marriage had weakened, I'd become a liability. I still required a nap in the afternoons, there were foods I could no longer digest, visitors tired me, l went to bed early. We couldn't leave the country because we could not get travel insurance for me on account of my pre-existing condition. "We could lose our shirts in a foreign hospital!" Ansel cried over and over. "Every penny we have!"

I had a hard time feeling at home in the apartment Ansel had bought, and he seemed resentful that I didn't appreciate his brilliance in snapping up this piece of real estate in the most expensive new apartment tower in this city, with its killer view of the river that everyone was fighting over, an investment that had swallowed up half our worth. At the house, we'd had our feet planted firmly on the ground, but here, it felt like gravity had let go, sent us floating up in space like helium balloons. Every time I stepped out onto the balcony, craving fresh air, craving *proof of life*, I was battered by the powerful winds that wrapped the building. I leaned over the rail to observe cars and people moving far below, so small that they seemed like wind-up toys. Then, I'd look across the parkland and I'd see Ansel's figure fly past, bright as a tropical bird in his Lycra costume, his bicycle wheels spinning like stars as he flew along the recreational path, under the spreading boughs of the red pines and the white pines, the river's silver rapids flashing beyond him. At times, I did think it unfair, this new athleticism of his, I thought it slightly unkind of him to flaunt his vitality.

I tried to regain my strength. I followed a dirt path behind the building, winding east, through tall bending grasses, to the mighty river. I made an effort to walk a hundred feet further every day. There was a place where I could sit down at a picnic table to rest in the shade of ancient willows, small waves lapping at my feet. We had three rainless weeks of forty-degree temperatures. The lawns grew brittle, the leaves in the trees yellowed prematurely and dropped. Everything around me was losing life. The burned grass along the river shattered, making way for fierce weeds that spread like wildfire, bursting with tiny, bright flowers, white or yellow or purple. Thistle, miniature daisies and morning glory, celebrating the heat and the drought. They were like Ansel, I thought: feeding off my illness. It seemed the more I weakened, the more he flowered. My waning was nurturing his rebirth.

Of course, I realized the cancer was still with me. Everybody knows chemotherapy does not kill cancer. It simply sends it to hide in another part of the body, where it lies in wait, ready to pounce just when you think you're safe.

I pictured cancer as a sleek, soundless predator, a panther, its emerald eyes bright with night vision, able to slink powerfully through the dark tunnels of my body. Sometimes I felt its very weight within me, curled up like a deadly feline.

As soon as we'd settled into the apartment, Ansel invited our son, Jericho, over, eager and proud to show off the view. I was surprised at the risk he was taking because, more than once, as a teen, Jericho had called Ansel a money-grubbing parasite, screwing investors to make himself rich. "He doesn't know *shit* about brokering," Ansel told me at these times, pacing with anger. "Wait 'til he has a dime or two to put into the market. Then he'll see the value of experts like me, won't he?" They clashed over everything – Jericho's hobbies, friends, school marks. Ansel was angry when Jericho went into English at university. He wanted him to study Economics. The two of them came to blows over it. Ansel got Jericho in a half-nelson on the kitchen counter and I had to pull him off by the hair. They faced each other, murderous, with the same red colouring and flaming tempers. Then, during my cancer, they had a brief rapprochement, united by a mutual anguish and fear. I'm ashamed to say that I felt jealous of their new bond. Also, I sensed it meant they thought I was finished. I resented that. I thought it bad luck for them to believe so, and I was full of superstitions by then. But as soon as my danger passed, they went back to their old hostilities.

Jericho came to the apartment and we followed him as he walked silently through the rooms, his expression reserved. Finally, he turned to us and said that what he saw sickened him: the brass gates downstairs, the marble foyer, the Tiffany sconces, the doorman in his grey coat and gloves, the Persian rugs in the elevators, our new sofa and chairs and dining table, the conspicuous display of privilege. Such is the righteous indignation of youth. Ansel tried to shrug it off, but could barely disguise his hurt. After Jericho left, he exploded. "He decided long ago to hate everything I represent. It's that simple. Who does he think he is? As if this place was bought with dirty money. He's all high and mighty now, isn't he, but what about when the will is read? He'll rush to the table then, won't he?" I tried to tell him that Jericho was just naive and idealistic and would be more practical someday. However, Jericho never came back to the apartment, he never brought the girlfriend, Coral, either, or the baby, Olympia, born just days before we moved in.

My church is right next door to our condo. Ansel does not attend. He says the Unitarian Church is a fake religion because its members are not obliged to believe in anything, even god, and I tell him maybe it is not a religion at all but a community, which is even better. I joined it because I prefer grey to black and white, I value ambiguity over doctrine. Ansel is a lapsed Catholic and he is very bitter about Catholicism though he was never molested by a priest or any such thing. I think his anger is misplaced. I suspect he is resentful because his family was so poor that the church was the only thing they had to turn to and he wasted his youth riding his bike to church every morning to play altar boy at seven o'clock Mass because he thought he wanted to be a priest. Eventually he became a stock broker instead, and I have never said as much, but it seems to me that money became his god.

I go over to my church on Friday mornings to arrange the flowers for Sunday services. It is a modern building with forty-foot windows rising in the shape of a prow, as though it were a great spiritual vessel sailing toward the river. The Portuguese woman is always there, dusting the pews and the pulpit and vacuuming the red carpet that runs up the aisles and over the hexagonal steps leading to what is not really an altar, more a stage. I hired her to clean our church thirty years ago. She is a small woman and over the years I've seen her grow shorter and thinner and stooped. Though she is seventy-five, her hair is still iron-grey, as though she carried with her from her homeland some ancient force. As a young woman, she worked in the olive orchards of Alentejo. I look now at her dark, arthritic hands and I picture the gnarled tree trunks and the twisted roots of the old country.

Her name is Genoveva, and each Friday when she's finished cleaning, she kneels down in one of the pews with her pail of dirty water beside her and her wet rags and a string mop and she is not embarrassed or ashamed that these have been her life's intimate tools. She crosses herself, her lips moving in prayer, for she is not of our faith, she is of course Catholic. Then, I sit down beside her in the pew and I feel very lucky to be in her presence. She has never learned English but is fluent in French. I try to talk to her, struggling along with the few words I recall from high school classes. So, even after all these years, I know very little about her life. She has a forty-year-old bachelor son living with her, that I do know. He suffers from depression and I can see that this causes her great pain.

"Dis moi quand tu veux prendre ta retraite," I've said to her many times. Tell me when you want to retire. Because at her age, she should certainly not be working, and I am afraid she is too conscientious and loyal and shy to say she wants to quit. But she tells me that she cannot retire because staying at home with her verbally abusive husband is too punishing. Once, confiding this, she began to cry and said that, in addition, some of her employers, such as I, were her friends and she would miss them terribly. This both surprised and filled me with guilt, because I don't give her a thought except when I see her there in the church and I never considered her in any way a friend.

I wondered what it would be like to feel that the only escape you had from marital abuse was wiping up people's filth, cleaning their toilets and kitchen sinks, removing the dust over and over again from this church and from the houses of wealthy people and their frivolous possessions. I suggested alternatives to working: she could go out for the day to her daughter's house, to a park or a movie, to her church, to a library or cafe, where she could sit and read a book, but she said she did not read. *Non, non, non,* she shook her head impatiently, perhaps annoyed that I understood her so poorly. *Non, non,* none of these things was imaginable. Sometimes she hugs me and murmurs into my shoulder, "*Je t'aime. Tu es comme ma soeur. Je t'aime beaucoup.*" You are like my sister. I love you. She clings to me, so shrunken that she feels like a sack of dry bones. Until recently I took this embrace for granted but, lately, I have come to cherish it because there has been an earthquake in my life.

Jericho's girlfriend, Coral, became pregnant before we even met her. For me, this came as a great surprise and a disappointment, because he'd always confided his most private experiences to me: his hopes, fears and failures, his first girlfriend, first sex. To be sure, he had Ansel's curly ginger hair, freckles, green eyes, but Jericho and I were kindred spirits. We were drawn to the same films, books, art. Coral was a high school dropout. "She's the opposite of us," Ansel told me. "That's why he picked her. It's obvious." I wondered if she'd got pregnant to entrap Jericho. Nevertheless, I embraced the idea of the baby, and in fact I was soon telling him that the unexpected promise of a grandchild was sustaining me through the chemotherapy. I said I was taking Olympia's birth, coinciding so closely with the end of my illness, as a sign that I'd survive. And indeed, before long, I was smitten with the child. When I held her tiny body in my arms, so perfect and full of promise, I felt myself healing.

One day, Jericho asked me to meet him at a coffee shop in the commercial strip not far from our apartment. As soon as we were seated, he got right down to business. Speaking quickly and nervously, his face flushed, he said that he and Coral were splitting up, that neither of them wanted to take responsibility for Olympia, or have anything at all to do with each other for the rest of their lives, so they had put the baby up for adoption. Interviews with prospective parents were already underway.

Of course, I was utterly heartbroken. This was more devastating news than when I found out I had cancer. I reached across the table and touched his hand. I begged him to let Ansel and me adopt Olympia. We'd raise her, I said, and if he ever wanted her back, she'd be there for him to take. But he recoiled at the suggestion.

"I wouldn't want Dad to be her *father*," he snapped impatiently, as though I should have known this.

"Your timing couldn't be worse," I told him.

"What do you mean?" he said angrily. "This isn't about your cancer. Everything's not about your disease."

"I'm sorry."

"Well, you guilt people out about it."

Was this true? I didn't know.

The baristas were dumping the thick white cups in the metal sink, they were grinding coffee beans, whirring the espresso machine. "It's so noisy in here," I told Jericho, trying to buy time. "I can't think. I can't hear you. Let's go over and sit in that park." There were benches in the shade. We could see them through the big windows.

"No, Mom. This isn't a social visit." *None of your tricks,* his expression said. He had always had a soft, boyish, kind face, but not that day. He was only twenty-two but he looked old and tired and hardened and defensive.

"You don't even know Olympia," he said.

"What do you mean? She's six months old. I've held her. I know her. She's my flesh and blood." I drew a tissue from my purse, dabbed at my eyes. "You can't just give her away. It will kill me."

"I knew you'd get emotional," he said with disgust. "I came here as a courtesy to you but now I regret it." He leapt up, knocking the table. It whirled on its round base and his coffee spilled and ran in a line toward me. I grabbed a napkin to catch the flow, and he took advantage of my distraction to bolt out the door. People stopped tapping away on their computers to glance over, people sitting nearby in leather armchairs lowered their newspapers to stare at me.

There was a long narrow park stretching west from the coffee shop, with a path winding in and out among young trees. This is where the streetcar had run, a hundred years before. They'd torn up the tracks and created this grassy corridor. I forgot to get on the local bus. I was in such a daze that I walked the three miles home on the cinder path, through this green passage, in the shade of the crab apple and ash trees, between rolling mounds. I reached our building, weak and shaking. And as the elevator lifted off, something strange happened. In that unsettling moment of suspension, the split-second interval of hesitation between earth and sky, that instant of nowhere-ness, I felt a malignant presence, a foreign seed, a hard kernel brilliantly shining, planted anew within me, bearing a deadly message.

"We're sixty years old, for Chris'sake!" Ansel exploded at me when I told him I wanted to adopt Olympia. He leapt up from the breakfast table, where we'd been sitting side by side, facing the wall of windows, so that we could both enjoy the panorama of the parkland, the brilliant river. He was dressed for his group ride along the water and over the lacy steel bridge, visible from our apartment, and up into the magenta hills. Every day he looked more youthful and physically explosive in his Lycra kits, the hairs on his muscular legs bleached by the sun, his face and arms bronzed.

"Plenty of grandparents our age have done the same," I told him. "It's not unheard of."

"This is ludicrous!" he said. "You can't even walk."

"That's not true," I answered, wounded.

"You said yourself you've never recovered your old energy. What if you get sick again?" he asked, though I'd told him that the chances of surviving breast cancer were the best, of all the cancers. "What if you – what if you die? Then I'll be saddled with that *kid*. I didn't retire so I could change diapers!" It was no refugee we were talking about here, he pointed out. It was a healthy child with good prospects for new parents. There were all kinds of fine people out there, dying to adopt.

"This isn't some civic project," he lectured me.

"Well, I know that." I had been a noted activist in the city, always involved in rallies, campaigns, fundraisers, sit-ins. I had thought he was proud of me for it.

"You're not going to get your picture in the paper for doing this."

By this time, I was on my feet too. Between us, on the dining room wall, hung four large black and white blow-ups of me, taken when I'd modelled for a big cosmetic company to pay my university tuition. In these, I had the waist-length hair of the day, smooth as syrup, the model's sexily parted lips, the false lashes, the large magnetic eyes commanding the camera. The photos were taken long before Ansel ever met me, but he insisted on hanging them, as though he fantasized that I was still that ingenue. Sometimes when we were talking, I'd see his eyes drift restlessly from me to the girl in the photographs. I could see that he had a crush on her. The contrast with my present appearance embarrassed me, my short hair grown in curly because of the chemotherapy, as though it belonged to someone else, all the softness melted from my face, my skin papery. I'd lost all notion of fashion long ago, and dressed now in baggy trousers, long shapeless cardigans, flat laced shoes.

He said, "You might as well say goodbye to your son, if you go ahead with this adoption. You know that, don't you?" Then he added, "This isn't the baby you lost, you know. This isn't Aileen."

I thought that unkind of him, to throw up my lost daughter at me.

"You're not going to bring Aileen back, doing this."

I said, "Maybe you just don't want Olympia because she's Jericho's child."

This wounded him but it was my turn to be cruel. He pulled on his cycling shoes, with their sophisticated buckles. For some reason these shoes had to match his clothes and his gloves and helmet and even his bicycle. "I think you're jealous of my life," he said. "I have my health, so to pay me back, you have to have this baby." I heard the cleats of his shoes clicking rapidly down the hallway to the elevator.

When I was thirty and married to a man named Richard, I gave birth to a baby with a hole in her heart. In the neonatal unit, I sat day after day, rocking and feeding Aileen and holding her while she slept. Nothing outside that room seemed important to me anymore, nothing seemed real. Making my way home in the evenings, I did not feel my feet touch the ground or notice the wind or rain or even the time of day. The hole was between the filling chambers of her heart. Her blood did not contain enough oxygen because the oxygen-rich blood mixed with the oxygen-depleted blood. She took on a blue tinge and sometimes her hands and feet swelled. She did lengthen but she remained thin and weak. I pressed my fingers to her throat to find the tiny tapping beat of her pulse. In time, I felt her grow lighter and lighter in my arms. She looked up at me as if to say: Are you not my mother? Why can't you save me? Why are you so useless?

The hole was too big. After eighteen months, they told me the hole was too big. They had hoped it would repair itself but it could not. Near the end, they put her on intravenous because she no longer had the will to take the bottle. This seemed to me to happen very suddenly, though perhaps it did not. I did not understand it, how an infant so small could appear to make such a profound and final and adult decision: to give up, to stop fighting. Now, I saw relinquishment in her eyes, an adult knowledge, and I felt her body relax, surrender. I had been convinced that it was not the doctors who would keep Aileen alive, but me. I had believed my love could deliver her but I had been wrong about that. All my desire for her to live could not make the blood pump more powerfully or more richly through her body.

The evening she died, I came home to an empty house, though I'd told Richard that the end was near and I'd asked him to stay close. He'd left a note saying he was in Toronto on business for the night. I may have suspected a lie. In the back of my mind, the hole in Aileen's heart had come to represent something more, it had become a symbol of our marriage.

At the cemetery, Richard's twenty-year-old secretary, Cynthia, came up and shook my hand. I thanked her for coming. She wore a chic black coat with a big curved collar and tall suede boots. Her long wheat-coloured hair flew back, and on her earlobes, large diamond studs glittered, a piercing brilliance I vividly remember on that grey day. Later I would find the bill for them in Richard's night table drawer. The three of us stood side by side as the tiny casket was lowered into the ground, Richard's shoulder touching not mine but Cynthia's. In all the months following Aileen's birth, he hadn't come to the neonatal unit even once. He said he wasn't cut out for that sort of prolonged ordeal. The day after the funeral, he moved in with Cynthia. "I've been grieving all these months too, you know, but you didn't even notice," he told me, chagrined. "Cynthia gives me comfort. You fell in love with Aileen and you forgot about me. You were too strong. You could have shown some need for your husband." He added gloatingly, "Cynthia is pregnant. We're going to have a healthy child."

Ansel said to me, "I know perfectly well you've been to a lawyer. I recognize that righteous look of yours. I haven't been married to you for twenty-five years for nothing. Who's going to pay his bills? I suppose that will be me."

The lawyer had said that, in the law, there is always an assumption that a family member is better suited than a stranger to love and care for a child. This gave me great hope. I filed an application to stop the adoption proceedings while I applied for an interim order of guardianship. The process would take two months. I didn't sleep well at night. I'd turn in the darkness, reaching for Ansel, forgetting that he'd shifted away in the bed, his back turned to me. I was dried up inside from the cancer. My tissues had grown brittle. I could not have sex anymore. It was too painful. But I still needed to be touched, I'd explained to Ansel. There were other things we could do, to be intimate, I said. But he wouldn't listen. He said he didn't care about sex anymore. I felt -- I felt --

"Maybe it's your depression making you do this," said Ansel one day.

"No."

"Is this your depression?"

"I'm not depressed."

"You said that -- "

I had said that some days, maybe most days, I looked forward to the moment each evening when I could lie down and go to sleep and just forget about everything.

"You said -- "

Jericho wouldn't answer his phone when I called. My emails to him bounced back. "He's blocked you," Ansel told me. "I can't say I blame him. What did you expect?"

August came, with its puffy clouds hanging so close to the apartment balcony it seemed possible to reach out and touch them.

The lawyer called and said we'd been successful in blocking the adoption. If Jericho would not consent to hand Olympia over, we would make a move to have the Children's Aid Society take temporary custody. "Is your husband on board?" he asked. I couldn't answer. I was trembling with fear and doubt.

"Are you limping?" asked Ansel in September.

"No."

"I thought I noticed you limping."

"No, I don't think so."

"What is it, then?"

"I'm just tired."

"Well, I hope you'll get that checked out."

I wrote letters to Jericho, many versions of the following: *I understand your point of view, so can't you try to understand mine too? After all we've been through together don't you think you owe me that much? All I'm trying to do is to keep you from losing what you will one day realize is the most precious thing you ever had. From abandoning your flesh and blood to the arms of strangers. You're young. This is the first big test life has presented to you. One day you're going to see that I have saved you from making a big mistake.*

I descended in the elevator, letter in hand, the weight of its message exhausting me as I carried it along the busy street to a red mailbox. I pulled the drawer open, listened to the envelope flutter down, like a faint pulse, and felt my own heart quiver with hope.

Weeks later, a thick manila envelope arrived in the mail. In it were my letters, all of them still sealed except for the first, which had been torn into small pieces and returned to its envelope. This cut me, but not in a destructive way. More like the surgeon's incision, carving the tumour from my breast, paring away the cancer, opening the way to life. I chose to see Jericho's statement as a healing moment and my resolve became all the stronger. Cancer had schooled me in loss. I was partnered now with it. It had become my inner strength.

The oncologist said, "How long have you had this pain?"

"I don't know."

"Months? Has it been months?"

"Yes, I suppose it's been months."

"Your husband hasn't come with you today."

"No."

"Usually he comes with you."

"He's away."

"Have you told him about this new development? The bone cancer?"

"Oh, yes."

"Because this is serious."

"Yes."

"Of course, you must tell him."

"I know."

"You will need his support."

"Yes, I'll tell him."

"And as we've said before, this is his disease too, in a sense, this is his journey as well as yours. I have found that life-threatening diseases bring out the best in people."

"Have you?"

"In most cases, yes."

"Is there something seriously wrong with your leg?" Ansel asked.

"No, nothing's wrong."

"Are you sure?"

"The physiotherapist said it's just a weak muscle. It's trivial. I can't stand your harping. Are you just trying to scare me?"

It snowed the first of November, just as it had the year Aileen died. I thought about this as I walked over to the church on Friday. I feared the approach of winter, the death of the leaves, of the gardens, the cold shroud of killing snow, the weakening of the life-giving sun. Beyond the sky-high windows in the church, the feathery flakes formed a delicate screen against the bare black trees, the whitening ground, the darkened river. I carried a bunch of carnations up onto the altar. I paused and looked up at the colourful banners hanging from the pitched wooden ceiling. *Joy. Peace. Love. Hope. Patience. Forgiveness.* I had been a force in this church, I'd raised funds for its construction, developed programs, conducted philosophical discussion groups, recruited members, chaired committees to build a seniors' home and a daycare on this very property. None of this, I thought, none of these good works or all the people I'd helped or come to know could protect me from my parasitic disease. This thought shook me. I steadied myself against the marble altar, took a deep breath. I was still going through the motions of making choices, when in fact I no longer had the liberty or power to determine anything, I was lying to myself that I still had influence or the ability to decide.

Genoveva carried her vacuum cleaner up the altar steps. She had missed three consecutive Fridays at the church. This had never happened before. I turned from my flower arranging and placed my hand on her fleshless shoulder. Her straight hair had thinned shockingly and had completely whitened and been crudely cut, as though she'd taken a scissors and attacked it herself, exposing her large ears, her veined temples. Her eyes were pained and her body all gathered in as though she'd been struck.

"Genoveva, what's wrong?" I asked, alarmed. "What's happened to you?" She broke down. She always spoke very fast and her French was rough and I could not always understand her, but I made out the words, *fils, surdosage, ambulance.* Son. Overdose. Ambulance.

"*Désolé,* Genoveva," I tried to comfort her, squeezing her shoulder. "I'm sorry." She wiped her eyes and, looking down at the floor, shook her head and turned back to her vacuuming. "Is your son home from the hospital now?" I asked her, in French.

She looked at me, incredulous, distressed at having to repeat herself, betrayed at the sympathy I'd expressed a moment earlier. "*Il s'est suicidé!*" she cried, anguished. "*Il est mort! Mort!*" Dead.

I felt a complete fool, not to have comprehended her the first time and she looked at me as though questioning whether, in thirty years, I'd understood anything at all that she'd ever said to me, and in fact I was often guilty of counterfeit and fakery, for many times while she spoke, I'd nodded or shaken my head sympathetically, listening to her but not quite grasping her rapid speech and too careless or hurried to ask her to slow down or repeat herself.

I lingered there, that afternoon, going through the motions of tidying the stacks of hymn books and updating the bulletin board and counting the flyers and replenishing the candles, killing time in order not to abandon her there in the empty church. She did not kneel down to pray. She emptied her pail and unbuttoned her apron and folded it very neatly into her purse and pulled her salt-stained boots on and her frayed coat and stretched scarf. I went over to her. *"Je ne suis plus vivant,"* she told me simply. *I am no longer alive.*

"And your husband?" I asked. "Is he a comfort to you?"

"He is all I have left," she said in French. "I must accept the way he treats me. I do not want to be completely alone."

We embraced, and I felt grateful that she needed me in that moment and I realized with surprise how I had come to need her. And then she said, again in French, speaking slowly now, "You have a son, don't you? Listen to him. Honour him. Hold him close. Because some day, he might be torn from you and that wound will never heal." *Jamais.*

The storm had been heavy. I put on my own coat and followed her out to her car and took the snow-brush from her hand and said, "Let me do this." She protested, not wanting any help, not caring about herself. But she was too defeated to resist, and while I swept the heavy white blanket off the roof and hood and windows of her rusty coupe, while it silently fell in great wet chunks to the ground, she stood there in the gathering darkness, sobbing raggedly, a handkerchief crumpled to her face, her feet locked in snow.

Honour

1

I do still drive out to the reservoir these summer nights. After supper, when the air, sweet with the ripeness of the day, somehow offers me hope, I get into my car. I make my way up to the north edge of Honour, where they put the dam in ten years ago, stopping up our humble Thames, narrow enough in these parts for a man to jump across. Before that, the only thing out that way were empty fields lying in a valley. But soon, pricey houses went in, ranged up a cliff overlooking the reservoir, and now it's become a recreational place, with sailboats bobbing and tipping and racing across the blue water and a strip of white manmade beach glimmering on the far shore.

I used to take Oneida out there just to demonstrate to her the engineering wonder of the dam. The brilliance of the massive steel embankments and piers and trusses. My heart pounded with awe and excitement at their size and genius. I pointed to the water tumbling and coiling and braiding powerfully over the gates into the foaming cauldron below, and we stood there silently in the refreshing spray, deafened and silenced by the roar of the cataract, our feet trembling with its vibration. It seemed to me as though the two of us were somehow suspended together in time and redeemed.

This was after supper, once we'd finished our tea, and we'd got into the car and woven through the deserted, strangely foreign, evening streets of Honour. I believe that Oneida at first hoped I'd taken her out there for the romantic sight of the clouds turning from orange to pink to mauve in the sunset over the water. And to be sure, we did try to time it so that we could watch the sun sinking below the blue horizon, but it had nothing to do with love. Soon I noticed that Oneida seemed less interested in the dam itself or the thundering water, being distracted by the distant sailboats flitting like gulls on the reservoir and the families packing up their cars after a day of swimming and picnicking on the far beach, and I wondered what she saw in them.

But I do have to admit that, once I'd parked the car in the narrow lot below the cliffs, I couldn't be bothered to wait for Oneida. I strode ambitiously ahead, leaving her to fight on her own against the punishing wind that always sliced off the water, her sweater hugged round her, and, because she is small and brittle and weak and handicapped, it would be some minutes before she reached me in the middle of the dam.

And sometimes, as the wind cut away at us out there on the bridge, I'd look over at her face, burnished by the coloured light, and I'd observe the sagging flesh of her cheeks and her withered mouth and the dark hairs springing like spiders' legs from its corners and the thatch creeping from her broad nostrils and her coarse hair driven straight up from her sublime forehead, which is high and wide and curved and white, like an ancient archaeological bone scoured and punished by soil and minerals and water and frost, and I'd wonder: who is this inarticulate, diminished woman I've tied myself to for half a century?

Some weeks ago, I called the police to our home. I'd returned from the market, a bouquet of gladiolas in my arms, and found the house empty. I looked in every room but Oneida was nowhere to be found. I sat down in my leather recliner and waited for two hours, my legs crossed, still wearing my straw fedora. From this chair, I can observe the street and I kept turning to look out, half expecting to see Oneida walk up the drive, a carton of cigarettes tucked under her arm. Finally, I picked up the phone and dialled 911. The young officer who arrived an hour later was tall and slender, with a graceful way of walking, long-legged and loose and slow, like a dancer. He went into every room as though he thought Oneida might suddenly spring out from behind a piece of furniture. The kitchen on the front of the house, with its two small windows like eyes watching the road, the living room behind that, beside it the master bedroom, then the narrow hallway leading down to the bathroom, to the side door with its little porch and clothesline, to the dark enclosed stairs, carpeted with cheap shag broadloom, climbing to the second floor. I followed him, puzzled and somewhat irritated, finally saying impatiently, "As I told you, she's not here. I looked everywhere."

Upstairs, under the steeply sloped ceiling of the back room, he said, "This is where your wife sleeps?" He looked at me strangely, so I explained, "She snores loud as a freight train, so I sent her up here." But I felt embarrassed, noticing for the first time how miserly and comfortless the room was, the poverty of the thin, home-made bed cover, pulled painfully tight as though to erase any evidence of human life, the crumbling green blinds dating back to the days of our girls, Oneida's pink velour swivel rocker, all faded and worn and stained, the television, small and ancient compared to my fancy set downstairs, the coldness of the bare strip flooring.

"Could you show me your wife's things?" he asked. In the bright, mid-afternoon light spilling in, the heavy wool of his blue uniform gleamed, the brass buttons shone.

"Things?"

"Items of daily use. Articles of necessity to her." Then I looked at the scarred side table, usually cluttered with her glasses, cigarettes, Bik lighter, rosary, tattered letters from the girls fastened together with an elastic band, torn envelope with photos of the children and grandchildren, large-print library book, magnifying glass, Holy Bible, tweezers, hand mirror, bag of humbugs, bag of butterscotch wafers. This nest of hers, this paraphernalia. All missing. Of course, I felt like a fool, because I'd always prided myself on my powers of observation.

"As you can see, Mr. Kennedy, all of her personal effects are gone. You yourself may have noticed this?"

"I don't know. I don't know. I might have."

"Where does your wife normally keep her clothes? Could you show me, please?" I led him back downstairs to a narrow closet in the master bedroom where I now slept alone. I drew aside the threadbare curtain printed with faded pussy willows, and found a dozen empty hangers. I pulled opened her dresser drawers. Gone were her stacks of neatly folded underwear, rolls of nylon stockings, nighties, slips, gloves, scarves, lipsticks, religious relics. "Where are her suitcases kept?" asked the policeman. "Where are her shoes?" Her coat? Boots, purse, umbrella, hats? "To be honest, Mr. Kennedy, I don't see any evidence of foul play here. No sign of violence, coercion, haste or confusion, chaos, doubt, accident, madness. This appears to me to be a very organized departure. A clear instance of a woman leaving of her own volition. An act of free will." In his hand he held a small pad, in which he hadn't made a single notation. Instead, he studied my face intensely.

I told him that what he was suggesting was pretty near impossible. "Oneida doesn't even know that people do such things. And our generation aren't leavers. My wife is a timid woman, Officer, a passive soul. She can't tell north from south. She waits for the world to come to her and it never does. What if she's lost her mind? That's not impossible, is it? Dementia? A brain-attack? She doesn't own much. What she has could fit into a cab. What if she's sitting on some park bench, not knowing who she is? Shouldn't you put out a missing persons bulletin?"

"Mr. Kennedy, I expect this is a family matter, not a criminal or a medical one. I don't believe your wife's come to any harm. She seems to have made a big and very well-organized statement here. However, you could take a little drive around the city parks to put your mind at peace. I feel uncomfortable asking this, but were you happy together? Did you have a good marriage?" Again, he looked at me closely, now with a soft expression. He paused. "This is an emotional moment," he observed.

"I'm not emotional."

His pale eyes pierced me. "Are you alright, Mr. Kennedy? Maybe you should sit down?"

Finally, passing the kitchen on his way out, he stopped and touched the bouquet of gladiolas on the table, still wrapped in their crisp cellophane. "Fresh," he said.

"I bring them home for her once a week."

I followed him to the front door. He turned to me. "May I ask how long you've been married?"

I said I didn't know exactly. Coming on to fifty years, I supposed.

"So, you could safely say you know your wife well?"

I'd no idea how to answer this.

"Do you have children? I suggest you call them. See if your wife told them about this. And, Mr. Kennedy, I recommend you go over the past weeks in your mind, the past few months. What things did your wife say to you? How did she look? There are always signs. Little clues. Body language. Changes in habit or mood. Glances. Silences. Put the puzzle pieces together."

2

After the officer left, I walked round the house again, my sole companion the sound of my own footsteps. Oneida gone? It wasn't possible. Had she told me she was going somewhere, that I'd forgotten? Or had she just neglected to tell me about a trip? I knew I was grasping at straws. The silence of the house crushed me. Once so familiar, the rooms now seemed hollow and traitorous.

We'd lived in this house, a Victory Home, for over four decades. It was one of thousands the government threw up cheaply during the war to house the fledgling families of soldiers. When we first came here, the place was a disappointment to Oneida. The day we moved in, she walked from room to room, the corners of her mouth turned down, remarking on the thinness of the walls and the smallness of the rooms and the cheap lead paint that was giving her a headache. But I was bursting with pride. They weren't easy to come by, these veteran's homes. I had to jump through hoops to land one. I didn't know what Oneida expected of me back then. On her hip, she balanced a toddler. In a carriage nearby slept a baby less than a year younger. Outside, three more children played, all under five. Oneida was thirty-seven years old. She'd have five more pregnancies over as many years, and two of those babies would die.

I remembered the fear in her eyes that day, that she had married a man who couldn't seem to hold down a job or curb his passions, so that there'd be no end to the flow of babies, and no food to put in their mouths. It was 1950. I'd been home from the war for four years. Other soldiers had come back and enrolled in college, courtesy of the government, lived a bachelor life in tenement houses, their fridges stocked with beer. I'd have given my right arm to do the same, but how could I, with a wife and two kids to support the day I demobilized? The prairie dustbowl and the Depression had ended my education at grade eight. Then the war stole six years from me. After that, all my working life, I was passed over for promotion by young upstarts who wouldn't know the butt end of a Lee Enfield if you handed them one. Why, some of them couldn't have told you who Hitler was or why this country is free.

At four o'clock, as was my habit, I headed out for my whiskey. It was almost as if the car started itself and drove automatically down Huron Street, over Dundas, past the market building to the liquor store. Like an old horse, it knew its way. I never bought more than a mickey at a time because I knew if I had more, I'd drink it all down in one go. Back at the house, I glanced over at the kitchen table, where Oneida usually sat at that hour, beneath her wall calendar showing the Sacred Heart breaking open his chest to reveal his blazing organ. She'd wait for me to pour her a glass, sometimes asking, "Why so little for me? Haven't you got a whole bottle there?" And I'd reply, "You're shy of a hundred pounds. You know you can't hold your liquor. You'll get tipsy and then how will you make supper?"

I felt the empty rooms of the house mocking me so I went outside and sat at the picnic table with my Canada Gold and drank it down glass by glass. I looked around at the gardens, which, since retiring, I'd made my hobby. I'd torn up the grass, barrowed in rich soil, banking it up, though not wastefully so, for a part of me feared if I piled it on too arrogantly, winds like those of my prairie youth would carry it away. It was May. My tulips dying off already, the iris opening up now.

I'd been full of ambition the day I quit working, but as it turned out, my heart had served me for sixty-five years and would no longer be my slave. It would pay me back for driving it so hard. The very first morning of my freedom, I set my foot to the blade of a shovel and drove it into the ground. I heard the protest of tiny grass roots, their fibres tearing.

Then, I felt an explosion of pain in my shoulder, and I crashed down like a felled tree, my cheek pressed hard to the earth. You may think that a man in crippling pain would be aware of nothing else, but I smelled the rich minerals of the soil, saw the grass shimmering close to my eyes, tall as a forest, a procession of ants crawling past, loud as an army, a ladybug toiling up the sharp valley of a blade that dipped and swayed with its weight. Then, through the screen of grass, I saw Oneida hastening toward me, her footsteps thunderous in my ear. I would never have believed that a woman so small could cause the earth to tremble so. For an instant, she towered over me, her blue apron, smelling of coffee, frying bacon, cigarettes, flapping in the wind. She dropped to her knees, her joints snapping and popping, and pressed her cool palm to my cheek.

"Trip!' she called. "Trip!" her voice coming from a strange, watery distance.

It was a neighbour who phoned the ambulance, noticing us there, two old people huddled in the dewy grass.

For a month after my hospital discharge, I was weak as a kitten. Confined to my bed, watching Oneida, across the hall, preparing my meals at the stove, I thought, *I will tell her right now, when she comes in with my tray of food, I will say that, just the way she pressed her hand to my cheek the morning the heart attack knocked me down, I knew that I wasn't going to die. Something of her character had flowed into me at that moment, a stillness, a strength I had not known she possessed. I will tell her what that gesture meant to me, I surely will.* But I kept putting it off and putting it off, the moment never seeming quite right. And so, of course, in the end, I never did.

The evening of Oneida's disappearance, I boiled a pot of potatoes for supper, doused them with butter, salt and pepper, and ate every last one. Then I settled into my recliner to watch TV. Looking over at Oneida's blue rocker again and again, I imagined I saw her there in the shadows, her figure ambiguous, obscured by the billowing sheers. I remembered her fingers sliding over the wooden beads of her rosary, the brass cross bearing the twisted figure of Christ resting in her lap, her lips moving, her breath powerful with the smell of cigarettes, coffee, silence. Twenty-five Hail Marys, five Our Fathers. "All that repetition," I once said to her. "Where does it get you?"

"It is my meditation, Trip," she answered impassively. For a long time, it seemed to me, she'd been content to carry on a dialogue with god and not a word to me. What, I'd often wondered, did she pray for? What was there left for her to desire so late in life? But now I did ask myself: why hadn't I looked at her more often or stopped to ask her what she longed for, deep inside?

Night fell. The house closed in around me. I put on my striped cotton pyjamas. In the bathroom mirror, my eyes blazed with fear. I removed my dentures, stared at my collapsed mouth. And though I'd slept alone in the marriage bed for five years, now it seemed an arid wasteland and the room a harsh prison. At two in the morning, I awoke. Beneath the bedclothes, picked out by the blue moonlight, my own form looked so shrunken now, compared to my youth, that the sight of it startled me, like a person spooked by a glimpse of his own corpse. Then, I became convinced I heard the floorboards creaking overhead and I felt such a yearning to creep into bed with Oneida, to take comfort in her warmth, that I shook with tears. Why this longing for her when it was I who'd sent her packing upstairs, a pillow under her arm? It had been so many years since we'd touched each other in intimacy or felt the heat of our bodies pressed together in the night that I didn't even know if we were capable anymore of such capitulation.

I got up and shuffled hopefully down the hallway, then upstairs, only to find Oneida's bed of course empty. The branches of the maple peppered the small window like a handful of stones. And I thought: *I never once came up here to visit her. Not once.* I stood there, the room dark as a tomb. Then, without premeditation, a wail escaped me. "Oneida!" I shouted, at the top of my lungs, like an angry child calling for his mother. But my voice died, muffled by the furniture crowding the room. My heart pounded, blood throbbed in my head, my legs trembled. Gripping the handrail, I crept shakily downstairs and crawled on top of the bedcovers, frightened and lonely for the first time in my life since the year my mother died.

The following morning, I went outside early. Nearby, a dog barked, a screen door slammed, a car engine burst into life. The houses beyond our high hedge no longer belonged to my contemporaries. Our old neighbours were all lying six feet under or tied to wheelchairs in nursing homes and so ignored or forgotten that they couldn't recall their own names. I pulled the garbage pails out to the curb. A new generation of children passed on the sidewalk, heading for school, stooped under backpacks bigger than what I carried during the war. They turned their heads and looked straight through me because I was an old man now and invisible.

I was no cook. At breakfast, my eggs, bacon, toast all came out charred, filling the room with black smoke. I recalled the first morning of my retirement when, lingering restless and disoriented in the kitchen, I reached out on impulse and touched Oneida's shoulder. We were caught together in the little passage between range and table. Her head came up from the stove, like an animal smelling danger. Between us there was a moment of both familiarity and estrangement. I myself did not know why I'd touched her. What this rash gesture meant and where, in a perfect world, I would have liked it to lead us. If only she would turn around and take my hand! We did not know what to do with this moment of intimacy. A word that was not even in use when we met. We had not said we loved each other since 1943. In her body, I sensed surprise, suspicion, flight. How had we come to be this way? When had we stopped smiling at each other? I thought I saw her tremble a little, like a leaf fluttering on a branch, and I felt ashamed. Why had I resisted her all my life, taunted her even, with my contrariness?

All day my mind played tricks on me. I sensed Oneida's presence in the house, certain I heard the rasp of the little wheel of her disposable lighter, the small crackle of her prayer book pages turning, brittle as onion skins, the soft lapping of water in the tub as she took her morning bath. I rushed down the hallway, my heart pounding with joy and gratitude, only to encounter emptiness. Once, toiling in the garden, I thought I saw her crossing the yard toward me and there stirred in my groin, like a hibernating beast waking in its dark cave, an old and dormant desire for her. I stood up to welcome her but then she turned toward the house, struggling, limping across terrain made lumpy with winter shiftings and hardenings. I covered my eyes for a moment, dizzy with confusion.

Two years ago, Oneida fell and broke her hip. When they drilled into her pelvis, the doctors found the bone soft as butter. *Butter!* They installed a pin but it slipped in the porous socket. Her leg shortened and now she wore a special shoe, its sole built up with four inches of rubber, the shape of a flatiron and just as unwieldy. A woman once so lovely as Oneida must have felt considerable dismay at this handicap. She'd never spoken of it, but I'd never asked her, had I? We seemed to have reached a stage in our lives where we couldn't expose to each other our deepest injuries, though one might have thought that two people married for fifty years should be the natural custodians of each other's most intimate wounds. Yet, it seemed possible to go on living with someone who had closed to you the doors to their profoundest sorrows because you were bound to that person by habit and fear and dismay and a most pathetic need.

3

We have eight girls. One of them manages a scientific lab in Antarctica. Another operates a horse barn on a Brazilian nature reserve. One teaches geography in Australia. One rides around at night in Toronto trying to get addicts off the street. Still another is a counsellor to Inuit on Baffin Island. Another resides in Calgary. From her bedroom window she can see the snow-capped Rockies shining like a procession of white elephants in the distance. The youngest settled in Ottawa. We have never been there. It is a long journey on a highway cutting through the Precambrian Shield, sheer cliffs, stunning in their beauty and power, I am told. One by one, our girls trickled away to university, their passage funded by government grants. Oneida and I were astounded. We'd expected them to become grocery store clerks, chambermaids, switchboard operators. We'd never seen a university, weren't even sure how one worked, where it took you.

Pride made me put off calling any of them, but one day, faced with another evening of silence, I picked up the phone late in the afternoon and dialled Ursa, the one on the West Coast. In her yard, she had told us, holly grows. Hard to imagine! Oneida and I have never seen real holly. Ursa has sent us pictures of her view of the Pacific Ocean. What I wouldn't give to have that! She was the most profound of my daughters, the most reflective and forgiving.

"You mother's taken off," I said. A pause. She asked me what I meant.

"She's flown the coop. Either she's lost her marbles or she's gone to live with one of you girls because, as you know, she has no friends. I don't understand why I wasn't let in on this."

"Hold on a minute, Dad. Let's not jump to conclusions," said Ursa. "We girls are in touch with each other all the time. If Mom was with one of us, I'd know it. And most of us are too far away for her to get to, right?" I pictured Ursa on the other end of the line. She looked exactly like Oneida, the dark hair and eyes, the olive skin, which was probably why I'd phoned her, over the other daughters. She also had Oneida's quiet class, her lady-likeness.

"What happened?" asked Ursa. "Did you and Mom have some kind of fight?"

"You know your mother doesn't have the first idea how to fight. Someone put this idea into her head. Someone brain-washed her," I said.

"I think we need to give Mom a little more credit than that. She has a mind of her own."

"Since when?"

"*Dad*," she said softly.

"Well, I don't know what kind of game she's playing."

"What if it's not a game, Dad?" she asked, patient but firm.

A cold wind swept through me. "She never said she wasn't happy here," I said in frustration.

"I wouldn't know about that. Dad, I've no idea if this has anything to do with Mom, but I've read that a lot of older women are leaving their husbands these days. So many that they're calling it an exodus. Apparently, they're looking for freedom or love."

"Well, I don't see why love would suddenly become so important to your mother. She's got along well enough without it for fifty years."

I heard a small, kind laugh and even I could see the absurdity of what I'd said and I smiled sheepishly.

"Well, I'm telling you, if she plans to come waltzing back in here easy as she danced out, she's got another think coming!"

"Maybe you don't mean that, Dad."

"After this stunt, I don't give a damn if I ever see her again." Though I heard the harshness of my own words, I didn't care. I'd always prided myself on being a black and white man.

Silence on the other end of the line. "Ok, Dad," said Ursa patiently. Then I felt ashamed. "Even so," she added, "I'll call around to the sisters, see if anybody knows anything or has an idea what Mom's done. In the meantime, take care of your heart."

"I'm fixed," I said. Didn't she remember? I'd had my double bypass.

"No," she said, "I mean the *other* heart."

I was shaking with fear when I hung up. I took a deep breath. Well, then, to hell with Oneida! I thought. What did I care that she was gone? Hadn't I always been my own man, a loner and a rebel?

4

I have only one friend, King Finney. Oneida never liked him. I was always forced to visit him in stealth, filled with guilt that I'd lied to her about where I was going. She believed his drinking was a bad influence on me. But I often wondered if she was just jealous of my long relationship with him and his wife, Pearl, and of our shared love for the prairie, which Oneida hated and feared and refused to understand. Also, she disapproved of the fact that King had lived off Pearl all his life.

"That poor woman," she'd say.

"She doesn't seem to mind," I answered.

"What choice does she have?"

I told her that King marched to the beat of his own drum, what these days they call a *rugged individualist.*

"He's lazy as a pet coon," Oneida said.

"He's done exactly what he's wanted with his life. What's wrong with that? Anybody would envy him."

"Only men get to be that selfish."

I waited a week after Oneida's disappearance to visit King, wanting to be able to put on a brave face, joke about it, even. I drove to the south edge of town and up a hill so perpendicular that my old car shook and coughed and stuttered and roared with strain. As usual, I was filled with expectation, as though the wind pouring over the hill's crest, blowing off the open fields in the countryside beyond King's house, was the dry, honest wind of Saskatchewan. Climbing out of the car, I felt my lungs quiver with it. Up there at the top was the sorriest collection of falling down places you could imagine, a neighbourhood nobody would pick to live in, and that's just why King liked it.

I didn't bother to go up to the door. I went around back to where I knew I'd find him, sitting on a torn web chair deep in the yard, on a ridge high above Honour. I stood before him. "You *would* pick the steepest goddamned street in town to park yourself on," I said.

He laughed. "No guru ever lived anywhere else." He gave me his thick, dry, strong hand to shake, the two of us silently happy as reunited twins. Though we'd known each other for near sixty years, and somehow landed here together, two thousand miles from our birthplace, we'd never openly called each other *friend*, for this was too intimate and fragile a word, and we were too proud and tough and shy to use it. He handed me his empty beer bottle and I went inside and got two more. It wasn't that King didn't work because he drank or that he drank because he didn't work. Beer was just part of him. He said he'd been born with one in his hand. He was the happiest man in the world because he'd never had to sweat or clock in on a job he hated or kiss some bastard's feet or sell himself short. He said if his life got any better, he'd have to hire someone to help him enjoy it. I used to bring our girls up there when they were little and they liked to sit on his knee and reach up and stroke the stubble on his square jaw. They sensed the contentment of his spectator life. On the drive home, they'd ask me, "How old is King?"

"Old as dirt."

"Is he your brother?"

"In a way."

"And that's why we call him Uncle?"

"Yes."

"But, is he *related* to us?"

I sat down with him that afternoon, pleased to be there and grateful for the life we once lived together way back, and for our fraternity and for this moment high above Honour. At our feet, the ground dropped sharply. No matter how many times I came there, I was always surprised to look down and see Honour nestled in a quiet valley. It never seemed like a valley when I was down there in it. But sure enough, there it lay, picturesque as a postcard, a little jewel with its forest of stone church spires and its dark canopy of trees shading the streets. From up here it hardly looked at all like the place I lived.

I told him Oneida had cleared out. "Took everything she owns. Looks like she's gone for good."

He searched my face, then he threw his head back and guffawed. "Congratulations, Trip. You're a free man, ya lucky bastard!" he cried. "It's what you've wanted all your life, isn't it? Now we can rent that Packard we've been jawing about for forty years and head west until we hit Saskatchewan." He wore a short-sleeved yellow shirt, nearly old as him, getting to the point of transparency, but crisply ironed. His shoes were polished and his nails neatly manicured. It was the old playboy in him, this attention to grooming. Really, he was little changed from our prairie days, his hair thick as a healthy wheat field, his shoulders square as the day I met him, though his once piercing blue eyes had clouded over.

I asked him if he thought Pearl would let him go and he said she'd be happy to see the back of him. I said no one else would have put up with a bum like him for so long.

"Still, she gets on my back," he said.

"You manage to shake that off fine."

We'd met on top of a freight car during the Depression, riding the rails in search of work. We'd watched each other's backs, shared what we could scrounge by way of victuals, got into plenty of rhubarbs together, just for the hell of knocking someone down. We ended up in the clinker a few times, punishment just for standing on a street corner looking hungry. *No blood on your hands without blood on mine. No jail time for you without jail time for me.* That was our pact. If we went hungry, King could always find the humour in it. Granted, he was one more for the handout than for the work to earn it and even then, he put more energy into acquiring the liquor than the grub. At the time, he was thirty-three years old and I was seventeen. I didn't know then that he'd make a career out of unemployment. He said the Depression was designed for him, that working was for chumps. Twenty cents a day for a forty-four-hour week was what they were paying unemployed men like us in Prime Minister Bennett's Relief Camps, one-tenth of the going minimum wage.

"You never owned your life after you married Oneida," King said that afternoon. "Some women eat men up."

"Well, I don't know," I answered dismally, feeling a troubling loyalty to Oneida. We sat there for a few minutes, looking down at Honour. Then I confessed, "I can't think what I'm going to do now."

"Enjoy life, is what!" roared King with mock impatience.

Then there was a heavy silence between us and I felt the tenderness and power of our lifelong bond.

"You've faced worse things than this," he said, more kindly.

"I know I have."

"When I met you in '30, you were a helluva man. I never saw a wall you couldn't climb over."

"I don't know."

"This is just a bump on the road, Trip."

"You're right."

"Celebrate, Brother! You're a free man, ya lucky son of a bitch!"

"I always thought Oneida was more interested in god than she was in me."

"God's a helluva lot better looking than you are, ya bastard!" We laughed.

Just then, around the corner of the house, walked Pearl, home from work, tall, lanky and graceless, all sharp angles, still a tom boy. She taught in a one-room school out in the country, a little throw-back place they never shut down, full of rural kids. She'd never earned her professional certificate, but they liked her out there, where she'd taught a couple of generations. She waved at us, seized the push mower from beside the porch and began to cut the grass. I jumped up and went over and tried to take it from her. "Let me do that," I offered.

"Don't shame me, Trip!" King called from his chair. "She's just showing off!" Pearl grinned at him. She held onto the mower, but she reached up and placed her hand for a moment on my cheek.

In 1939, I owned a general store on the prairie. One day, a couple burst in the door. Instantly, I recognized King, whom I hadn't seen in three years. I asked them up to my apartment for a stir fry supper, which we washed down with a couple of bottles of Dewar's. I thought King had found himself a swell girl: leggy as a colt, ready for adventure and hungering for a man. Not much to look at, to be sure. Buck-toothed enough, as they used to say, to eat corn on the cob through a picket fence. King didn't have a penny in his pocket and she was squandering a small inheritance. She was crazy about him. Back then, he could have passed for Earnest Hemingway, a bearded, barrel-chested, silver-tongued devil full of bravado. He was pushing forty and she was thirty and, by the standards of the day, a spinster. They loved to drink and drive fast and keep moving. She was smarter than he and they both knew it. She was attracted to his devil may care attitude. She made the mistake of thinking he'd outgrow it.

After she'd finished the grass-cutting, Pearl came over and ruffled King's hair fondly and asked, "How's my old philosopher today?" He told her I was a newly minted bachelor and we filled her in. "Stay for supper, then," she begged. Before this, I'd always been reluctant to leave, their spot above Honour seeming untroubled by the world. But I did not want to be the object of their pity. And didn't their words cast judgement on how I'd lived my life, the choices I'd made, the family Oneida and I had raised, the value of those things? So, I said I had a meal on the stove.

"If you're looking for company, I'm here all the time," King called over his shoulder as I left.

"We can count on that!"

"Spend all day with me if you want," he said, but we both knew I wouldn't know how to sit still.

"Why do you have to run off?" Pearl asked unhappily, following me across the yard.

In the kitchen, she said, about Oneida's disappearance, "This looks to me like a gift." I set my empty beer bottle down on the counter. "Oneida held herself above me and King," said Pearl. "We never saw her here. What's supposed to be

so wrong with us? Maybe we were just too prairie for her."
I wondered why women stewed about things they couldn't
change and looked everywhere for insult and injury.

"She didn't think that way," I said gently.

"Go on, Trip. She was so stuck up she'd drown in
a rainstorm."

"She was a homebody, is all," I said, surprised to find
myself defending Oneida.

"I would never have left a man like you."

I didn't know what to say to that. "I felt pretty damned
lucky when I met her," I rejoined.

"She was an Easterner through and through. She never
gave the prairie a chance."

I found her words harsh. "She grew up here in Ontario.
Oneida needs the familiar."

"Funny she ran off, then." Pearl was wearing denim over-
alls, heavy laced shoes. She seemed to me to have become
sexless, she'd forfeited her feminine side to expediency. I
wondered if, for most of their life up here, she and King had
lived more like brother and sister than man and woman.

I went out to the road with her at my heels. I started up
the engine and threw the car into gear. Pearl's hand fell on
the windowsill, delaying me. "The day I met you, I was just
a silly girl," she said. "Why do they let people make such
big decisions when they're young and so cavalier about the
future, Trip?"

I thought she looked weary and toughened in a way that is not attractive in a woman.

5

At five o'clock one evening, I was drawn out to the dam. On the bridge, I watched the ropy water shoot over the gates, yellow and green and purple. I felt its energy in my blood. If only in my life I'd been let to flow, I thought, go where my heart wanted to take me. All around me on the bridge, red caution signs were posted and they'd strung barbed wire everywhere because teenaged boys from Honour had, whether through naivete or recklessness or foolish dares or belief in their own immortality, dived off this bridge and cracked their heads open on the submerged rocks below. Others had deliberately leapt to their own deaths. I wouldn't have admitted this to anyone, but as I stood there, I saw, as though suddenly separated from myself, my own body fly over the balustrade and arc down suicidally into the deadly waters. The image scared the living daylights out of me.

I stood there filled with regret and shame at having abandoned Oneida so often to struggle along the dam alone, a woman tiny when I met her, shrunken now to the size of a child. I found myself longing for the mothball smell of her sweaters. I turned and saw her face for a moment, softened by the mist, her expression saying, *It's cold out here. I just fixed my hair and now it's ruined. The reflections hurt my eyes.* All of this I deeply missed. Well, enough of that.

I slid my dark glasses on and looked up at the costly houses stacked on the shale cliff. I picked out the one I knew, a bungalow belonging to a widower from our parish, Stan Dragland. Its expensive stone, I'd been told, was imported from Oregon. Its glossy white columns shone and its roof projected out like the shining wings of a new airplane. I shaded my eyes to get a better look and saw, crossing Stan's stone terrace, which was boldly cantilevered over the cliff, a small figure limping heavily. I knew that gait at once. Why, it could only be Oneida! God damn! I blinked and looked harder. Then, Stan, appearing more confident and erect than I'd seen him in years, crossed the terrace and handed her a drink, its amber tint caught like a jewel in the sun and I felt a jab of remorse at how miserly I'd always been when doling out Oneida's small share of whiskey.

Now, all the pieces of the puzzle fell together. Fool was I not to have seen it sooner!

"*Bastard!*" I shouted, but the roar of the cataract chewed up my cry. The wind was knocked out of me, as though I'd received a blow to the chest. I gulped air and grabbed the handrail. My trouser legs snapping like flags in the wind, my thin jacket battering my ribs, the decorative feather in my fedora twisting with a high whistling sound, I struggled off the dam, huffing, my knees near useless. I floored it all the way home. Dragland! That son of a bitch! He wasn't half the man I was! In bed that night, I resolved to change the door locks in case Oneida thought she could ever come back.

But by morning, I'd calmed, of course, and decided to leave things be.

Over the years, Stan Dragland's wife, Fayme, had had the idea of fixing up one house after another, selling it at a profit to buy a bigger one. Stan played her lackey. Handy at drywall, welding, painting, tiling, laying carpet, he did the improvements, nights and weekends. Eventually the construction dust and asbestos and toxic fumes perforated his lungs. By then he was prematurely grey, deaf from the scream of drills and grinding tools, stooped as an old man, arthritic in the knees, a chronic cougher. He had to go on workers' compensation from his day job. No one ever thought he'd outlive Fayme. Now that she was dead, he had that spanking new bungalow up on the cliff all to himself, with lacquered hallways shining like rivers, Chinese carpets thicker than the heel of your hand, picture windows curving out to capture the radiant waters, the floating clouds, the sailboats flickering like white handkerchiefs on a blue sea. I'd always known Oneida would have given her eye teeth for a place like that.

After Fayme's death, Stan started to show up at our place with greater and greater frequency, pulling his oxygen tank behind him, his moist breath fogging up his plastic mask. He'd find me working in the garden and when I gave him the cold shoulder, he'd inquire whether Oneida was in, and he'd go inside. After he'd cleared out, I'd enter the house, find Oneida at the ironing board.

"What did that loser want?" I'd ask her.

HONOUR

"What loser?"

"You know who I mean. That Dragland. Why's he coming around here all the time?"

"It's not all the time."

"Seems like every other day. Has he nothing better to do with his miserable life?"

"He's lonely."

"We're not even his friends. If he didn't go to our church, I wouldn't give him the time of day."

"He has a hard life."

"Hard, my foot."

"The poor man can't breathe."

"What the hell does he talk to you about?"

"You know," Oneida paused, the iron in her hand spitting steam, "I don't even remember."

Though I swore I wouldn't do it, the day after I saw Oneida up at Stan's, I found myself running my finger down the columns of the phone book looking for Stan's number. He picked up after one ring.

"Is Oneida Kennedy there?" I asked.

"Who wants to know?"

"You know damned well who this is, Dragland. Put her on."

"She doesn't want to talk to you."

"Says who? Says her or says you? You can't keep me from speaking to my own wife."

"Let's just say she's indisposed at the moment."

311

"I'll stay on the line until she isn't."

"You may not live that long."

"I've a notion to come over there and knock you into next year!" I shouted.

"That would be assault, Trip," he gloated, emboldened by having captured my wife. "You wouldn't want to be arrested, would you? Goodbye, Trip."

I hung up, sweating with rage and humiliation. There I sat in my customary chrome chair at the chrome kitchen table. Looking around me, I felt I did not know this cold place. I felt so utterly appalled by this alien room, in which my eight daughters had taken their meals as children, most nights barely acknowledged by me, all of them filled with hurt and fear at my indifference and temper. At the thought of this, I despised myself.

6

Dear Mother

Why did you not say goodbye?

How could you go rattling off in the darkness with nothing but your back for me to behold from the upstairs window, your figure held so painfully stiff against the jolting of the cart that it chilled my heart? Only this for me to remember? Why did you let father tear you away without a word to me, startled and trembling in my bed, frightened by the commotion I'd heard in the hallway at midnight, the quick footsteps on the stairs, doors slamming, the whinnying of our horse, Hank? Then, Betty and I alone in the profound and terrifying darkness, deep in the countryside, the fire in the stove dying, and the next day, me keeping vigil at the kitchen window, six years old, watching for sight of the buggy in the lane, while Bunny, still in her flannel nightgown, her hair in plaits, stoked the stove, made me porridge and then for lunch warmed up for me a piece of pork pie, assuring me all the while: She'll be back, Sonny, don't you worry, it was only a little pain. The doctor will give her some medicine and she'll be right as rain.

No message sent, no neighbour looking in. Weren't you worried about us? The wagon didn't appear until just before supper. Of course, it was only Father, looking stricken, your place beside him empty. Bunny ran out to get the news. They spoke and father brushed past her roughly. Once inside, he went straight to the sideboard, drank down three glasses of whiskey, one after the other. Where is Mother? I asked, trembling. Your mother died on the operating table, he growled without looking at me. From the doorway, Bunny said, She's not coming back, Sonny. I laughed, nervous and confused. That can't be, I said, my voice quivering. It's true, Sonny, said

Bunny, dry-eyed, her face solemn, her figure like stone, as though she saw her burden before her. But she wasn't sick! I shouted. She was fine yesterday. You said yourself she just had a little pain! Then, Father crossed the room in two strides and struck me across the face.

Did you know that, on the weekends following your death, strangers came to our house, one couple after another? Bunny and I were brought forward in our Sunday best. Father had told us: When they ask you a question look them straight in the eye. What were our names? the strangers wanted to know. How old? Can you read? Can you write? Turn around. Touch your toes. Reach high over your head. Bend from side to side. What's the heaviest thing you can lift? Father was quick to assure them, You wouldn't have to take them both, you understand. They can be split up. I didn't know what was happening. Bunny went to the kitchen to make more tea for these visitors. I followed her. What are these people coming here for, Bunny? I asked her. I don't know, she said. Is Father trying to give us away? I don't know. She wouldn't look at me. I gripped her arm hard, thrust my face into hers. Tell me, Bunny! Yes, she conceded. He's put us up for adoption. He's not giving us away. He's selling us. She turned and hugged me, stroked my hair, tears flooding her face, the first she'd shed since you died. I felt her trembling. I don't want to be separated from you, Sonny, she wept. I don't want to lose you!

Do you want to hear the advertisement he'd put in the paper? Two obedient children up for adoption or general use. Separately or together. Girl, eight, strong, a conscientious worker. Can run a house good as an adult. Boy, six, well formed, sound of muscle and bone, servile, a quick study, fit to be trained for a man's labour. Price negotiable.

If only you'd said goodbye, Mother. Surely you suspected, surely you knew, from the severity of your pain, that you might never see me again. Why did you let Father rush you out? What few moments would it have taken to come into my room before leaving, to kiss me, tell me you loved me? That, at least, I could have held in my heart, carried around all these years like a garden, instead of thirsting in this desert.

Mother!

7

When Oneida found out she was pregnant with our sixth child, she retreated to our bedroom and cried for a whole day, while the children cowered in the living room, their brows knitted with fear, their faces adult with worry. The eldest went to her and asked, "What's wrong with you? Are you sick? Are you going to die?" which only made Oneida weep the harder. When I arrived home from work, I stood in the bedroom doorway and barked, "Stop that crying. Pull yourself together and make supper. You're frightening the girls." Looking back now, I realize that Oneida had no one to talk to about her despair, no one to console her. At that time, she had a child nine months old, another eighteen months, three others under six, for I kept at her, plunging myself inside her as soon as she got home with a new baby in her arms, and the next thing, she was back in maternity clothes.

If I had not wanted eight children, why had I turned to Oneida night after night, reckless with passion and need, reaching for her soft, warm body. Those years, the world seemed such a hard and cold place with nowhere for me in it. I'd no thought for who Oneida was or what she wanted. Is it any wonder that she grew rigid when she felt my hand sliding up between her thighs? In bed, we became strangers of sorts, with no shared language. Our entire lives were played out in that cold room, with our hollowed-out mattress and our thin blankets and the heavy smell of apples rotting in the grass, drifting in through the window screen.

I hear talk these days of the need to satisfy a woman. Men had no notion of that back then. And even if I'd known, how can you please a woman frightened of her own body? The church did that, the Pope preaching abstinence even while his priests and bishops and cardinals unbuttoned their fine habits to plunder girls and boys, exploiting the innocent for their own secret and sinful pleasures while denying a man the right to lust after his own wife. Oneida would not practise birth control, being afraid of hellfire, and I did not tell her that her Catholic conscience was gradually killing us.

The baby Oneida did not want, a boy, died three days after he was born. Oneida was so sick that the doctor postponed telling her. She'd turned blue and they'd rushed her down to x-ray and found that she had a collapsed lung. To be honest, my first instinct was relief that the child had died, for it meant one less mouth to feed. I met the parish priest at the cemetery, the tiny white plywood coffin, not much bigger than a shoe box, in my hands. We stood together on a rainy slope in a bitter wind, the autumn trees bare around us. The priest was a stocky man with a quarterback's shoulders, a head of thick white hair, a big hairy hand cutting the air with his sign of the cross. A small hole had been dug. It was when I placed the coffin in it that I felt utterly ashamed of my relief that this baby had died.

Oh, God, read the priest, *whose nature is always to have mercy and to spare, we humbly beseech Thee on behalf of the soul of thy servant, Michael, whom Thou has bidden this day to depart out of this world: that thou wouldst not deliver him into the hands of the enemy nor forget him forever but command him to be received by the holy angels and taken to paradise his home, that he may put his faith and love in Thee, he may not undergo the pains of hell, but possess everlasting joy.*

While Oneida recovered in the hospital, I hired a woman, Miss Solo, who lived in a small neighbouring town, to care for the children and run the house for a dollar a day. I was working in a body shop during the week and peddling Fuller Brushes door to door on the weekends. It would be eight o'clock by the time I got home after visiting Oneida. The children would be in bed and my supper on a plate in the oven. I'd eat and then drive Miss Solo home. The day of the burial, Miss Solo put her hand on my shoulder in the kitchen and said softly, "How did things go at the cemetery, Trip?" Her sympathy undid me, so exhausted and in need of comfort was I. I leaned on the counter and wept, and she put her hand on my head and drew it down onto her shoulder. I let myself lean into her. She was a tall, big-boned woman, cheerful and uncomplaining. She rocked me until I'd stopped crying and then without a word we moved together toward the bedroom. She was not the head-turning beauty that Oneida was, but her body was strong and she was not prudish or stingy with her womanhood. We clung to each other all night. In my dreams I heard the words of the priest in the cemetery: *The Lord is close to the broken hearted, and saves those who are crushed in spirit.*

The next morning, filled with shame, I promised myself I'd drive Miss Solo home the moment I arrived after work, but by evening my resolve had weakened. This went on for weeks, the two of us entwined at night beneath Oneida's picture of Our Lady of Perpetual Help, with her long dog bone nose, her rosebud mouth, a painful crick in her neck, her sorrowful eyes sliding toward us, her long fingers elegant as flower petals, her blue cloak exploding with a pattern of gold stars. Once or twice, our oldest, Greer, came downstairs early in the morning and found Miss Solo already preparing breakfast and me still in my nightshirt, drinking coffee at the kitchen table. Though only six, she threw me a look of reproach, her eyes suspicious. "When is Mommy coming home?" she asked.

Oneida was kept in the hospital for a month. She was suffering not just the collapse of her lung but profound melancholia because of the death of Michael. On Sundays after church, I took the girls over to see her, all of them dressed in the wool hand-me-down snowsuits that Oneida's sister sent from the States. Back then, children weren't allowed to visit hospitals. Hand in hand, we walked across the sparkling hospital lawn, our feet breaking through a brittle crust to the soft powdery snow beneath. Oneida's room was on the first floor. Greer and Ursa were tall enough to see in on their own. The other three, I lifted one at a time to the window, their faces shining and their blonde hair curling out from beneath their bonnets. Oneida was expecting us. The nurses, who loved her for her quiet, sweet spirit, fixed her up for the occasion. Mommy! I can see Mommy! the girls cried. Our visits seemed a tonic and each week Oneida's lips looked redder and her hair shinier and her face fuller and her skin more radiant. The littlest ones cried when we had to leave and they cried all the way home in the car and I gripped the steering wheel and whipped myself for my infidelity. But I did not reform.

Finally, there was talk of Oneida's discharge. I asked her if she was sure she was well enough to come home. Don't rush out of here before you're good and strong, I urged her. We're managing okay. But this only aroused her suspicions. "Why are you telling me to stay here?" she asked. "Why don't you want me to come home?" A couple of days later, a car drew up to the house. Oneida had asked a parish woman to bring her home. "I would have come for you," I told Oneida. "Well, I'm here," she said firmly, "so take note."

Miss Solo stayed on for another week to help out. She washed the sheets and tucked Oneida in. Observing the household comings and goings from the same bed Miss Solo and I had shared, Oneida seemed to know that something had gone on between us. Perhaps I overdid it, keeping a conspicuous distance from Miss Solo, never meeting her eyes. Oneida did not ask me about it, perhaps knowing I wouldn't tell her the truth and without doubt realizing she had no financial means to separate from me and to provide for herself and the girls.

8

Dear Mother,

*Did you know that a month after you died, I came
down with a mysterious illness? Sickened with grief,
I could not eat and grew too weak to get out of bed.
Bunny called Dr. Champion in. He had a brow steep
and rugged as a mountain slope, a narrow fringe of
beard on his jawline that made him look like an Old
Testament prophet. Father told him, There's nothing
wrong with that boy that a good kick in the pants
wouldn't cure. The doctor said, It's the shock of his
mother's death. Call it melancholy, call it a breakdown,
but the boy's genuinely sick, Trip. He's skin and bones,
don't you see? You can't take your own catastrophe out
on that child. Let him heal.*

*Bunny asked Father if she could take time off school.
She taught me reading and math, and took her own
studies by correspondence. She made custard for me,
rice pudding, bread pudding, cocoa, anything to build
me up. Winter came and she covered me with a heavy
patchwork quilt. Snow twisted against my window. I
became her child and she my mother. I stayed home
for a whole year, gradually growing stronger, my heart
slowly healing. In September, she and I mounted Hank.
I sat behind, my arms wrapped around her waist, my*

*cheek pressed to her sturdy back. We rode the five miles
to the one-room school. We dismounted and Bunny
led me by the hand into the classroom. She said to the
teacher, "This is my brother. We call him Sonny but his
real name is Trip".*

After my heart attack, Oneida thought I should abandon the
idea of gardening. Up until I retired, I'd worked for twenty
years weighing freight trucks out on the Trans-Canada
highway, entirely exposed to the weathers, both in summer
when the heat of the asphalt nearly melted the soles off my
shoes and in winter when the wind was like ice poured into
my veins. Before that, I'd been a grease-monkey, well-driller,
car salesman, encyclopedia salesman, assembly-line man,
custodian, truck driver. Out West, in my youth, a wheat
farmer, ploughman, harvester, bridge-builder, cowpuncher,
ditch-digger, lumberjack, roofer, handyman. Not to mention
a gas station owner and a farm equipment supplier, right
here in Honour, following the war. Both times, I lost my shirt
with these ventures, and it left a bitter taste between me and
Oneida, for she had neither the stomach for risk nor a shred
of faith in me.

I told her that any man who could fill all those shoes was
up to the task of creating a garden. Now, seven days a week, I
busied myself weeding, cultivating, fertilizing. I hadn't gone
to church since my heart attack. I knew this upset Oneida.
She said I'd made nature my god and that I spent more time

kneeling in the garden than I ever did in a church pew, and I could only answer, "What's wrong with that? Who made nature, if it wasn't god? Someone has to take care of his creation, don't they?" Unwilling to praise my flowers, she said, "Twenty years ago, I couldn't even get you to cut the grass." *Bitter, bitter!* Why, I wondered, did we begrudge each other our small victories? Why did we so fear losing ground? Seek advantage over each other? Keep a tally of injuries? Too many wounds, too many wounds!

"You're out there day and night," she complained.

"What is there for me in this house?" I answered.

She blinked at me, wounded I could see. Why did I respond that way? Why this posture of harshness and indifference to her? She'd stepped off the train out West, an hourglass figure in a Kelly-green suit, a dusky beauty with thick black hair, big brown eyes, a smile so dazzling that the first time I saw it across a dance floor, my knees turned to jelly. The broad, arresting gaze of a film star – a dead ringer for Olivia de Havilland. Everything about her ran deep, body and soul. She turned heads alright. There wasn't a bachelor in the district who didn't fancy her, doctors and lawyers even, but I got the jump on them all, didn't I, arriving at her door with flowers before she'd hardly unpacked her bag. Why, then, would I now want to make her feel like a beggar?

9

"I think your mother has had a change of heart," I tell Ursa on the phone. I say that I saw Oneida wave to me from Stan's terrace.

"You still go out to the dam?"

"Dragland's got no monopoly on that view," I say. "Maybe she's actually a prisoner up there, looking to be rescued."

"Dad, Mom's called some of us. She didn't mention anything about being kidnapped."

"I tell you, I saw her motion to me to come up there."

"Maybe the sun was in your eyes?"

To be honest, Ursa's voice is almost that of a stranger to me because, like my other daughters, she lives far away and when she's called it's always been Oneida who spoke to her. "You don't like talking on the phone," Oneida would explain to me after hanging up without passing the receiver over. "I never said that," I told her. One of my daughters once told me, "You're not easy to talk to, Dad. You never answer a question straight. You always turn it into some joke, as though you're afraid of something. You twist it around and point it back at the asker. I don't know why you have to be so closed."

It seems fathers have changed. I see them out there now, carrying babies in their arms and whispering sweet words in their ears, kissing their soft cheeks over and over, entirely smitten. No one ever gave me the chance to do that or told me I should want to. I don't remember ever having the time to hold a baby in my arms.

"I just can't imagine why she'd take up with that *nothing*," I tell Ursa on the phone.

"Maybe she wanted to feel special to a man."

"I can't see your mother being so foolish."

No reply.

"If she doesn't want to come back, that's fine with me," I burst out, my pride stinging.

A pause. Oneida always said I could twist the truth into a lie or a lie into the truth easier than the wind bends a sapling.

"I know, Dad. That's what you said," Ursa answers patiently. I picture behind her the shining Pacific, her laurel hedge, her pond blooming with lotus, thick with swimming Koi.

"Hell will freeze over before I ask her back," I say.

Silence.

"Do you think it's about a house?" I ask more calmly.

"Would Mom be that shallow?"

"I gave her the best I could."

"And she appreciated it."

"Why did she leave then?"

"I can't answer that."

"Do you think they – her and Dragland -- you know – sleep – ?"

"In the same bed? I don't know Dad. Maybe you should ask her."

"How would I do that?" Then, I break down and weep for the first time.

"Dad. Dad," Ursa says softly, her own voice cracking in response, and this only makes me shake the more and blubber like a baby into the receiver.

Ursa waits. "I guess the important thing is to keep moving forward," she says finally. I don't even know what that means or how I'd go about it. Some days I can barely put one foot in front of the other.

All night, Oneida passes through my dreams. In one, she appears beside me on the bridge of the dam, her thin cardigan pulled tight as a skin around her, shivering. *I didn't know,* she says, bewildered as a child, *no one told me about the wind.* In another, I go upstairs in darkness, watch her sleeping peacefully in her bed, no snoring, none of the bedlam that made me drive her up there, just the profound and private respiration of a woman I no longer know. In the silvery moonlight, the excellent curve of her cheekbone, of her great nostrils, her formidable arc of brow. I awake, choked with longing, shaking with tears. *Fool! Weakling!*

Dear Oneida,

Since you left, I have spent a lot of time thinking about the decades we spent together, our beginnings, our love for each other, and how that may have deteriorated over the years, the ways I may have mistreated or ignored or misunderstood you or let you down, all of which I now thrash myself for, like a martyr with a cat 'o nine

*tails. Your absence has pained me deeply. I am nobody
without you. I acknowledge that at times I have been
a hard and unfeeling husband. But, truly, I have seen
the error of my ways, I have taken ownership of my
sins, and now I am a reformed man. If you can find it
in your heart to forgive me and return to my arms, I
promise I will in future treat you with the love, kindness
and consideration that you have always deserved.*

Your loving and devoted husband, Trip.

I look up from the letter, see Oneida's face in my imagination. The fear of me she's had all her life. It shames me to
remember it. She always knew I could argue circles around
her, that I was skilled at long silences, could become a wall of
stone. I'm not proud of this but I can't seem to pull it out of
me, nor can I change the past.

I cross Honour and drive up the narrow switchback road
hugging the cliff, past retaining walls of imported stone,
shrubs pruned in the shape of giraffes and elephants, to Stan's
house. I confess I've fantasized about the fragile cliff collaps-
ing and Stan's place sliding down into the reservoir, him with
it. But, by now, I know such feelings of envy and destruction
are harmful to my health. I step up onto the porch, which is
flanked by two pairs of pretentious white columns, like the
entrance to a temple. I am reaching out to slip the envelope
through the letterbox, when Stan opens the door, looking
less hunched, less impotent and defeated than he once was,

not so brittle, not so one-foot-in-the-grave. The smell of a baking apple pie wafts out to me, I hear an oven door shut. When I peer past his shoulder, Stan draws the door close behind him. I think I see a movement in a nearby window, a small figure stepping away quickly into the room's shadows. Stan snatches the letter from my hand, smirks at me, taps it on the knuckles of one hand, grins, revealing his blue false teeth. "I'll have to screen this," he says. "I wouldn't want anything to upset Oneida."

Nothing comes of any of this.

Dear Mother,

Now I am alone in this house. I've had time to turn over in my mind all the mistakes I've made in my life. The ones I knew about and the ones recently revealed to me. Sins of commission and sins of omission. Were you alive now, you might be disappointed in me. I hate to think it. This is not a time in my life when I expected to be between things. I no longer have something I always thought was wrong for me. And, now that it has been stolen, I find myself needing to analyse the reasons, so that I can begin to celebrate that it's gone and stop wondering if I'm to blame. At this moment, I have everything that I deem essential, yet all seems lost.

10

"Trip, you son of a bitch!" King cries when I finally visit him again. "I haven't seen you in three months! What the *hell*?"

I laugh and sit down opposite him. He sobers. "I thought you'd be over more often. I expected you every day. I imagined it'd be like old times."

"I've been sorting out the house," I tell him, unwilling to admit that I did not want him to be disappointed in me or think me less of a man, in my grief.

"And?"

"Let's just say for the last while I haven't known half the time if I was coming or going."

A pause. "Maybe I let you down," King says apologetically.

"If you did, it'd be the first time in your life."

"I never meant to disparage Oneida. What would *I* know about your needs?"

"*You* know, alright," I reassure him unconvincingly.

"You had a lot more to lose than I ever did," he says, and then he takes a big regretful sigh that shakes his chest. "You know that first time you met Pearl? We'd been careless and she was pregnant. She wanted to settle down, raise a family. But I told her she was talking to the wrong man. I didn't want no kid. She got rid of it. I didn't even ask her how. We never spoke about it again. I was a heartless bastard back then. Maybe I still am now. I'm close to eighty and what do I have to show for it? No kids, no grandkids."

He begins to cry, big tears rolling down his old spotted face. He glances over at me in wonder and embarrassment.

"King," I murmur, and I go over and stand beside him, my hand on his head. His scalp burns with emotion. I feel his old thin shoulders shaking and I realize how fragile he's become. He takes out a handkerchief and blows his nose. Then the seriousness is over. "Come on," he growls, "enough girl talk. Run in and fetch us some beers."

Before I go in, I say, "Are you alright? You look pale and tired."

"Change of weather. These seasons are a bugger."

"What about seeing a doctor?"

"Wouldn't know what to say to one. Anyway, he might take beer off the menu."

I go inside and open their ancient fridge. I pause to look around at the old kitchen, the broken linoleum, the dark, rancid smelling wooden counters, the faded paint. Nothing has changed here in fifty years. He and Pearl have been standing still all this time.

At first, I can't see King when I go back outside. I think he's disappeared into the bushes to relieve himself, as is his habit. But as I get closer, I notice his body slumped on the ground in front of his chair, his legs twisted. I run to him, turn him over, lift his head, which seems impossibly heavy. "King!" I cry. "What happened? Where's the pain?" He makes a weak gesture toward his chest. "I'll call an ambulance," I tell him, but as I try to rise, he grips my arm hard and his eyes say,

Don't leave me." He pulls me closer. "Friend," he whispers, and lets out a sigh, his eyes falling shut.

Then, I hear a cry right behind me, and Pearl crashes to the ground beside us, heavy-boned, awkward. "King! King!" she weeps, pressing her cheek to his forehead. I am somehow surprised to see her so utterly broken, for she's been the coper, the provider, never a crack in her shell. I hold King's hand, put my arm across Pearl's shoulder. We are locked together, the three of us huddled on the ridge, connected now for half a century. Our bodies are hot, they burn with life and death, desire and loss. We cannot let go. It does not seem possible our union could be broken. I feel like I will split in two. Below us, Honour blazing with autumn colour, a fresh breeze sweeping up the ravine. Big yellow leaves drift down onto our shoulders. Too late now to say how we feel. Why, I wonder, do we hide our love so for each other?

Nobody comes to King's funeral. He didn't know anyone. All he ever had was his own company. But at the cemetery, there stands Oneida, a few yards off. I am as shocked by her beauty as I was the day I met her. Clearly, her life with Stan has made her happy. She looks younger, her complexion glowing. I force myself to be pleased for her. If life on the cliff overlooking the reservoir has wrought these changes in her, so be it. I am proud of myself for this thought. Maybe I am moving on, after all. It is a cold and windy day. She is wearing a mink coat, not in an ostentatious way, but with understatement, a quiet class. The garment becomes her, its thickness and weight, the gleaming pelts. After the prayers, she walks over to me smoothly and I remember Ursa saying that Stan was paying for a physiotherapist to correct her gait. "I never hated them," she tells me. "King and Pearl."

"You didn't?" We stand there together, under a tree. I don't want her to leave. At the curb, Stan waits for her in an idling car.

"That was just something someone put in someone's head. After that, there was no undoing it."

And though, out of pride, I'd promised myself I'd never ask, the words slip out nevertheless. "Why did you leave?"

She looks me in the eye, but kindly. "Stan notices me," she says. "He tells me I'm beautiful. That's all you had to do." I feel a pain in my chest, which is not the mechanical pain of my heart going haywire again, but a deeper, mysterious and unexpected ache.

After everyone's gone from the cemetery, Pearl holds me back.

"I thought the old bugger would outlive us all," she confides, clear-headed now, seemingly recovered from her disintegration. "He once said to me, 'I haven't accomplished a damn thing in my life and I'm proud of it.' He didn't hold any store in success. He was a wise old fool. You know, Trip, I lived my whole life with a drunk. I do believe it's important for me to be able to admit that now. After all is said and done, King was a drunk." She touches my arm, looks at me earnestly, "Let's you and me get out of here, Trip. Go back to

Saskatchewan together. There's nothing holding either of us here now. We both love the West and we miss it. We feel the same way about a lot of things. We're a good fit. There's no future here for either of us." I feel shame for her disloyalty to King and pity for him, his body barely cold in the ground.

I remember him saying to me once, "Pearl's sweet on you, you know," and I answered, "Oh, go on!" and he said, "Always has been."

I tell her I can't do that. I couldn't have explained the reasons, except that I do not love her, though of course I don't say this.

"I've adored you all these years," she says. "You know that."

I answer, no, I didn't know it. I say I care for her but only as a friend. I say I don't think I've ever done anything to suggest different. This is not the time, I say, to go chasing fantasies. We are too old.

She steps back, her face hard, her eyes wounded. "You and King were like a pair of lovers, you know," she says bitterly. "I was always on the outside."

11

A heavy cleansing rain begins to fall, filling the house with the perfume of wet soil, earthworms, fallen leaves. The rooms chill. I go to the thermostat, turn it up to twenty. I've grown accustomed to the empty house. In untold ways I'm better off alone. I have no one harping at me about my cholesterol or the volume I play the TV at. I watch whatever programs I want. *The Longest Day, Flying Tigers, The Greatest Battle, Convoy, Sergeant York.* No longer do I awake at night, frightened, my body a hollow chamber, quaking and ringing like a cast iron bell with the pounding of my heart. I'd gone looking for our Bible. Every day I read from it. I hold much of it suspect, the writings of old, bearded men. Still, it seems to bring me comfort. *For we know that if the earthly tent we live in is destroyed, we have a building from God, an eternal house in heaven, not built by human hands.*

So do not fear, for I am with you, I remembered the priest reading on the cemetery hill, the day we buried my only boy. *Do not be dismayed, for I am your God. I will strengthen you and help you. I will uphold you with my righteous hand.*

Now, it is as though my chest has been broken open, I am like an old dried-up tree that ruptures and from its powdery centre a dark bird flies out, and finally the acute pain I've felt is gone.

One day, I get up and, I don't know why, but I feel like a different person. Fresh and happy and unscarred as a newborn child. Recovered. Reborn. All my sorrow suddenly passed, like a spent illness. I feel harrowed. Stripped bare and strong, like the trees outside the windows, bristling with their hardened-off buds. Happy in my rawness, prepared for winter on my own. In the kitchen, the sun slanting in through the window strikes the jar of marmalade on the breakfast table, making it shimmer like a jewel. My sectioned grapefruit sweats with its juices, my cup of strong coffee shines black as a well. All is fine with the world.

I go outside in my gardening trousers, my plaid flannel shirt and suspenders, my felt hat. I feel full of energy, optimistic, like the young Trip on the prairie. A delicate fog lifts off the wet grass as from a deep, still river, like the ghost of some ancient spirit stirring. The miracle of it stops me in my tracks. It sets me trembling strangely for a moment with regret and loss and longing. These potent emotions are not what I'd expected to move me at this point in my life. No. Peace, fulfillment, reconciliation are what I believed I'd know. But I shake off these thoughts.

Zealous as a lover, I work away all morning on the backyard, a fan rake, both light and fine, waltzing in my hands like a sensitive and cooperative partner. Its springy tines quiver and sing as it sprays my ankles with soil, the cuffs of my trousers filling with flecks of clay. Clay clings, cold and slippery, to the soles of my shoes. I welcome this feeling of being grounded, at one with the earth.

Now, I notice that it is ten thirty. In my love affair with the yard, I have nearly missed my morning tea. I go into the house through the side door, wash my hands at the bathroom sink, pass down the hall. Then I see Oneida sitting in her navy velveteen chair by the living room window. *Ha!* I laugh to myself. I will not be fooled. I'll have no truck with ghosts, apparitions. I remove my hat and hook it on the post of a kitchen chair. I take a loaf of Wonder Bread out of the fridge, the jar of peanut butter. I drop a tea bag into the pot, stand at the sink, filling the kettle, turn to place it on the burner, though, despite my disbelief, my fingers tremble.

Then I see Oneida again, standing now in the kitchen doorway. I turn the burner to high. Finally, I sigh, pluck up my courage, prepare to face my demons. With deliberation, I walk toward her, certain that she will vanish, as she's done so many times before. The closer I get, the more her figure will fade, I know this, until it entirely vanishes, like a fog. The wall clock ticks out its hollow judgement. Then I am close enough to touch the phantom. I reach out, expecting my hands to slide right through it.

But, no. Oneida's thin shoulders, solid, corporeal, meet my fingers. Even so, I will not credit it. No miracles here. My mind tells me: do not believe sensation, do not trust your heart, don't let hope take a foothold. Still: I quake with wonder, my whole body shaking as from an earthquake. Then I begin to weep, a shameless old man turned child again, my face twisted, my body trembling, my eyes brimming with tears. I had not dared to think this moment would ever come and now that it has, I am unprepared and defenceless.

"Yes," says Oneida. "I'm real."

12

I am too wise, or perhaps too afraid to ask Oneida why she came back. But, in time, she tells me that the lofty view from the cliff began to sicken her. She did not require so grand a perspective on the world. Also, she says, Stan regarded her limp as a flaw, something ugly, and he wanted it fixed. This gave her pause for thought. She did not want to change her walk, it was part of her, she says, her story. She says Stan doted on her, he wanted to be her vassal. She did not need to be worshipped. "I am not so soft as that," she says.

By silent agreement, we never return to the dam to gaze down at the foaming waters, in the shadow of Stan's bungalow high on the shale cliff. We give up whiskey and I instantly feel a marvellous vigour and clarity. In the evenings I leave my chair, gently pull Oneida from hers. We sit side by side on the couch, pressed together, holding hands. Her small form beside me is simple, warm, forgiving. I turn to ask her which program she'd like to watch. Around her mouth and eyes and temples I see all the beauty life has wrought in her face.

I am humbled and grateful. I am unworthy of her, I know this. She had made a brilliant escape, only to come back to me. I do not deserve it. I do not merit her return. Will I be able to tell her this? Some day? I hope so. I will try.

CPSIA information can be obtained
at www.ICGtesting.com
Printed in the USA
LVHW021941080322
712936LV00019B/814/J